Queens

Queens

A History of the Most Diverse Place on Earth

LAWRENCE R. SAMUEL

Cover art credit: Queens 7 Train: Adapted from Wikimedia Commons, cc-by-sa-2.0 license, The All-Nite Images from NY, NY, USA. Map of Queens: Lionel Pincus and Princess Firyal Map Division, The New York Public Library. "Hagstrom's map of Queens N.Y. City." New York Public Library Digital Collections.

Published by State University of New York Press, Albany

© 2025 State University of New York

All rights reserved

Printed in the United States of America

No part of this book may be used or reproduced in any manner whatsoever without written permission. No part of this book may be stored in a retrieval system or transmitted in any form or by any means including electronic, electrostatic, magnetic tape, mechanical, photocopying, recording, or otherwise without the prior permission in writing of the publisher.

Links to third-party websites are provided as a convenience and for informational purposes only. They do not constitute an endorsement or an approval of any of the products, services, or opinions of the organization, companies, or individuals. SUNY Press bears no responsibility for the accuracy, legality, or content of a URL, the external website, or for that of subsequent websites.

EU GPSR Authorised Representative:
Logos Europe, 9 rue Nicolas Poussin, 17000, La Rochelle, France
contact@logoseurope.eu

Excelsior Editions is an imprint of State University of New York Press

For information, contact State University of New York Press, Albany, NY
www.sunypress.edu

Library of Congress Cataloging-in-Publication Data

Name: Samuel, Lawrence, author.
Title: Queens: A history of the most diverse place on Earth / Lawrence Samuel,
author.
Description: Albany : State University of New York Press, [2025] | Series:
Excelsior Editions | Includes bibliographical references and index.
Identifiers: ISBN 9798855801439 (pbk. : alk. paper) | ISBN 9798855801422 (ebook)
Further information is available at the Library of Congress.

Contents

Introduction	1
Chapter 1. The Revolutionary Movement	21
Chapter 2. The Common Good	53
Chapter 3. The Golden Door	85
Chapter 4. The International Express	109
Chapter 5. Tomorrow's America	135
Notes	159
Selected Bibliography	181
Index	183

Introduction

Although I grew up in Nassau County, right next to the Queens border, I have a strong personal connection to the borough of New York City. In 1964, when I was seven years old, my family went to the New York World's Fair in Flushing Meadows Corona Park. As I recount in my book *The End of the Innocence*, the fair was an unforgettable experience that helped to shape my vision of the world. In those pre-internet days, the world's fair, with its reckless crossing of the boundaries of time and space, opened my eyes to the infinite possibilities that lay beyond the Long Island suburbs.[1] Because of that, I owe a great debt to Queens, and I cannot help but smile whenever I pass by or visit the grounds and see the Unisphere or the crumbling towers of the New York State Pavilion (which is thankfully now being restored).

This work is intended to pay down some of that debt. *Queens: A History of the Most Diverse Place on Earth* charts the historical residential development of the borough from the 1920s right up to today. The work focuses on what can be said to be the borough's most remarkable aspect—its profound diversity. Tracing the historical evolution of the borough in terms of the groups of people who have lived there adds much to our understanding of not only Queens and New York City but New York State, the United States, and even the world. The value of diversity in all its forms is being increasingly recognized, making this work a timely and important one. *Queens* is also inherently multidisciplinary, crossing over into the territories of social history, cultural geography, urban studies, the built environment, border studies, demography, anthropology, studies of race/ethnicity/class/religion, and other fields.

Queens strives to be recognized as a valuable addition to both scholarly and trade literature dedicated to the history of the borough. While there are

Figure I.1. My mom, older brothers, and I (lower right) at the New York World's Fair in Flushing Meadows Corona Park, Queens, in 1964. For me and many others, the event was an unforgettable, even life-altering experience. *Source*: Author photo.

Figure I.2. My dad, older brothers, and I (foreground) at the fair. We left my three-year-old brother at home, and he still hasn't forgiven us for that. *Source*: Author photo.

Figure I.3. The Unisphere, the principal symbol of the 1964–1965 New York World's Fair. At 140-feet in height and 120-feet in diameter, it was the largest representation of Earth at the time and is one of the few surviving structures of the fair. *Source*: Carol M. Highsmith, *1964 New York World's Fair Site in Queens, New York*, between 1980 and 2006, photograph, Library of Congress Prints and Photographs Division, Washington, DC, https://www.loc.gov/pictures/item/2011631096/.

at least a handful of excellent histories of Manhattan, a definitive history of Brooklyn (Thomas J. Campanella's *Brooklyn: The Once and Future City*), and a superb history of the Bronx (Evelyn Gonzalez's *The Bronx* [2004]), a contemporary, borough-wide history of Queens does not yet exist.[2]

There have, however, been some excellent studies of specific dimensions of the borough's history. Steven Gregory's *Black Corona: Race and the Politics of Place in an Urban Community*, for example, showed how African Americans gained empowerment through activism in that neighborhood.[3] Warren and Judith Sloan's *Crossing the BLVD: Strangers, Neighbors, Aliens in a New World* took a fascinating look at the lives of some Queens residents,

Figure I.4. The New York State Pavilion at night, one week before the fair's opening in April 1964. The roof of the Tent of Tomorrow, to the left, is long gone. The Observation Towers still stand but are in ruins. *Source*: Warren K. Leffler, *New York World's Fair*, 1964, photograph, Library of Congress Prints and Photographs Division, Washington, DC, https://www.loc.gov/item/2016646526/.

while Claudia Gryvatz's *The Neighborhoods of Queens* was a guide to no less than ninety-nine neighborhoods in the borough.[4] R. Scott Hanson's *City of Gods: Religious Freedom, Immigration, and Pluralism in Flushing, Queens* explored the captivating history of one of them, Flushing, from the colonial period to the post-9/11 era.[5]

While a sweeping history of Queens has not appeared in decades, Arcadia has published quite a number of books about some aspect of the borough, all of them prioritizing images over text. These include Rob

Mackay's *Famous People of Queens* (2023) and *Historic Houses of Queens* (2021); Richard Panchyk's *Queens through Time* (2022), *Abandoned Queens* (2019), and *Hidden History of Queens* (2018); Richard Panchyk and Lizz Panchyk's *Dead Queens* (2021); Kevin Walsh and the Greater Astoria Historical Society's *Forgotten Queens* (2013); Christina Rozeas's *Greeks in Queens* (2012); Jason Antos's *Queens (Then and Now (2009)*; and the Greater Astoria Historical Society and Roosevelt Island Historical Society's *The Queensboro Bridge* (2008).[6] In addition to these, Arcadia has published a bevy of books about specific neighborhoods or sites in Queens, including Douglaston-Little Neck, St. Albans, Corona, Glendale, Kew Gardens, Jackson Heights, Fresh Meadows, Jamaica, Jamaica Estates, Laurelton, Flushing, Shea Stadium, College Point, Long Island City, the Rockaways, the 1964–1965 New York World's Fair, and JFK Airport.

The lack of a definitive history of Queens is surprising given the borough's compelling story, especially with regard to its transformation from a quasi-suburb of Manhattan for the White middle class into what is widely considered the most diverse place in the country, if not the world. Viewing the history of the residential development of Queens through the lens of the people who have chosen to live there over the past century represents a valuable contribution to the existing body of work. Most important, perhaps, the potential for improving intergroup relations is implicit in the project. People who believe that they are unique, or who think that their experience is uniquely painful or even unprecedented, are likely to discover common threads from this study that have the capacity to serve as a cultural bridge.

It's safe to say that Queens deserves such a study. For various reasons, Queens can be seen as the Rodney Dangerfield of the five boroughs of New York City, lacking the glamour of Manhattan, the hipsterness of Brooklyn, the toughness of the Bronx, and the small-town feel of Staten Island. Ever since F. Scott Fitzgerald described the dump in Willets Point as the "valley of ashes" in his 1925 *The Great Gatsby*, in fact, Queens has not been given a whole lot of respect. Television certainly hasn't done Queens any favors; our image of the borough's residents has been indelibly imprinted by the rather obtuse Bunkers of *All in the Family* and the bourgeois Heffermans of *The King of Queens*.

Unfortunately, for many Americans, even New Yorkers, Queens has just been the place one goes to catch a flight (JFK in Jamaica or LaGuardia in East Elmhurst). Some may know that arguably the greatest pianos in the world are made at the Steinway & Sons Factory in Astoria (and have been since the early 1870s). Jazz aficionados may be aware that Queens (particularly the Addisleigh Park neighborhood) had been home to hundreds of African American artists including Fats Waller, Billie Holiday, Dizzy Gillespie, Louis Armstrong, and Ella Fitzgerald. Finally, with dozens of cemeteries, the borough is also commonly seen as the place to visit one's dead relatives (my people are in Elmhurst) or perhaps spend eternity oneself.

Queens is, of course, much more than that. In his *Hidden History of Queens*, Richard Panchyk calls Queens not just "diverse and wondrous" but New York City's "most intriguing borough."[7] Take a ride on the No. 7 subway train and one instantly realizes how diverse the borough really is; its mashing of global cultures makes it a true crossroads of the world. And while stereotypical, the working-class image of Queens is well deserved and, I think, a good thing; most of its residents do what needs to get done in order to get by, and there's no shame in that.

Need it be said, there are some very attractive parts of Queens (the Willets Point ash dump has thankfully disappeared). For more than a century, people from near and far have flocked to Aqueduct Racetrack in

Figure I.5. Architect Eero Saarinen's fabulous TWA terminal at Idlewild Airport sometime between 1956 and 1962. *Source*: Balthazar Korab, *Trans World Airlines Terminal, John F. Kennedy (originally Idlewild) Airport, New York, New York, 1956–62. Exterior*, between 1956 and 1962, photograph, Library of Congress Prints and Photographs Division, Washington, DC, https://www.loc.gov/item/2018673375/.

Figure I.6. The modernist American Airlines terminal at Idlewild Airport in August 1963. With the assassination of President Kennedy three months later, the airport would soon be renamed in his honor. *Source*: Al Ravenna, *American Airlines Terminal at Idlewild Airport*, 1963, photograph, Library of Congress Prints and Photographs Division, Washington, DC, https://www.loc.gov/item/2011645166/.

Figure I.7. A Pan Am Boeing 707 "jumbo" jet at Kennedy Airport with the control tower in the back, May 1973. As with the auto traffic on the Long Island Expressway, the Environmental Protection Agency had concerns about the effects of air pollution emanating from air travel. *Source*: Arthur Tress, *Pan Am Jumbo Jet at the John F. Kennedy Airport, May 1973*, photograph, National Archives Identifier 547959, Local Identifier 412-DA-5472, National Archives at College Park-Still Pictures (RDSS).

Figure I.8. The No. 7 train (the Flushing Local and Express) pulling into Seventy-Forth Street. The No. 7 has deservedly been nicknamed the International Express. Source: The All-Nite Images, *Queens: 7 Train from Queensboro Plaza to 74 Street*, Wikimedia Commons, CC BY-SA 2.0.

South Ozone Park, a lovely place to watch a horse run around an oval at considerable speed. The grand golf courses of the 1920s may be gone, but a number of quiet sporting links remain in the borough. Rockaway Beach may not have rivaled Coney Island in terms of pure numbers but was and continues to be a beloved stretch of sand and boardwalk amusements. (North Beach too was a popular place for sun and fun until the area was redeveloped for LaGuardia Airport in the 1930s.)

And while it may lack the pedigree of Manhattan's Central Park and Brooklyn's Prospect Park (each designed by landscape architect extraordinaire Frederick Law Olmsted), Flushing Meadows Corona Park is an oasis for both locals and visitors from near and far. Every fall, the best tennis players in the world hit balls at the USTA Billie Jean King National Tennis Center (the US Open moved to the site from the gorgeous West Side Tennis Club at Forest Hills in 1977), and for decades the New York Mets have made their home just steps away at Shea Stadium and now Citi Field. That

Figure I.9. Aerial view of Aqueduct Racetrack from the west in August 2013. *Source*: Joe Mabel, *Aerial View of Aqueduct Race Track from the West 01; White Balanced*, Wikimedia Commons, CC BY-SA 2.0.

Figure I.10. A hand-colored postcard of Rockaway Beach from the early twentieth century. While the scene looks much different today, Rockaway Beach remains a popular destination for urbanites in the summer. *Source*: *Boulevard at Arverne, Rockaway Beach, L.I.*, Miriam and Ira D. Wallach Division of Art, Prints and Photographs, Picture Collection, New York Public Library Digital Collections, https://digitalcollections.nypl.org/items/510d47e2-8df3-a3d9-e040-e00a18064a99.

spot and many of the borough's beaches, attractions, parks, museums, and neighborhoods are often not given the credit they should, and Queens fully warrants recognition for the beautiful place it was and remains.

∼

The history of the area to be known as Queens is unarguably rich and complex, something entirely fitting given the present state of the borough. Until the early twentieth century, Queens, situated on Long Island, was a mostly isolated and rural area dotted with various towns. For centuries, it was home to Native Americans who lived in small bands farming the land, hunting the forest, and fishing the waters. Some tribal names still exist in some form today: Jamaica was named for the Jameco Indians, Rockaway after the Reckowacky Indians, and Maspeth for the Mespeatches Indians. Those names disguise a tragic legacy, even more so than the land grabbing: a smallpox epidemic in 1658 brought by Europeans reportedly killed two-thirds of the area's Native American population.[8]

Figure I.11. The Women's Tennis Championship at Forest Hills in 1924. Helen Wills Moody won the event. *Source*: Bain News Service, Publisher. *Forest Hills, Woman's Champ*, n.d., photograph, Library of Congress Prints and Photographs Division Washington, DC, https://www.loc.gov/item/2014717596/.

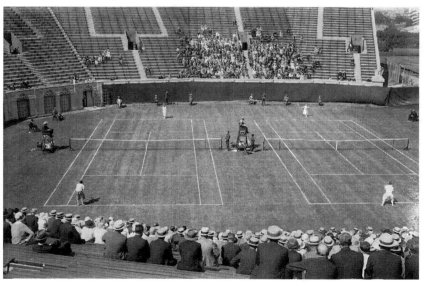

Figure I.12. A New York Mets game at Shea Stadium in the late 1960s. The team had a losing record from 1962 to 1968 but the following season finished 100–62 and won the World Series. *Source*: Wikimedia Commons, CC BY-SA 4.0, Dada1960.

It was the early seventeenth century when the area was discovered by European explorers, beginning with Henry Hudson's sighting of the Rockaways in 1609. Just five years later, Astoria, Hunters Point, and the Dutch Kills area of Long Island City were settled after Adrian Block, commissioned by the Dutch East India Company, sailed through Hell Gate into Long Island Sound. Bayside and Little Neck were settled in 1637, and the following year William Kieft, the third Dutch governor, "thought it well to secure more land for the West India Company from the Indian Chiefs," as a 1920 book published by the Queens Chamber of Commerce diplomatically put it. That purchase, whose cost is unknown, added the territory of what would be Queens to the earlier acquisition of the Island of Manhattan from Native Americans by that same company.[9]

In 1664, Governor Peter Stuyvesant surrendered New Amsterdam to the British, and the city was renamed New York (Long Island became Yorkshire). Queens County was established as one of the original ten counties of New York on November 1, 1683, said to be named after Catherine of Braganza, the Queen of England and wife of King Charles II.[10] Queens was then three times its current size, encompassing all of Nassau and part of Suffolk Counties, yet it was home to just ninety-three families.[11]

Many more villages would be settled by Europeans over the course of the following decades, with the area's original inhabitants often in conflict with the Dutch over occupancy of the land. (The relationship between Native Americans and the English was considerably less hostile.) African Americans first settled in Queens in the late seventeenth century, and they would represent 10 to 12 percent of the borough's total population for the following two hundred years. Queens would play an active role in the Revolutionary War; residents leaned heavily toward Tories, but there were Whigs as well.[12]

The British occupied Queens for seven years following George Washington's defeat in the Battle of Long Island in Brooklyn in 1776, but their military presence was no more by 1783 with the American victory. Significant numbers of Irish immigrants soon took the place of the British, however, the result of overpopulation and a potato famine in the former's homeland. This could be considered the beginnings of the diversification of Queens, which would ultimately become its defining feature.[13] The population of Queens was just 5,393 in 1790, according to the nation's first census, but things would soon change dramatically.[14]

In the early nineteenth century, roads (the main ones called *turnpikes*) and ferries made Queens more accessible, good news for farmers taking their produce to markets, and Jamaica became the first incorporated village in the county in 1814. The new roads also aided travel to and from the pair of horse racing tracks in Queens (the Union and the Eclipse), which were proving to be quite popular and showed visitors the natural beauty of the county. Woodside, Woodhaven, and Douglaston were soon settled, and in 1836 the first Long Island Railroad (LIRR) train brought passengers to and from Jamaica, its population almost doubling that decade. "The urbanizing forces that would eventually overwhelm rural Queens first became apparent in the 1830s," CUNY history professors Vincent F. Seyfried and Jon A. Peterson posited.[15]

Indeed, it was then that real estate people recognized the opportunity to be had and money to be made by developing suburban villages. Factories too began to spring up in Queens, as the land was much cheaper than in Manhattan. As well, due to the passage of the Rural Cemetery Act by the state government, Queens, with its open spaces, would soon become home to a significant population of the deceased. Burial grounds were not permitted in lower Manhattan for health reasons, leading to the creation of Calvary (1846), Evergreens (1848), and Cypress Hills (1852) cemeteries.[16]

The growth of Queens was augmented by another large wave of immigrants from Ireland, most choosing Astoria, but some, Jamaica and

Figure I.13. A section of Calvary Cemetery in March 1983, which appears to have not changed much over the decades. *Source*: Camilo J. Vergara, *Calvary Cemetery, Queens, N.Y.*, 1983, photograph, Library of Congress Prints and Photographs Division, Washington, DC, https://www.loc.gov/item/2009633512/.

Figure I.14. Another image of the sprawling Calvary Cemetery, one of many burial grounds in Queens. *Source*: Camilo J. Vergara, *Calvary Cemetery, Queens, N.Y.*, 1983, photograph, Library of Congress Prints and Photographs Division, Washington, DC, https://www.loc.gov/item/2009633538/.

Flushing. And in the early 1850s, more than half a million Germans settled in New York City, fleeing economic hardship and political unrest. Many of them put down roots in western Queens (via Brooklyn), just as hundreds of thousands of people from dozens of ethnic groups would do over the next century and a half (often for the same reasons).[17]

With much open space remaining, villages continued to appear in Queens after the Civil War. Between 1865 and 1890, "the initial urbanization of western Queens was largely completed," according to Seyfried and Peterson in "A Brief History of Queens." The population jumped from 45,468 in 1870 to 56,559 in 1880 and 87,050 in 1890 as farms were converted into building lots. Glendale (1865), Corona (1870), and Queens Village (1871) were settled, and Ozone Park (1882), Morris Park (1884), and Hollis (1884–1985) were laid out for development by visionaries who had little doubt that the county would attract still more people. Most were coming from increasingly crowded Manhattan (where "skyscrapers" were beginning to appear) and, in the case of Ozone Park, from Brooklyn. Bellerose (1887), Richmond Hill (1888), Howard Beach (1890), and Edgemere (1892) were next in line (the developer and promoter of Edgemere not shyly describing it as the "New Venice").[18]

On January 1, 1898 (following a nonbinding ballot among borough residents in 1894), Queens County became part of Greater New York City, composed of the western "wards" of Flushing, Newtown, Jamaica, and the Rockaway peninsula. (The eastern half of the county became Nassau County the following year.) The population of Queens was 152,999 in 1900, yet greater growth lay ahead.[19] Forest Hills (a far superior name to its previous one, White Pot) was developed by Cord Meyer in 1906 and soon drew more affluent Jews from Manhattan's densely populated Lower East Side. Congregation Tifereth Israel opened its doors in Corona in 1911, and the synagogue became a catalyst for more Jews to move to Queens. The following year, the LIRR added Kew Station stop, encouraging the creation of Kew Gardens (originally Hopedale), an adjacent neighborhood to Forest Hills.[20]

The population of Queens had reached 284,041 by 1910, owing much of that growth to the opening of the Penn Tunnels under the East River that year and the Queensboro Bridge over it the previous year. With a host of vehicles using the bridge to cross the river, "this span ended the isolation of the borough's road system at precisely the time when mass use of the automobile was getting underway in the United States," Seyfried and Peterson wrote.[21] Now literally linked to Manhattan, Queens would soon lose much of its farmland as industry and people marched in. "For Queens, the new Queensboro Bridge dramatized the change from the nineteenth century to the twentieth," wrote Janet E. Lieberman and Richard K. Lieberman in their 1983 *City Limits: A Social History of Queens*, the physical connection to the rest of the world bringing with it "modern technology, new people, and growth occurring at a dizzying pace."[22]

Figure I.15. The Queensboro Bridge around its opening in 1909. *Source*: *Queensboro Bridge*, 1909, photograph, Library of Congress Prints and Photographs Division, Washington, DC, https://www.loc.gov/item/2002706025/.

Figure I.16. Much festivity surrounded the opening of the Queensboro Bridge, including this June 1909 parade. *Source*: *Parade Opening Queensboro Bridge*, 1909, photograph, Library of Congress Prints and Photographs Division, Washington, DC, https://www.loc.gov/item/2016652416/.

Figure I.17. A view of the much built-up Welfare Island and East River from the Queensboro Bridge in 1941. *Source*: Arthur Rothstein, *Welfare Island from Queensboro Bridge. New York City*, 1941, photograph, Library of Congress Prints and Photographs Division, Washington, DC, https://www.loc.gov/item/2017774891/.

Over the next few years, the transportation grid of Queens would be additionally transformed, as Queens Boulevard (1914), the Queensboro Subway (1915), the No. 7 train (1917), Hell Gate Bridge (1917), and bus operations (1920) all came into being.[23] These new ways of traveling "brought virtually the whole of Queens within the suburban commuting zone of Manhattan," Seyfried and Peterson wrote, "greatly inflating land values and stimulating home building."[24] In short, Queens as we know it today had been born.

While that race through three hundred years of Queens history is certainly interesting, each village of the borough has its own captivating story to tell, none more so than Flushing. Flushing (which was made the borough's county seat after becoming part of New York City) was settled by the Dutch in 1628 as part of the Colony of New Netherland, but British colonists from Massachusetts were granted land there in 1645.

An important part of the history of Flushing took place soon after that, a result of Governor Peter Stuyvesant's placing restrictions on how residents worshiped, specifically a ban on Quakerism in favor of the Dutch Reformed Church. Local citizens revolted, leading to the Flushing Remonstrance of 1627, a petition directed to Stuyvesant to allow them to worship as they liked. (The petition made a case for freedom of worship not just for Quakers but for Jews, Presbyterians, and Baptists, as well as for Turks and Egyptians.) That document "remains the most eloquent defense of religious freedom in all of American history," wrote Kenneth T. Jackson in his introduction to Copquin's *The Neighborhoods of Queens*, and foreshadowed language put forth in the Bill of Rights of the United States Constitution. Stuyvesant fined and jailed those who disobeyed his ruling, but the Dutch government would overrule him, the beginnings of what would be a very long history of tolerance in Flushing and, with notable exceptions, all of Queens.[25]

The British colonists who had relocated to Flushing from Massachusetts had been farmers, and the village would remain predominantly agricultural for more than two centuries. Nurseries were established in the village in the mid-eighteenth century, making Flushing well known for its trees, plants, and flowers, some of which were brought to markets for sale. The population of Flushing when Queens became part of New York City was twelve thousand, with the center of its business district located at Northern Boulevard and Main Street (until the arrival of the subway shifted the district to Main Street and Roosevelt Avenue).[26] Today, Flushing/Whitestone is the second largest neighborhood in New York City by population and is 55 percent Asian and 17 percent Hispanic.[27]

Not just each village but the entire county of Queens, much like Manhattan, Brooklyn, the Bronx, and Staten Island, had its own distinct identity before the consolidation. "Prior to 1898, each borough had a unique settlement morphology," observed Ines M. Miyares, adding that "the pre-consolidation history of Queens is linked to rural, agricultural Long Island."[28] It wouldn't be long, however, before both borough officials and real estate speculators recognized that Queens could be home to much more than farms and flora. "Sections of Queens had already been laid out by 1909, with the Queensboro Bridge completed and transit lines ready for a flood of new inhabitants," noted J. M. Tyree. Indeed, the population of the borough would quadruple over the next two decades, leading the American historian and sociologist (and Queens native) Lewis Mumford to label such development "the disease of growth."[29]

Disease or otherwise, the growth of Queens in the early decades of the twentieth century included about a thousand African Americans. In their research, Richard and Janet Lieberman of LaGuardia Community

INTRODUCTION | 17

College found that there was a Black middle-class community in Queens before World War I, a surprising finding that they reported in their book *City Limits*. "Blacks had a more significant role in the development of the borough as was previously recognized," Richard Lieberman told the *New York Amsterdam News* in 1983, as it was generally held that significant numbers of African Americans left crowded Harlem for Queens in the 1920s. After conducting oral histories with and studying documents of older Queens residents whose ancestors settled in the borough in the late nineteenth century, however, the researchers learned that a Black middle class had existed even earlier.[30] More such research into the amazing past of Queens is warranted in order to uncover stories that add to our understanding of the place and potentially challenge existing scholarship.

～

This work picks up the story immediately after World War I, when the Queens that we know today came to be. Between the World Wars, real estate developers "discovered" the borough across the East River from Manhattan, viewing the mostly open land of Queens as an ideal place to create a quasi-suburb for the White managerial class. Taking advantage of a short commute to Manhattan (relative to that in the true suburbs of Long Island, Westchester, and New Jersey), hundreds of thousands of people settled in Queens, attracted to the new houses and apartment buildings popping up in dozens of neighborhoods. (The population of the borough doubled between 1920 and 1930.) The "garden city" concept of urban development in Forest Hills Gardens, Sunnyside Gardens, and Jackson Heights was especially popular among more well-to-do White Protestant families, with exclusionary covenants in place to bar recent immigrants, Jews, and people of color.

The African American experience in Queens between the world wars was, however, quite different. Parts of the borough were highly segregated, and sparks often flew when Black families tried to move into predominantly White neighborhoods such as Elmhurst. As well, housing built for the African American market was often flimsy, and the Ku Klux Klan was a visible presence in the borough in the 1920s and early 1930s. Discrimination against African Americans was common, and Blacks fought for equal rights, notably in healthcare—an early example of the civil rights movement that would blossom after World War II.

Although World War II put things on hold, the development of Queens for the White middle class accelerated in the postwar years. Large garden apartments, single-family houses, and high-rises filled up much of

18 | QUEENS

the remaining vacant land.[31] While William Levitt would become famous for building Levittown in Nassau County, it was Queens-based Alfred Gross who pioneered the concept of "whole community" (vs. individual house) development. Between the late 1920s and early 1930s, Gross built about 2,500 houses in Laurelton to create what many agreed was the nation's largest community of moderately priced homes. In 1948, Gross was using the same formula to build a garden apartment community in Glen Oaks Village.[32]

Such communities were typically redlined, but the demography of Queens had already begun to shift. Beginning in 1940, large numbers of West Indian immigrants moved into the borough, soon followed by Chinese due to the repeal of the Chinese Exclusion Act. In the decade following World War II, German immigrants leaving their war-torn homeland found a new homeland in Queens, while the War Brides Act of 1946 allowed Chinese Americans who had served in the war to bring their wives to the States. The United Nations set up camp in the New York City Building at Flushing Meadows Corona Park between 1946 and 1950, a fitting location given that the borough was on the way to becoming a real-life example of united nations. A sizable population of Japanese immigrants first settled in Queens in the late 1950s, further diversifying the borough.[33] The 1964–65 New York World's Fair, on the same spot as the 1939–40 World's Fair, was presented as a celebration of global culture, portending things to come in the borough.

The Immigration and Nationality Act of 1965 (reversing the restrictions of the 1924 National Origins Act) proved to fundamentally alter the demographics of Queens, more so than anywhere else in New York City and perhaps even the United States. Fittingly, President Johnson signed the act at the base of the Statue of Liberty, opening the country's "golden door" to groups who had for decades faced strict quotas for entering the country. Hundreds of thousands of Whites from southern and Eastern Europe, Asians, and non-Whites settled in Queens in the late 1960s and through the 1970s, choosing the borough for its affordability, family connections, and employment opportunities.

The range of groups who emigrated to Queens over these years was startling despite a decline in the borough's population in the 1970s (the first in its history). In the 1960s, many of the first major wave of South Asian immigrants came to Queens, as did hundreds of thousands of Russians fleeing Communist oppression in the early 1970s. Through the 1970s, Chinese and Korean immigrants began buying property in Flushing, where real estate remained a relative bargain.[34] The diversification of Queens was hardly over, however.

In the 1980s and early 1990s, troubled economies in Mexico and Colombia motivated many of those countries' citizens to emigrate to New York City, including Queens, and seek employment. It was not surprising then that in 1992 Queens was judged as the most ethnically diverse area in the world. By the end of that decade, the No. 7 train, which traversed northeast through the borough, had earned its nickname, the International Express. At the same time, however, a backlash against the extreme diversity of Queens surfaced; billboards stating that unchecked immigration was "eroding our quality of life" appeared. Those with a greater understanding of what the nation was about countered, saying that it was in fact the diversity and multiculturalism of Queens that made the borough special.[35]

Immediately after 9/11, an even greater ethnic and racial backlash emerged, this one against Middle Eastern and South Asian Queens residents. There was no stopping the continual diversification of Queens, however. Over the past couple of decades, local Hispanics and Asians have been elected to the Queens City Council and the New York State Assembly, a clear sign of those groups' ascending political power. As evidence, a bill was introduced in the City Council in 2005 to grant voting rights to noncitizens in municipal elections.[36]

The demographic transformation of Queens over the past half century has been well documented by the US census. In 1970, 85 percent of the population of Queens was White, but by 1980 that percentage had dropped to 65 percent (18 percent of the borough's population in 1980 was African American, 14 percent Hispanic, and 5 percent Asian).[37] In some neighborhoods, the change was even more dramatic; the White population of Elmhurst-Corona dropped from 98 percent in 1960 to 67 percent in 1970, 34 percent in 1980, and 18 percent in 1990.[38] In her 2004 study of Jackson Heights in *Geographical Review*, Miyares parsed how that neighborhood morphed from an exclusive suburban community for native-born Whites to one defined by "ethnic hyperdiversity."[39] And in his 2005 essay for the *Antioch Review*, Tyree labeled the borough "the United Nations of Queens," an apt way to describe the place.[40] Today, some eight hundred languages are reportedly spoken in New York City, according to the Endangered Language Alliance, with more spoken in Queens than anywhere else in the world.[41]

Why did Queens become such a prime site of pluralism? What economic and social factors drove the transformation of the borough? How do ethnicity, race, and the immigrant experience play into the sociology of Queens? Such questions are addressed in the following pages, revealing key insights into the constructs of both national and personal identity.

CHAPTER ONE

The Revolutionary Movement

Queens is destined to be New York's greatest borough.

—John J. Halleran, *New York Herald Tribune*, 1927

In May 1920, it was announced that two thousand lots in the borough of Queens would be sold at auction in two weeks. The land was located in Jamaica Estates, within what was referred to as the hill section of Jamaica due to the area's rolling wooded hills and ravines. With Jamaica Estates near a Brooklyn Rapid Transit (BRT) elevated and subway station, a Long Island Rail Road (LIRR) station, a trolley line, and Hillside Avenue—the main automobile route through Queens to Nassau and Suffolk Counties at the time—it was believed that the lots would be particularly attractive to the growing number of commuters considering buying property. The sale was presented as "an extraordinary opportunity for home seekers, speculators, and investors" by the well-known real estate broker Joseph P. Day in promoting the auction. With a piece of property to be had "at bargain prices," he added, the bidders had the "proverbial opportunity of a lifetime."[1]

Many would indeed seize the opportunity, adding to the population of the New York City borough. Queens thrived in the 1920s, the result of various social and economic factors that drove more people to the borough that had been linked to Manhattan with the opening of the Queensboro Bridge in 1909. Immediately after the Great War (World War I), Queens, with its abundance of farmland, was understandably seen by land speculators as too good of an opportunity to go ignored. Syndicates were formed

Figure 1.1. Under the elevated ("el") train on Jamaica Avenue in November 1944. *Source*: Gottscho-Schleisner Inc., *Jamaica Ave., Jamaica, New York. I*, 1944, photograph, Library of Congress Prints and Photographs Division Washington, DC, https://www.loc.gov/item/2018722822/.

to back builders, the true beginnings of the borough that we know today.

Taking advantage of its close proximity to Manhattan—an important thing for commuters—many urbanites decided to relocate to Queens through the 1920s. Then, as now, one could get more space for one's housing dollar than in Manhattan and Brooklyn, and there were many neighborhoods from which to choose. Well off White Protestant families were apt to settle in one of the new "garden city" developments that offered suburban-like living without having to leave New York City. Such communities did not welcome certain people based on their race, religion, or ethnicity, however, a form of discrimination that would persist for decades.

Running parallel to that story is one of the larger African American experience in Queens in the 1920s. Parts of the borough were highly segregated, and sparks often flew when Black families tried to move into predominantly White neighborhoods such as Elmhurst. As well, housing

Figure 1.2. Another image of the normally busy shopping area in Jamaica near the el in 1944. It being wartime, goods were scarce. *Source*: Gottscho-Schleisner Inc., *Jamaica Ave., Jamaica, New York. II*, 1944, photograph, Library of Congress Prints and Photographs Division Washington, DC, https://www.loc.gov/item/2018722823/.

built for the Black market was often flimsy, and the Ku Klux Klan was a visible presence in the borough. Discrimination against African Americans was common, and Blacks fought for equal rights, notably in healthcare—an early example of the civil rights movement that would blossom after World War II.

A Note of Optimism

Jamaica Estates was hardly the only neighborhood of Queens being developed in the early 1920s. Quite a few modest houses were being built in other parts of what had been designated as the borough's fourth ward, comprising Jamaica itself, Kew Gardens, Woodhaven, Richmond Hill, Hollis, and Morris Park. (At fifty-six square miles, the ward was about two and a half times the size of

Manhattan.) "Here, as in other sections of the borough, the housing bureau of the Queensboro Chamber of Commerce has found a note of optimism prevailing among the real estate and other far-seeing businessmen," the *New York Herald Tribune* noted. It wasn't a boom—a good thing given that a bust often came next—but such development was taken as a positive sign in the uncertain economic period following the Great War. And while Queens had been home to thousands of people for decades (actually centuries), most current residents were renting apartments; developers were thus happy to see that potential homeowners were taking the borough seriously as a place to live. Banks and theaters were also being constructed in the fourth ward, an additional reason for developers to be optimistic.[2]

More confidence in the future of Queens came with the news that the Prudential Insurance Company made its first-ever loan on real estate in the borough. The $540,000 loan was made to the Queensboro Corporation to build what was being called "garden apartment houses," a rather new concept in real estate development. These garden apartment houses would be located in Jackson Heights, an area in which the Queensboro Corporation owned some one hundred city blocks. "We accepted the loan because of the growing importance of that borough as a center of population and industry," explained a Prudential executive, the postwar housing shortage in Manhattan having much to do with the company's decision to make such a big loan ($8.3 million in today's dollars). What was different about the Jackson Heights garden apartment houses was that their tenants would own the units rather than rent them, blazing the trail for what would evolve into co-ops and condominiums.[3]

In her 2004 article for *Geographical Review*, Ines M. Miyares explained how many developers had been inspired by Ebenezer Howard's 1898 book *Garden Cities To-Morrow*. With affordable land in Queens available after World War I, developers looked to the borough to apply the principles outlined by Howard. Forest Hills Gardens and Sunnyside Gardens were each based on the concept, with the Jackson Heights development adding the new element of ownership to the model. Wedding "town and country," as Howard had put it, would create an ideal synergy of urban and rural lifestyles. Forest Hills Gardens would be sponsored by the (nonprofit) Russell Sage Homes Foundation and become home to middle- and upper-class residents (most escaping teeming Manhattan). Sunnyside Gardens, on the other hand, drew working-class families.[4]

True to form, a concerted effort was made by the Queensboro Corporation to bring nature into an urban environment when developing the

Jackson Heights garden apartment houses. Grass, shrubs, and flowering plants could be found in front of the buildings of Laburnum Court, and as its name suggested, there were interior garden courts as well (designed by professional landscape gardeners). Walks and open plazas with benches were also part of the interior courts, adding to the feeling that one was in the country rather than part of New York City. Living rooms contained working fireplaces, another nod to country life, although elevators were a distinctly modern feature.[5]

Restricting the Jackson Heights garden apartment houses to White Protestants was a key part of the selling and buying proposition. "The costs of the apartments and the exclusionary covenants prohibiting sale or rental to blacks, Jews, or Catholics—the latter a euphemism for immigrants—in the original deeds created an attractive community for white middle-class and upper-middle-class Protestants desiring to suburbanize without the long commute to communities farther east on Long Island, in New Jersey, or in Westchester County," Miyares wrote.[6] That the buildings in Jackson Heights (considered "the largest co-operative apartment house group in the world") were restricted was sometimes overt and sometimes not so. Residents have the "opportunity to mingle with those of a social status congenial to theirs," observed Lawrence Elliman, a partner of the real estate brokerage Pease & Elliman, in 1922, a hint at the community's exclusive nature in terms of race, class, ethnicity, and religion.[7]

Queens was a hot real estate market not just on a city or state basis but a national one as well. In 1920, $38 million was spent on new construction in Queens, a number surpassed by only five cities in the entire United States.[8] By the summer of 1921, $1 million a week was going toward new buildings in the borough, and the number was continuing to rise as more construction companies saw the opportunity that was Queens.[9]

As in the past, development was clustered around subway and train stations, although the area between the once distinct villages of Queens was now being filled in with houses and apartment buildings. The low cost of land was clearly driving the growth, as was the conviction that property values would rise. Lots in Queens just twenty minutes by train from Pennsylvania Station were much cheaper than those requiring the same amount of travel time in upper Manhattan, Brooklyn, or the Bronx. Land was selling well in Flushing, Floral Park, and St. Albans, villages considered to be suburbs at the time, and the Metropolitan Life Insurance Company was buying property near the Bliss Street subway street, which it planned to develop into apartment rentals.[10]

In 1922, a milestone was reached when the reportedly last remaining large tract of farmland was divided into 1,500 lots that were then placed on the market as Forest Hills West. "Farm after farm, large as well as small, has been taken in the revolutionary movement that has changed Queens from New York's vegetable garden to a great expanse of small homes, flats, factories, and building sites," the *New York Herald Tribune* noted. (Cabbages and potatoes had been commonly grown in the borough.) Anticipating the arrival (and departure) of commuters, the LIRR was starting train service to Forest Hills West. Not far away, plans were in the works to widen Queens Boulevard to two hundred feet, as merchants and tradespeople believed it was the avenue best suited for retail business in the borough.[11]

The year 1923 was a very good one for development in Queens, with more buildings erected in the borough than anywhere else in the country save for much larger cities of Chicago and Los Angeles.[12] There was every indication that more buildings and more people would come, however. The extension of the Queensboro subway west from Grand Central to Times Square in Manhattan and, even more so, the connecting of the BRT with the interborough IRT line in 1923 boded well for further development of Queens. Two areas in particular—Astoria (named after the elder John Jacob Astor without consulting him) and Elmhurst (after the trees)—would benefit in terms of population growth, experts (correctly) predicted, as it was now easier to get to and from Manhattan and Brooklyn. The linking of the BRT with the IRT would also save passengers money; it would no longer cost an extra fare (a nickel) to transfer lines.[13] Hopes were for an interborough parkway, which had been conceived a decade earlier, that would connect Queens with Brooklyn by automobile.[14]

Who was moving to Queens in the early 1920s? The Queensboro Chamber of Commerce asked that very question in 1924 and completed a survey to find the answer. Interestingly, at least 75 percent of new residents were purchasing property rather than renting. One- and two-family houses priced between $7,500 and $15,000 were the most popular, confirmation that it was families with moderate incomes who were most attracted to the borough. The bulk of the buyers were, as the *New York Herald Tribune* noted in 1924, "of the middle classes, or thrifty mechanics who have not allowed their increased earnings to slip through their fingers."[15]

Direct references to race were scarce in the mainstream press, although there was little doubt that the purchasers of property in Queens were over-whelmingly White. Again, sales of cooperative apartments in Jackson Heights were entirely White, just as they were on Park Avenue in Manhattan. In each location, their popularity was "due in a measure to the highly restricted character of the neighborhoods," boasted Frank Ray Howe, a vice president at the Queensboro Corporation. Put simply, a certain segment of White people did not want to have African Americans, Jews, or members of certain ethnic groups as their neighbors and were willing to pay a significant amount of money for that perceived privilege.[16]

A Certain Sentiment

Although unlikely to be found in Jackson Heights, African Americans were very much part of the cultural fabric of Queens in the 1920s. African Americans had called Queens home for centuries, but their numbers increased dramatically due to the Great Migration. From the 1910s to the 1970s, millions of Southern Blacks moved to the Midwest and Northeast for better lives, with New York City the destination for some. Many settled in Harlem in upper Manhattan and Bedford-Stuyvesant in Brooklyn, although those neighborhoods quickly became crowded (and later dangerous), impetus for thousands to relocate throughout the five boroughs during much of the twentieth century.

The African American real estate market in Queens in the 1920s ran parallel to and occasionally intersected with the one serving the larger White community. By the mid-part of the decade, many Blacks had benefited from the robust economy and were seeking to buy property in the borough. Jamaica, and to a lesser extent Corona, represented the heart of the African American community in Queens, making that neighborhood the choice for most. Builders, whether White or Black, recognized that there was a legitimate market in Jamaica for, as they were commonly called, "colored buyers."[17]

A number of African American real estate brokers too recognized the opportunity to be had in Queens. One was William J. Weir, who by 1925 had a number of agents (and his wife) working for him.[18] Another was Jamaica-based John J. Hill, whose business practices extended well beyond making a commission as quickly as possible (something ascribed to quite a few in the field). Hill profoundly explained his philosophy to the *New York Amsterdam News*:

> Our condition in this country is such I believe that a certain sentiment should play its part between our people as a race. I haven't lost a thing by looking out for the interest of my

people in the purchase of real estate. I want to see my people well housed. I want to see them in prospering communities and living in wholesome surroundings. I want to see them looking forward without the discontent that comes from practices that in the past have left many of them discouraged. If I can do my part in helping towards this end and still manage to make a livelihood, I am satisfied.[19]

Recognizing the need for decent housing for his people (especially given the overall shortage after the war), Hill had some years back persuaded a construction company to build fourteen houses on George Street and another two on Dewey Avenue for "colored people." These were said to be the first set of houses designed specifically for African Americans in Jamaica. Fifty more such houses were being erected in 1925 in Jamaica, with William J. Weir appointed as the broker. The homes were selling before they were finished, a clear sign of the demand for good housing for African Americans in Queens.[20]

Jamaica had become the most popular place for African Americans from Manhattan and Brooklyn to relocate for the very same reasons that Whites were attracted to Queens. It was an easy hop to Manhattan by subway, the LIRR, or trolley, and property remained relatively cheap compared to most other parts of New York City. As in Harlem, more Blacks were buying property on streets in Jamaica that had previously been all White. More often than not, should one African American family buy a house on such a street, neighbors quickly put their house on the market for "colored buyers."[21]

As part of New York City, Jamaica had the same school system as that in Manhattan, a source of comfort to families moving from that borough. (School buildings were also newer in Jamaica.) There were six African American teachers in the Jamaica school district (plus a few substitutes) as the 1925/26 school year began, with more likely to come with the opening of the new Jamaica High School. Men from Jamaica had traditionally worked as porters or messengers in lower Manhattan, but job opportunities opened up in Long Island City, a burgeoning area of manufacturing. With the widening of Queens Boulevard and other projects, there was construction work too for African American men. Blacks were being hired by the LIRR as watchmen at grade crossings (accidents at the gates were frequent), positions that had previously been held by new immigrants.[22]

With rents getting ever higher in Manhattan, including Harlem, it was easy to recognize the attractiveness of Jamaica. "Colored men in the real estate field in Jamaica with a vision of the possibilities have interested white builders with large capital," the *New York Amsterdam News* noted. E. & J. Dorf, a large lumber merchant in Queens, had gotten into the home building business for the African American market. The houses sold quickly, and the company decided to put up twenty more. Again, it was William Weir who got the exclusive to sell them; the man advertised regularly in that newspaper, and it appeared to be money well spent. The lumber company was beginning to think bigger, eyeing a spot in the Merrick Park section of Jamaica (near the new high school), which could accommodate two hundred homes.[23]

While such development was business as usual in mainstream real estate circles, it was unprecedented with regard to African Americans. By the end of 1925, it was believed that Jamaica, Queens, was the only suburb in the United States predominantly populated by Blacks. The Milla-Cohn Company, which built homes for both Whites and Blacks, had secured fifty-two additional plots in Jamaica on which to construct houses for prospective African American homeowners. "Many colored men and women suffering the inconveniences of flat life will be inhaling the healthful ozone of the country and pottering around in their own yards," *New York Amsterdam News* reported. With six rooms, steam heat, parquet floors, breakfast nooks, electric kitchen appliances, and built-in ironing boards, the homes were indeed a dream come true for those who could come up with the down payment and afford the monthly payments.[24]

Jamaica remained a magnet for African Americans as financially motivated developers created more housing for them. "The Jamaica of today is a colorful mass of surging humanity," a journalist for the *New York Amsterdam News* observed in 1927, particularly on the town's south side. White real estate agents steered Black homebuyers to that area to try to keep Jamaica segregated, although significant numbers of both Polish Americans and Italian Americans resided there as well. African Americans began moving into Merrick Park, on the south side, around 1910, and the area continued to thrive. The NAACP had recently formed a branch in Jamaica, and the organization would soon play an important role in the pursuit of racial equality across the borough. The total number of African Americans residing in Queens was now estimated to be twelve thousand, with thousands more expected to settle in the borough over the following year.[25]

While Jamaica was the epicenter of the African American community in Queens in the 1920s, Corona was, as the *New York Amsterdam News* put it, "also making a bid to better class of race home seekers." (Corona had been developed on the crown of a hill, hence its name.) Like Jamaica, Corona was well connected to Manhattan by mass transit and was indeed attracting Harlemites wanting more breathing space. In September 1925, twelve hundred of Corona's five thousand residents were African American, with about half of that twelve hundred owning or in the process of buying their homes. Corona's interdenominational Congregational Church served as the hub of the Black community, both religiously and socially, and the Corona Building & Loan Company was helping prospective homeowners get financing. There were few (if any) Black members of the West Side Tennis Club in Forest Hills Gardens, but the Corona Tennis Club had been organized in 1921 by Mrs. Daisy C. Reed, an African American who continued to serve as its president.[26]

With those amenities, plus the fact that a nice two-family home (brick or frame) could be had for $10,000 and a single-family home for half of that, one could see why Corona was a desirable place to live, regardless of one's race. (To that point, Corona was not segregated, a rare thing in those days.) Seeing a show by the Aldridge Players, a drama club, was a popular thing to do; the group was led by Frank Wilson, a well-known playwright. If that weren't enough, Flushing Bay was just a short hop away, a great spot for beach activities and boating.[27]

It's understandable that Corona continued to draw residents, many of them coming from congested Harlem, which in addition to its space constraints had air quality judged to be unhealthy because of the crowded conditions. By February 1927, the African American population in Corona had risen to about three thousand, with two-thirds owning their homes. These houses were not "across the tracks," as they were in many communities, but interspersed among middle-class White-owned houses. The town was getting bigger as more people arrived; the number of retailers and banks were growing along with the population. In addition to the Congregational Church, there were the Episcopal Mission and First Baptist, and the public schools in Corona were modern and considered racially tolerant.[28]

Somewhere on Long Island

Decidedly not racially tolerant was the Ku Klux Klan (KKK, or the Klan), which, as in many other areas of the country, had a visible presence in Queens in the 1920s and early 1930s. The KKK enjoyed marching in parades to promote its message of hate toward non-White Protestants and received permission to take part in the 1927 Memorial Day parade sponsored by the

Jamaica Council. (Sheets and pointy caps were allowed but not masks.) Upon learning about a planned counterattack, however, something that could lead to a full-fledged riot, police attempted to stop the Klan from marching. The police effort failed, however, and the KKK (one thousand Klansmen and four hundred Klanswomen) took part in the parade as planned, although considerable fighting broke out between the group and police for hours.[29]

The incident caused quite a stir, not surprising given the fact that the KKK was not a popular organization in culturally diverse Jamaica. (The Queens chapter of the KKK was based in Ridgewood.) The fraternal organization Knights of Columbus had withdrawn from the parade, not about to march alongside such a hateful group. Apparently in response to the inhospitality shown to them by the police and the Knights of Columbus, Klan members lit a twelve-foot-high cross in Briarwood at Briarwood Road and Queens Boulevard the night of the parade. Local residents tore the cross down and extinguished it.[30]

That might have been the end of the regrettable story, but it wasn't. Another parade—this one to be held on the Fourth of July—was fast approaching, and the "invisible empire," as they were sometimes called, had every intention of marching in their white regalia. This time, however, the Klan's petition to be part of the festivities was denied by police commissioner Joseph A. Warren, who understandably feared there would be disorder should they be allowed to march. The KKK found a lawyer to begin court proceedings to try to get a permit, however, not ready to give up the fight.[31] Despite the attorney's plea, the ban on the Klan was upheld. In place of marching in the Fourth of July parade (which traveled though Woodhaven, Richmond Hill, and Jamaica), the KKK spent the holiday in an open lot "somewhere on Long Island," according to the leader of the local chapter.[32]

Despite the ugly affair, Queens' image as a good place to live regardless of one's race remained strong. Those in the real estate business anticipated that property values in the borough would continue to climb and urged potential buyers to get in on the action before being priced out of the market. Hollis had become a popular neighborhood for ex-Brooklynites, and Flushing was expected to boom because of the planned subway extension all the way to Main Street. The Rockaways couldn't match Coney Island in terms of amusements, but those wanting to live near a beach where they might find a small area of sand on which to sit were increasingly opting for the Rockaways.[33]

While there had been substantial growth in both population and new construction, real estate professionals remembered how the opening of the Queensboro Bridge virtually put the borough on the map. "Queens is in need of more bridges and tunnels," stated Edward A. MacDougall, president of the Queensboro Corporation, aware that his business depended heavily on the ability for people to drive to and from the borough quickly. History showed that both sales and property values rose where there were good transportation options, and he urged city officials to further link Queens to Manhattan, and perhaps the Bronx, by going over or under the water.[34] Bus service had recently been added in a section of Jackson Heights, and houses within a block of that route were selling well.[35]

By 1926, the post–World War I housing crisis in New York City was declared over. Rather than the government, it had been private interests—developers—who had made housing available to all, except for the lowest paid workers. There was considerable interest in Metropolitan Life's project in Long Island City, where rooms rented for $9 a month. (A five-room apartment would thus rent for $45.) More of this kind of project was needed (there was a waiting list of 25,000 applications), but there were legal restrictions regarding how much "low-income" housing could be built and, not incidentally, developers saw more money in single- and two-family homes.[36]

The growth of Queens through the 1920s had much to do with the slow but steady migration of Manhattanites uptown. "The geographical position in relation to the shifting population of Manhattan has undoubtedly been responsible for the advancing real estate market and growth of the borough," noted Carl G. Skog of the Queensboro Corporation. In decades past, Brooklyn was the logical place for disenchanted Manhattanites to relocate, as it was just east of Manhattan's population hub. But since then that hub had moved northward, making Queens appear attractive to Manhattanites seeking what was considered a suburban lifestyle.[37]

A look back at the evolution of Queens since the turn of the twentieth century put things in useful perspective. In 1905, the population of the borough was 180,000, and in 1926 it was almost a million. The growth of Jackson Heights, which was located on the north side of Queens, was especially impressive. In 1906, a family of precisely five people occupied the single farmhouse on the 325 acres of land that would be developed, by the Queensboro Corporation, into the one-hundred-city-block community reserved for six thousand White Protestants. It took half a day to travel to Manhattan, involving a horse and wagon on dirt roads and a dodgy trip across the East River. In 1927, it took twenty-five minutes via the subway tunnels under the river, a true miracle of engineering. In another twenty years, some were predicting, Queens would overtake Brooklyn in population, something inconceivable in the early twentieth century.[38]

32 | QUEENS

Much was made of how the Queensboro Bridge altered the trajectory of Queens, and deservedly so, but the rapid transit lines built six years later arguably had a bigger effect. "Like the opening of the Queensboro Bridge, the beginning of operation of trains through the Queensboro subway on June 22, 1915, marked a distinct epoch in the history of Queens," stated Judge Frank F. Adel, president of the Queensboro Chamber of Commerce. "It was a recognition that the borough was an integral part of the city, destined to play an important part in its future history," he added. There were more than one hundred million riders on the north and south lines in 1926, many of them commuters to and from Manhattan. (The line had recently been extended to Fifth Avenue and Times Square.) The development of Queens closely followed the path of the trains through the borough, clear evidence that the subway had indeed reshaped its built environment. The line extension to Flushing had been delayed a few months because of construction issues, but property values in the neighborhood were already rising.[39]

A Fairy Tale

Queens' past was certainly an interesting one, but it was the borough's future that was seen as truly exciting. John J. Halleran, former member of the Tax Board of New York City and a Queens real estate authority, believed that the recent progress made in the borough was just the beginning of even better things to come. Part of the reason that Halleran envisioned Queens as the greatest borough in New York City was that there was still undeveloped land. Queens would also benefit from the automobile, which had already changed the concepts of time and space, as one could now travel further distances relatively quickly. Because of that, Halleran expected a revitalized Flushing to attract more well-to-do shoppers from the north shore of Nassau County who had been going to Manhattan to buy things. As well, the recent erection of the fourteen-story Bank of Manhattan "skyscraper" on the Bridge Plaza in Long Island City was a harbinger of literally bigger things to come in that area.[40]

With its innovative tenant ownership plan, Jackson Heights too was predicted to continue to grow in the years ahead. Dozens more new shareholders were taking occupancy in apartments in Linden Court, Hampton Court, Hawthorne Court, the Chateau, Willow Court, Plymouth Court, Greystone Apartments, and the Colonial Apartments in 1927. Owners paid about $4,500 for their stock, which could then be resold to a new tenant.

The Jackson Heights Plan, as it was now being called by the Queensboro Corporation, had begun in 1912, when cooperative ownership was virtually unknown in the United States. The ability to own shares in the development (vs. the apartments themselves) at the same cost of renting in Manhattan was proving to be a winning formula. The garden-style layout—and the knowledge that one would not have people of color, Jews, or Catholics as neighbors—was icing on the cake.[41]

Need it be said, not all parts of Queens were as posh or exclusive as Jackson Heights.

In 1926, a lawyer representing a group of African American homeowners in Flushing made an appearance in Queens Supreme Court regarding the construction of their houses. The houses were "constructed very largely of paper," their complaint read, with a court action planned against the builders. Doors were being blown open by the wind, and in one case a doorknob went through a wall. When one of the houses had caught fire, firefighters refused to walk on its roof to extinguish the flames for fear of falling through. The houses somehow passed inspection (money was often exchanged to guarantee such an outcome), but a subsequent inspection revealed that the roofs were indeed made of papier-mâché instead of the recommended material, asbestos.[42]

The following year, State Senator James L. Whitley and his team decided to visit Queens after learning about some of the houses that been recently been built in the borough. Whitley's goal was to have the Tenement House Act revised, as there was little to prevent more unscrupulous builders from putting up flimsy structures to minimize costs. Many such houses had been constructed, it was revealed, and collectively they were considered the worst fire trap not just in New York City but in the entire country. Even if the houses didn't burn to the ground, they would almost certainly attract only those people who couldn't afford to live anywhere else, suggesting they would be the slums of the future.[43]

While the shoddy houses were obviously a problem, the fact that so many African Americans, previously paying egregious rent in Manhattan, became property owners in Queens is an amazing story. The post–World War I housing shortage in New York City had been especially hard on low-income Blacks, as profiteers gouged the most vulnerable. In 1927, just $500 was typically enough for a down payment on a house in Jamaica (about $9,000 in today's dollars), and monthly installments were close or equal to rent payments to a landlord. Jamaica was becoming less dependent on Manhattan for work or play, and old buildings were being demolished to make room for bigger, modern ones. Real estate bargains were said to be getting hard to find in Jamaica, however, making the warnings to "buy now or be sorry" appear to be more than hucksterism.[44]

By 1928, it was clear that the borough's "revolutionary movement" was slowing down, and that too many new houses had been built for Jamaica's White population. The population of the town had reached 135,000, including some 10,000 African Americans. Of those 10,000, reportedly 90 percent were homeowners, an astounding statistic if true. With an oversupply of houses, however, developers were more open to making even more African Americans homeowners. Less scrutiny was paid to a Black family choosing a house in a White neighborhood of Jamaica, and banks' lending policies toward African Americans had become more lenient as fewer loans were being made overall.[45] More homeowners meant more payers of property taxes, after all, and assessments were being levied against all residents to pay for the many improvements being made to the town, notably roads and utility infrastructure.

Although Corona was (generally) happily integrated and Jamaica mostly so, the same could not be said for Elmhurst. Many Whites in that town did not take kindly to a Black family moving in and were not reluctant to express their feelings on the matter. When two African American families moved onto Ninety-First Street between Thirtieth and Thirty-First Avenues, White neighbors made threats of violence against them. Five patrol officers had to be assigned to protect the families after rocks were thrown through the windows. The White neighbors put signs in their windows and yards that read "Negroes—stay away, you're not wanted" and "No colored need apply" and, led by the Elmhurst Manor Community Council, tried to buy the Black families out.[46]

Queens real estate executives and elected officials were hardly ready to stop aggressively promoting the borough in order to extend its phenomenal growth (and make money in the process), however. A barrage of statistics were produced and disseminated in the media boasting the rise in property values (72 percent) and the number of new buildings constructed (125,242) between 1922 and 1927.[47] The level of boosterism could reach magical proportions. "The story of the rapid rise in real estate values in Queens Borough in recent years reads like a fairy tale," Percival Mullikin glowed in 1928. Fortunes had been made "overnight" and property owners "have awakened to find themselves suddenly rich," the PR rep for the Queensboro Chamber of Commerce happily reported.[48] The population of the borough had increased 115 percent between 1920 and 1928, but a bigger rush was coming, as the remaining land would be developed and more transit lines and roads built.[49]

THE REVOLUTIONARY MOVEMENT | 35

Figure 1.3. A 1928 map of first ward of Queens. *Source*: Lionel Pincus and Princess Firyal Map Division, New York Public Library, *Index Map to Volume One. Atlas of the Borough of Queens. Ward 1. City of New York*, New York Public Library Digital Collections, https://digitalcollections.nypl.org/items/05b55110-5b74-0131-f009-58d385a7b928.

Figure 1.4. A view of Randall's Island and Queens from the twenty-seventh floor of River House at Fifty-Second Street in Manhattan in 1931. *Source*: Samuel H. Gottscho, *River House, 52nd St. and East River, New York City. Queens, from 27th floor*, 1931, photograph, Library of Congress Prints and Photographs Division Washington, DC, https://www.loc.gov/item/2018739263/.

This was classic real estate hyperbole, but the puffery got a dose of realism with the October 1929 news that ground had been broken for the long-planned Triborough Bridge. (The idea had been first raised in 1916.) It would take about four years to build the $24 million span connecting Manhattan, the Bronx, and Queens, but all agreed that the bridge would allow drivers to more speedily make their way around much of New York City. Astoria Park was chosen by engineers as the location of the bridge in Queens, and again historical comparisons were made to the opening of the Queensboro Bridge and the rapid transit lines that linked the borough to Manhattan.[50]

No one in 1909 could have anticipated that another bridge linking Queens to one or more boroughs would be considered necessary in just twenty years. The population of Queens was then 250,000, however, and the borough had yet to be "discovered" by real estate developers. Also the automobile was in its early days, and since then millions of tin lizzies had been sold. At a total length of 16,850 feet, the Triborough Bridge would be enormous, with its foundation made strong enough to support an upper deck should traffic demand its construction. All kinds of challenges in building the bridge lay in store—the stock market had just crashed, ushering in the Great Depression—but work would begin soon.[51] It was the beginning of another new era in Queens, and a fitting end to its Roaring Twenties.

An Enforced Holiday

"The last frontier in Queens is about to be attacked," the *New York Herald Tribune* rather startlingly announced in January 1930. What was the cause of such alarm? An almost virgin forest of 370 acres—the last of its kind in the borough—was on the verge of being developed. The tract between Flushing and Jamaica had been a lumber camp, the sole surviving one in New York City. Trees were still cut there, in fact, and the logs processed in the onsite sawmill, a throwback to an earlier time.[52]

Should the Board of Estimate approve acting borough president John J. Halleran's plan for the area, however, the forest would be no more. Neatly arranged streets had been laid out on Halleran's map, which real estate developers would have to use when building their houses. There was one other remaining forest in Queens—Hillside Park, which was owned by the city—but that too would likely fall into the hands of developers if what's past is prologue.[53]

After a great run in the late 1920s, real estate in Queens was taking what Fred G. Randall termed "an enforced holiday." Every year since 1925, record after record had been broken in terms of the value of property sold, mortgage loans taken out, and buildings erected. The stock market crash of October 1929 put a rude stop to all that activity. Now, in 1930, there was no money to lend, slowing new construction considerably. (Some buyers were paying all cash.) Real estate professionals believed that the "holiday" would be short one, however, and that Queens was in a strong position for future growth.[54] The Triborough Bridge and Midtown Tunnel were destined to make Queens even more accessible, and a myriad of other projects (notably the Queens Boulevard subway and the upper deck of the Queensboro Bridge) were in the works, which boded well for the borough.

All agreed that the 1930s would be a good decade for Queens if it was even remotely similar to the 1920s. The transformation of Queens in the Roaring Twenties was nothing less than remarkable, evidenced by the fact

Figure 1.5. The Triborough Bridge, linking Queens, Manhattan, and the Bronx. *Source*: Historic American Engineering Record, *Triborough Bridge, Passing through Queens, Manhattan & the Bronx, Queens subdivision, Queens County, NY*, 1968, photograph, Library of Congress Prints and Photographs Division Washington, DC, https://www.loc.gov/item/ny1799/.

Figure 1.6. The Triborough Bridge and Randall's Island, the river-bound plot of land amid Queens, Manhattan, and the Bronx. *Source*: Historic American Engineering Record, *Triborough Bridge, Passing through Queens, Manhattan & the Bronx, Queens subdivision, Queens County, NY*, 1968, photograph, Library of Congress Prints and Photographs Division Washington, DC, https://www.loc.gov/item/ny1799/.

Figure 1.7. A female toll taker at the Queens Midtown Tunnel around 1943. She and eleven other women had replaced men who had enlisted or went to work in war plants. *Source*: Alfred T. Palmer, *New York, New York. Mrs. Joilet Jones [. . .]*, 1943 [?], photograph, Library of Congress Prints and Photographs Division Washington, DC, https://www.loc.gov/item/2017872111/.

that its population had doubled. It was almost hard to remember what the borough was like immediately after the Great War. In 1920, there were no fewer than 565 farms in Queens, whose acreage (14,148 acres) comprised about one-eighth of the total acreage of the borough. Almost all of those farms were now communities with much higher property values as houses, apartment buildings, churches, schools, theaters, and businesses. Many of the new residents had come from Manhattan and the Bronx seeking "open spaces," a fast-disappearing commodity as Queens itself became more urban.[55]

Also disappearing with the development of Queens were the geographic lines between the borough's many villages. Before the building frenzy of the 1920s, towns were quite distinct and generally disconnected. (Trolleys and a rather primitive LIRR were the main transportation options.) The construction of thousands of houses, apartment houses, and businesses had changed that, with the village boundaries now running into each other. The term "sprawl" had yet to be applied in real estate, but that is essentially what took place as borders became increasingly blurred. While the borough had been developed far more and in a shorter span of time than anyone could have anticipated, pride was taken in the fact that the oceanfront had been largely left for recreational purposes.[56]

The hard times of the Depression were affecting many Queens residents in profound ways. A third family could often be found living in a two-family house as a way for the owners to make some much-needed income. This was a violation of the Multiple Dwelling Law, which classified a dwelling in which three families lived under one roof as a tenement. That law had been passed in 1901, however, and houses built in the 1920s were much bigger than apartments built in the late nineteenth century.[57] Despite being illegal, many an attic was being used as a "bootleg apartment," so many in fact that it was impossible for the city's Tenement House Department to locate them all. The old law needed to be amended, even city officials believed, if only because the current one was unenforceable.[58]

A peripheral problem of residents living in such apartments was that they were unlikely to be counted in census figures. The population of Queens, as with the other boroughs of New York City, was thus underreported to some extent, although it was impossible to say by how much. The official count of the 1930 census revealed that the "native white" population had increased from 351,985 to 793,530 over the previous decade while that of the "foreign born" had risen from 111,676 to 266,150. The number of African Americans in Queens had increased from 5,120 to 18,609—a more than tripling of that population. Queens had become more diverse in terms of both ethnicity and race, a trend that appeared likely to continue.[59]

The church was an important component of everyday life for African Americans in Queens; 5,156 Black residents in the borough (out of 18,609) were reportedly churchgoers, a 1931 survey revealed. There were forty-three Black churches in seven denominations (the statistic alone making it clear that the borough's religious institutions were not integrated at the time), with Baptists leading the way with nineteen churches. Eighteen of the forty-three Black churches were in Jamaica and South Jamaica, four were in Corona, and another four were in Flushing. (Jamaica, Corona, and Flushing had the largest Black populations.) There were also a number of "storefront" churches, although these were not counted in the survey.[60]

The 1931 survey, conducted by George S. Hobert of the Greater New York Federation of Churches, revealed other interesting facts about African

Americans in Queens. It was the worst days of the Great Depression, but Blacks in the borough were doing relatively well, at least in terms of where they lived. There were few tenements compared to the other boroughs, and three-fourths of African American residents now owned their homes (although they were heavily mortgaged). The properties were valued between $7,000 and $12,000, about average for the borough.[61]

Although the heyday of the Klan was in the 1920s, in Queens and elsewhere, members occasionally made their ugly presence felt in the early 1930s. In November 1932, five hundred members of the "bedsheet bigots," as the *New York Herald Tribune* referred to the group, had taken to attending Sunday services at the Grace United Christian Church in Long Island City, which happened to be located in the Black section of that neighborhood. Any get-together of the Klan was at some level odd, but these were especially puzzling. They were surprise visits, for one thing, an exception to the Klan's historic reliance on announcing a mass gathering well ahead of time to get as much publicity as possible. As well, the group made no mention of its feelings toward people of color, Jews, or Catholics. Rather, it was Communism that now presented the main threat to its version of the American way of life. Leaflets proclaiming "Communism will not be tolerated" were distributed outside the church, along with others stating that "the Klan rides again." Similar leaflets had recently been distributed in Jamaica, South Jamaica, Ozone Park, Richmond Hill South, and other communities (by boys paid fifty cents to do so). All of these communities had a decent-sized Black population, however, and no Communist meetings were known to have taken place in any of them.[62]

It was unlikely that any members of either the city's Department of Hospitals or the Queens County Medical Society were bedsheet bigots, but some believed that each organization discriminated against both Blacks and Jews. The staff of the new Queens General Hospital had been named in 1933, but, curiously, none were African American and Jewish doctors. Dr. J. Edward Lowry and Rabbi Joshua L. Goldberg pointed this out to the hospital's grievance committee, but an investigation into the matter revealed no favoritism, according to the committee's report. There were a number of prominent Black doctors in Queens County, some of them members of the medical society, raising the question of what qualifications they didn't possess to earn a position on the staff.[63]

Dr. Lowry had raised that very question earlier at a meeting of the Corona branch of the NAACP, which was becoming more active in fighting discrimination of various sorts in Queens. The Jamaica branch of the

42 | QUEENS

Figure 1.8. Building Y of the Creedmore State Hospital in Queens Village in 1933. Like other hospitals in Queens and the other boroughs, administrators were reluctant to hire African American physicians. The psychiatric institution that was founded in 1912 still exists. Source: Historic American Buildings Survey, *Creedmore State Hospital, Building Y, 80-45 Winchester Boulevard [. . .]*, 1933, photograph, Library of Congress Prints and Photographs Division Washington, DC, https://www.loc.gov/item/ny1981/.

NAACP too was busy; it was looking into the matter of African Americans being excluded from jury service in the county. Jurors commissioner William Blake denied the charge, saying, "There is no such thing as a color line in the drawing of jurors." In fact, African Americans had sat on juries in both County Court and the Queens Supreme Court, Blake pointed out, challenging the claim that they were being underrepresented in jury selection. (Besides being a resident of Queens, one had to be over twenty-one years old, own property, and be able to read and write to be eligible for jury duty.)[64]

Others felt that relief from the Depression was not being provided on an equal basis. The Fourth Assembly District Women's Democratic Club of Queens, a predominantly White organization based in Jamaica that combined politics with welfare, tended to ignore the residents of South Jamaica, a predominantly Black community, according to magistrate Benjamin Marvin. South Jamaica needed food, clothing, and other essentials during the economic crisis, Marvin told the group at its tenth anniversary party in 1933, every bit as much as the "needy whites" that were receiving such relief from the club.[65] The local organization was, however, acting consistently with most New Deal programs, which routinely discriminated against Blacks, a concession President Roosevelt made to get the legislation through Congress.[66]

The Flushing Plan

It's safe to say that African Americans were not welcome at another club in Queens that went by the name the Friends of New Germany. The group, which was part of the Ridgewood Grove Sporting Club based in Glendale, consisted of "Hitlerites," that is, those who subscribed to the philosophies of the Nazi Party, which was firmly in power in Germany by 1934. President Roosevelt had ordered a boycott against the importing of German goods as a response to Hitler's antisemitic doctrines, and it was this issue that served as the basis for members of the Friends of New Germany to get together in April of that year.[67]

There was clearly no shortage of Hitlerites in the New York City area at the time, as 4,500 of them squeezed into the Ridgewood Grove Sporting Club hall, with another thousand having to stand outside the building. Presiding over the ceremonies was Louis Zahne, who proposed a resolution calling for an end to the president's boycott "in the interests of continued friendly relations between the United States and Germany." All but one of the attendees voted yes to the resolution (some actually said "jawohl"), with the lone dissenter promptly pummeled and then literally thrown out of the hall by the uniformed "guards of honor."[68]

Compared to what was about to take place outside the hall, however, things inside were relatively peaceful. Just a few blocks away at the Queens County Labor Lyceum, a much different kind of group was holding its own meeting—a group that consisted of the Jewish War Veterans, the Blue Shirt Minute Men (an anti-fascist organization), the Communist Party, and the American Committee to Aid Victims of German Fascism. When that meeting ended, the attendees decided to walk over to the Ridgewood Grove Sporting Club to make their feelings known about the boycott and Nazism in general. Police had been tipped off about the close proximity of these very different meetings, and more were called in when it appeared there could be trouble.[69]

It was difficult for the more than 150 police officers to completely separate the coalition of Jews, anti-fascists, and Communists from the thousand or so Hitlerites lingering outside the hall, however. "The opposing forces in the street jeered at each other and engaged in numerous fist fights," a journalist on the scene wrote. A "stench bomb" was thrown, but with the two groups so close together it did not have the desired effect. (The bomb thrower was arrested, as were four others, on the charge of disorderly conduct.) Intermittent fighting continued in the neighborhood during and following the Hitlerites' meeting, after which everyone went home.[70]

As Joachim Remak discussed in a 1957 article in *Journal of Modern History*, the Friends of the New Germany first began in 1933 as the Friends of the Hitler Movement. It was an American offshoot of the German Nazi Party whose mission was to disseminate Nazi propaganda in the United States. Both German and American citizens belonged to the group, which in 1936 evolved into the Amerika-Deutscher Volksbund or German-American Bund. The Bund's most infamous rally was held on February 20, 1939, when more than twenty thousand people gathered at Madison Square Garden. Despite attracting such a large crowd, the Bund's efforts backfired, according to Remak. "The Bund's attempts to rally the German-Americans to the Nazi cause failed ingloriously," he wrote, thinking the organization instead "helped to alert America to the Nazi danger."[71]

Until then, however, it would be international peace and harmony, or at least the pursuit of it, that would reign in Queens for the remainder of the 1930s. "The greatest world's fair in history" was coming to Queens, announced a page-1 story in the *New York Times* in September 1935, a commemoration of the 150th anniversary of the full establishment of the United States Government. (George Washington had become president in 1789, with his inauguration in New York City, which was then the capital of the United States.) The chosen site for the fair was a thousand-plus-acre tract of land stretching from Flushing Bay to Kew Gardens. The opening date was set for the ambitious project—April 30, 1939—with two six-month seasons planned, the latter in 1940. The estimated $40 million investment was undoubtedly a large one, but it was considered money well spent. Such a world's fair would stimulate the economy of not just New York City but the entire nation, it was believed, thus helping the country recover from the lingering Depression.[72]

Figure 1.9. The decidedly futuristic Trylon and Perisphere at the 1939–1940 New York World's Fair in Flushing Meadows. *Source*: Gottscho-Schleisner Inc., *World's Fair [. . .]*, 1939 or 1940, photograph, Library of Congress Prints and Photographs Division Washington, DC, https://www.loc.gov/item/2018750315/.

Many approvals had to be made for the bold enterprise, of course, and New York City's contribution would be development and use of the land in Queens. The city already owned much of it and planned to obtain the remainder by condemning neighboring properties. After the fair, the area would be turned into Flushing Meadows Park, it was revealed, further incentive to get the go-ahead from city, state, and federal officials. (There actually were open meadows along Flushing Bay at the time.) The site was also chosen for its waterfront, which allowed large boats to port, and for the new bridges, parkways, and subway to Jamaica that were already in progress.[73]

Most important, perhaps, city parks commissioner Robert Moses was strongly in favor of what was called "the Flushing plan." Moses had already begun work on developing the area into a park and golf course, as he was determined to rehabilitate the site that had been known as the Corona Dump (even though the site was in Willets Point), Fitzgerald's "valley of ashes" in *The Great Gatsby*. Moses and the rest of the fair's steering committee imagined "a new white city" rising on Flushing Bay, a reference to the beautiful

Figure 1.10. Fairgoers could also catch a glimpse of the World of Tomorrow at the art deco Ford Motor Building. *Source*: Gottscho-Schleisner Inc., *World's Fair, Ford Motor Building. Entrance*, 1939, photograph, Library of Congress Prints and Photographs Division Washington, DC, https://www.loc.gov/item/2018735496/.

World's Columbian Exposition in Chicago in 1893. There was much to be done over the next three and a half years, however, the first step being filling in large areas of marshland so roads and structures could be built.[74]

As soon as the Flushing plan was announced, real estate activity in Queens jumped, as speculators anticipated land values, especially for business property, would rapidly increase due to the upcoming fair. Values were already slowly rising as the general economy improved, but this was expected to be a major boost for the borough. That the fair would cover such a large area was particularly exciting for the real estate community. The western end of Flushing was doing well with home building, but the Kew Gardens-Forest Hills area was lagging, making it likely that those neighborhoods would benefit most. Work had begun on the Grand Central Parkway Extension to connect with the Triborough Bridge, an additional reason to be bullish on real estate prospects, both commercial and residential, in that section of Queens.[75]

A year later, the Great Depression in the recent past and the world's fair in the near future, new home developments were popping up across

Queens. Six hundred homes were going up in Bayside Hills on what had been the Belleclaire golf course; the developer, Gross-Morton, was blazing the trail of mass construction, a model that Levitt & Sons would perfect on Long Island after World War II. (The latter had recently developed Strathmore-at-Manhasset on the North Shore of Nassau County.)[76] Flushing and Jamaica were active as well in 1936, not surprising as they were not far from what would be the new Flushing Meadows Park in a few years.[77] Some in the business were cautioning against overbuilding in the neighborhoods surrounding the fairgrounds-to-be, however, worried especially about the number of large hotels and apartment houses that were being constructed. Would there be high demand for them after the fair ended in the fall of 1940? they wondered. Would this be another bust following a boom?[78]

The Heart of the Negro Section

Until then, however, it was full speed ahead for the making of Queens. John H. Morris, the president of the Long Island Real Estate Board, certainly was enthused, even delighted, to see the plotlines of Flushing Meadows Park (later Flushing Meadows Corona Park) take shape. From a bird's-eye view, its location couldn't be better, he believed, as it served as a geographic bridge between Manhattan to the west and Long Island to the east. (It was also roughly the geographical center of New York City.) In actual distance, the park would be just three miles from Manhattan's Central Park, Morris noted, predicting the new park in Queens would even outdo Frederick Law Olmsted's nineteenth-century masterpiece. "It will surpass Central Park in perhaps every aspect for which a park is created," he said in 1938, the bonus being that there was much land remaining around it ripe for development.[79]

Boosters of Queens took every opportunity to tell the world how much housing had already recently been created in the borough. Queens was "the greatest home-building center in the nation," the Queensboro Chamber of Commerce claimed after compiling building permit statistics for 1938. Queens accounted for a full quarter of all new residential construction in the United States for the first eight months of that year (and 74 percent of that in New York City), its data showed, and 14 percent of the nation's total in dollar value. These numbers didn't include construction projects for the upcoming world's fair, making that icing on the cake.[80]

Queens was in fact drawing national attention for its phenomenal growth since World War I and for what promised to be a tremendous international event. The fair in Queens would bring "better trade relations and improve business conditions," MacDougall foresaw, something of considerable value to the country as the situation in Europe worsened. Queens would be brought onto the global stage over the next few years, a long way from the borough's marginal status just twenty years earlier. "During 1939 and 1940 visitors in great numbers will see for the first time the new Queens transit facilities—parkways, bridges, tunnels and other improvements, costing several million dollars," he proclaimed, seeing nothing but greater progress for the borough.[81]

Things were not as majestic in another area of Queens, however. Just a short distance from where the World of Tomorrow was being created, a "slum clearance" project was being planned, with a low-cost housing development to rise in its place. The predominantly African American neighborhood of South Jamaica was considered one of the worst areas in the city, state, and nation, with FDR himself approving an appropriation of more than $2 million to clear the "ghetto." (The United States Housing Act of 1937 was the legislation that paved the way for such projects.) The United States Housing Authority considered using the funds for a similar project in Harlem but opted for Queens, with the world's fair no doubt playing a role in its decision. (The Harlem River Houses had been completed a year earlier.) Millions of visitors might pass through Jamaica (it was just 6.3 miles away along the Grand Central Parkway) and think less of Queens, New York City, New York State, and the United States after seeing the racial and economic divide.[82]

The site for the development, which was planned to house 448 low-income families (about 1,600 people), had not yet been chosen, but it would be, as the *New York Amsterdam News* described it, in "the heart of the Negro section." (Irish Americans too lived in the area.) Demolition of a number of blocks of "sub-standard dwellings" would be required, but that was a fraction of what Robert Moses had proposed in his own plan for the area. Moses, who despised what he considered urban blight of any kind, envisioned the construction of 16,000 rooms at a cost of more than $16 million with parks, playgrounds, street widenings, a school building, and fire and police departments bringing the estimated cost to almost $20 million. One could see why the "power broker" wanted to essentially obliterate South Jamaica and put up something entirely new. The overcrowded, unsanitary area, especially around the railroad tracks, was "a slum of the most dejecting kind," according to the newspaper, with widespread prostitution just one of its many social ills.[83]

THE REVOLUTIONARY MOVEMENT | 49

By April 1939—just when the world's fair opened its gates—the three-square-block site for the South Jamaica project had been selected and work had already begun. Although condemned on the basis of being unfit for human habitation, the tenements that would soon be razed were still mostly occupied. The owners of the seventy-five properties, who had been holding out for higher prices, were warned that they had better sell them fast lest they lose their whole investment. (They had previously refused to make any repairs.) Local civic organizations, including the Jamaica Council of the NAACP, had lobbied for such a project for several years and were thus happy to see that it was underway.[84] Mayor Fiorello LaGuardia and the recently appointed New York City Committee on Negro Welfare were also glad that action was being taken as overflow from Harlem continued

Figure 1.11. Mayor Fiorello LaGuardia (left), conferring with Col. F. C. Harrington, the new Works Progress administrator, in December 1938. Although diminutive in stature, the "Little Flower" (Italian, *Fiorello*) was a larger-than-life character during his dozen years as mayor of New York City. *Source*: Harris and Ewing, *New York Mayor Confers with New WPA Administrator [. . .]*, 1938, photograph, Library of Congress Prints and Photographs Division Washington, DC, https://www.loc.gov/item/2016874645/.

to spill over into South Jamaica, as well as Bedford-Stuyvesant, Brownsville, and the Navy Yard sections of Brooklyn.[85]

Not happy about the project was George Harvey, borough president of Queens. Harvey, who appeared to be an avowed racist—he was even alleged to be a member of the KKK—voiced his objections on the basis that streets would have to close because of the construction, creating "a traffic hazard." Alfred Rheinstein, chair of the City Housing Authority, responded to Harvey's complaint by informing him that improving the neighborhood (and borough) was the larger goal and that the area would ultimately be safer for both vehicles and pedestrians. (No traffic problem had resulted from the construction of the Harlem River Houses or at another project in Williamsburg, it was pointed out.) Based on his record, Harvey simply didn't want good money spent on providing African Americans with modern, fireproof, affordable rental apartments (complete with central heating, hot water, electric refrigerators, and gas stoves), some surmised, even if they were residents of his borough.[86]

Now that the public housing development in South Jamaica was going to be built, however, local African Americans wondered if they could get jobs on the nine-and-a-half-acre construction site.[87] An average of three hundred workers each day would be needed over a period of three or four months, a nice source of income for those lucky enough to be offered employment. As well, being employed was one of the requirements to be selected as a tenant for what was now being called South Jamaica Houses, with other considerations including family size, number of rooms currently occupied by the family, current rent amount, and the previous year's income.[88]

Getting an apartment at the South Jamaica Houses would be especially fortunate given an increasing housing shortage not just in Queens but across the country. Both renting and buying properties was becoming more difficult with war having been declared in Europe in September 1939. "People remember what housing conditions were during the World War," remarked Frank S. O'Hara, a Jackson Heights realtor who had been president of the Real Estate Association of the State of New York, speaking of World War I. It was looking increasingly clear that the United States would have to enter this new war at some point, in which case almost all new construction would have to be put on hold so building materials could be used for military purposes. Simply finding a place to live would become a challenge if what's past is prologue, as Americans mobilized to join the defense effort.[89] Another season of the world's fair was in the wings, but the world of tomorrow was beginning to look like a perilous one.

THE REVOLUTIONARY MOVEMENT | 51

CHAPTER TWO

The Common Good

Peace through understanding.

—Theme of the 1964–1965 New York
World's Fair, Flushing Meadows Park

In February 1960, Governor Nelson Rockefeller announced that a new cooperative apartment complex would be built on the site of the 170-acre Jamaica Racetrack, which had shut down the previous year. Within two days, three thousand requests for applications poured into the offices of the United Housing Foundation, the sponsor of the huge housing development.[1] The project would be called Rochdale Village, named after the town of Rochdale, England, notable for conceiving the "Rochdale principles of cooperation," whose aim was to serve "the common good." With the complex's affordable pricing and attractive housing for working-class families with moderate incomes, it could be seen why there was so much interest in what was perceived as "a city within a city." When Rochdale Village opened in 1963, it was the largest private housing cooperative in the world, and it remains a highly desirable place to live.[2]

Serving the common good was certainly an honorable aim, and something that the entire borough of Queens strived for through the World War II and postwar era. Queens was already the most diverse borough of New York City, an ideal foundation for both race and ethnicity to emerge as major points of contention, particularly as related to housing. The struggles taking place over these years in Queens symbolized what the nation as a whole was going through as it tried to fulfill the Founding Fathers' noble ideals grounded in democracy and equality—a pursuit that proved to be a highly challenging one.

We're Americans

For Queens, the new decade got off to a very exciting start—the opening of a tunnel connecting the borough with Manhattan in November 1940. Although $68 million was spent to build the giant tube ($1.5 billion today), it was considered to be a wise investment given the saved time driving between the two boroughs. Commuters from Jackson Heights could be in midtown Manhattan in twelve to fifteen minutes and back home for dinner in the same amount of time, assuming they owned a car. (It was uncertain whether buses would be allowed to use the tunnel.) As well, getting to and from Grand Central Terminal, Penn Station, and the Broadway district had become easier and quicker than using the Queensboro Bridge. Real estate values in Queens were expected to rise as the borough became more desirable for those from other parts of the city seeking more living space but thinking Long Island, Westchester, Connecticut, and New Jersey were a little too far from town.[3]

To that point, the Queens-Midtown Tunnel, as it was called, was expected to increase the population of the borough, perhaps dramatically. While the population of Queens had not grown in the 1930s at the same rate as in the 1920s (100 percent), there were 20 percent more residents in the borough in 1940 than there were in 1930, according to the new census figures. Queens was benefiting as the population of New York City continued to shift eastward. Of all new homeowners in Queens between 1936 and 1940, according to the Federal Housing Administration, 44 percent were borough residents while 19 percent came from the Bronx, 18 percent from Manhattan, 18 percent from Brooklyn, and 1 percent from Staten Island.[4] Queens was also becoming increasingly diverse; beginning in 1940, large numbers of West Indian immigrants moved into the borough, soon followed by Chinese immigrants due to the repeal of Chinese Exclusion Act.[5]

Real estate people in Forest Hills and Kew Gardens were especially excited about the new vehicular tunnel, as those neighborhoods were just a little south of where it fed from Manhattan into Queens. It was a twenty-minute drive to and from Manhattan, quite a short commute for those wanting live in the "suburbs" but stay within the city limits. The new

54 | QUEENS

1,687-acre Flushing Meadows Park was just a few minutes away, although as of yet just the New York City Building with its winter sports was open for visitors. Forest Hills High School had opened in 1937, yet more reason why local brokers expected to be seeing more families wanting to rent or buy in the area. Unlike the bridges linking Queens and Brooklyn to and from Manhattan, which were free, there was a toll for the tunnel (twenty-five cents, which remained the price until 1972). Authorities presumed there would be plenty of drivers willing to pay a quarter, however, as it was likely that the three-minute ride saved both time and gasoline.[6]

There were many other reasons why there were more new homes built in Queens in 1940 than in any other county in the United States. Most of the new single-family houses in Queens were priced around $5,000, which qualified buyers for a Federal Housing Administration mortgage, and they were available in the latest styles and on larger plots. In the 105-square-mile borough, there were 34 neighborhoods (Astoria being the most populated by far), 90 Roman Catholic parishes, 241 Protestant churches, and 50 Jewish centers. For the automobile-less, there were express subways, 139 LIRR stations, and 40 bus routes. Finally, Flushing Meadows Park was just one of 50 parks in the borough, the most popular among beachgoers being Jacob Riis Park on the Rockaway Peninsula.[7]

In addition to the 6,511 single- and two-family houses built in 1940 in Queens, numerous apartment buildings were rising. By the spring of 1941, almost every apartment was being rented as soon as it became available, the beginnings of what would be a wartime and postwar shortage of living space in the borough and in many parts of the country. Builders would work with architects, landscapers, and interior decorators to create aesthetically pleasing structures, something that Queens had been recognized for since the formation of the Jackson Heights garden apartments in the 1910s.[8]

Following the Metropolitan Life Insurance Company's surprising success with low-priced multiple housing in the early 1920s in the Thomson Hill section of Long Island City, apartment building developments spread throughout the borough, with no sign of the trend slowing down.[9] In fact, builders were working overtime to complete as many as projects as possible while they had the materials to do so, as the national defense effort had begun. Workers from across the country were heading to areas where the tools of war were produced, including Queens, Brooklyn, and Nassau County.[10] Alongside the busy market for apartment rentals, buyers were willing to pay more for a house than they would have before the war buildup, even $20,000 if that's what it took.[11]

The rush to build and purchase a new house soon proved to be warranted. In August 1941, FDR signed Executive Order 8875, creating the Supply Priorities and Allocations Board, which drastically limited new residential construction in the United States. Only housing deemed essential to the defense effort could be initiated, with price restrictions and a complicated application process also put in place. Fortunately, however, both Queens and Brooklyn were in a designated "defense area," meaning a certain number of new houses could be built in those boroughs if they were to be used by people who were contributing in some way to the war effort.[12]

In Queens, the impact of the war in Europe could be felt well beyond the universe of real estate. Ethnic Americans demonstrated their loyalty to the United States in many ways, perhaps none more so than those of Italian heritage. After staying neutral, Italy entered the conflict on the side of the Axis powers in June 1940 when Benito Mussolini, the country's dictator, declared war on France and Great Britain. Just two weeks following that decision, ten thousand Italian and Italian Americans used their annual Society of St. Paolina celebration in Long Island City to show which side they were on. "We're Americans," many participants told reporters, a notable feature being the lack of native costumes at that year's event, making that declaration as clear as possible.[13]

Greeks in Queens took a different tack by demonstrating support for their native country. The Italian Army invaded Greece in October 1940, followed by a German invasion in April 1941. Two weeks after the Germans occupied Greece, fifteen hundred Greek Americans gathered at the Greek Orthodox Church of St. Demetrios in Astoria to observe Easter. A march through the Greek section of Astoria preceded the service, with ten thousand spectators waving American, Greek, and British flags. (Great Britain had defended Greece in the latter invasion.) Supervising the proceedings was Captain David Zimms of the Astoria police precinct. "Mention that I am of German descent," he told a reporter at the scene, adding that his two patrolmen, Joseph Gatto and Joseph Sulmonetti, were of Italian descent. "There is no race hatred in Astoria," Zimms stated. The highlight of the day was the donation of an ambulance for Greece, which local residents had contributed money toward.[14]

A couple of months later, an old-fashioned, All-American block party was held in Laurelton, Queens, for five hundred soldiers from Mitchel Field and Fort Totten. (Twenty-five sailors from the USS *Seattle* joined the festivities.) Sixty-four families along 229th Street between 130th and 131st Avenues hosted the party by making enormous quantities of home-

56 | QUEENS

cooked meals. A local member of the New York office of the United Service Organizations had orchestrated the event, but it was the residents of the street who prepared and served the food. An Italian American supplied "a typical Italian menu from antipasto down," including a gallon of chianti. None other than the Tommy Dorsey Band headlined the block party, with the soldiers and sailors jitterbugging with young women who lived on the street. The penultimate part of the bash was the stringing together of a very long conga line, followed by the singing of "The Star-Spangled Banner."[15]

Lots of Fun

The bombing of Pearl Harbor and the entry of the United States into the war in December 1941 obviously redirected the trajectory of everyday life in Queens and elsewhere in the country. Americans instantly became "war-minded," and residents of the borough contributed to the effort in a myriad of ways. There are clear signs that 1941 was a major turning point in the history of Queens, as it gained national and even international attention due to its many defense plants. The war would ultimately change the makeup of the population of the borough. New residents of Queens had for decades come almost exclusively from the four other boroughs of New York City, but that had changed in 1941, according to a survey made by the Forest Hills-Kew Gardens Apartment Owners Association. In the twenty-five apartment houses in that neighborhood, 13 percent of the tenants had recently arrived from other states, with another 2 percent coming from foreign countries (including Switzerland, Batavia, and Cuba). Many of the former were undoubtedly defense workers, and most of the latter were European refugees.[16]

Also recently arriving in Queens from Europe was one Kurt Frederick Ludwig, a professional Nazi operative. Ludwig created a spy ring by recruiting a handful of people sympathetic to the Nazi cause from various German American groups in Queens, including the youth section of the Bund. The ring gathered material such as the position and movement of Army personnel, location of military airports, and armed forces morale and relayed the information to the enemy abroad (in secret writing). The group was caught, however, and put on trial for espionage in February 1942.[17] One of the members of the ring was Lucy Boehmler, an eighteen-year-old Maspeth high school student who told the judge that she worked as a Nazi spy for $25 a week because it was "lots of fun."[18]

THE COMMON GOOD | 57

Figure 2.1. Students at Flushing High School doing "commando" training as part of their wartime physical education courses in October 1942. *Source*: William Perlitch, photographer, *High School Victory Corps [. . .]*, 1942, photograph, United States Office of War Information, Library of Congress Prints and Photographs Division, Washington, DC, https://www.loc.gov/item/2017694742/.

A few months later, near LaGuardia Field, the homes of seven German "enemy aliens" were raided by the FBI as they too were suspected of espionage. Quite a variety of contraband—radios, cameras, binoculars, guns and ammo, German marks, and Nazi propaganda—was confiscated. When questioned after being brought to Ellis Island, the men said they refused to fight for the United States as they had relatives in the German Army, with one stating that he hoped Germany would win the war. The Navy, meanwhile, had recently taken over the Brewster Aircraft in Long Island City, as it appeared that most of its employees were enemy aliens.[19] Between December 1941 (the entry of the United States into the war) and October 1943, the FBI had arrested almost two thousand German aliens in New York City, one of them a Queens housewife who claimed she was a second cousin to Rudolf Hess.[20]

Of course, most German Americans in Queens and elsewhere were as patriotic as anyone else, but anti-German sentiment was pervasive. The

Figure 2.2. A victory garden in Forest Hills, June 1944, where local residents grew fruits and vegetables to augment the nation's wartime food supply. *Source*: Howard R. Hollem, *New York, New York. Victory Gardening at Forest Hills, Queens*, 1944, photograph, Library of Congress Prints and Photographs Division Washington, DC, https://www.loc.gov/item/2017865736/.

younger generation, who had been born in the United States rather than in Germany, were particularly inclined to distance themselves from their ethnic heritage because of the war. That was made clear in December 1942 in the case of the German Second Reformed Protestant Dutch Church in Elmhurst. The church had been around for more than a century, established by prosperous German farmers in the early nineteenth century, but the congregation had in recent years shrunk significantly as its younger members lost their allegiance to German culture. The church decided to become a Reformed Dutch congregation, and the transfer was made official by a court order.[21]

Things were much worse for Japanese Americans, particularly on the West Coast, where thousands were being incarcerated in camps. Even in New York City, however, those of Japanese descent were viewed suspiciously and mistreated, more so in fact than those of German or Italian heritage because of Pearl Harbor, racial prejudice, and it being illegal for Asians not born in the United States to become naturalized citizens. In the early 1940s, the

Japanese community in New York City was small and dispersed, with about fifteen hundred people of Japanese descent (half that of a few years back). One of them was Yoichi Hiraoka, a famous xylophonist who lived in Kew Gardens. After Pearl Harbor, however, Hiraoka, who had an American wife and two children born in the United States, could no longer work because he was Japanese, as federal law stated.[22] One thirty-five-year-old woman of Japanese descent who had been born in the United States hung herself in Malba, Queens, in 1944 after being continually subjected to verbal abuse and the stoning of the house where she worked as a maid.[23]

It could be easily seen how those of German, Italian, and Japanese heritage felt the need to publicly demonstrate their patriotism during the war years. Seeing an opportunity, three unscrupulous entrepreneurs invited a number of Queens storekeepers and businessowners of German, Italian, and Hungarian descent to join a "patriotic society." (The Kingdom of Hungary was also part of the Axis.) For just $25 or $50, one received a certificate attesting to their loyalty to the United States, which they could proudly display. In their pitch, solicitors insinuated that unless their prospects formally proclaimed their loyalty, they could be perceived as engaging in Nazi or fascist activities, making it not surprising that sales of the certificates (which read "The love of country will always be the ruling influence of my conduct") were brisk. The whole enterprise was a racket, and the three men were arraigned on a number of charges in Queens Special Session Court in September 1942.[24]

An authentic display of patriotism among ethnic Queensites took place in June 1944 at a German American bond rally in Ridgewood. There was in fact a German American War Bond Committee for New York State, which had already raised tens of millions of dollars. The committee pledged to raise $10 million for the Fifth War Loan, kicking off the drive at the RKO-Madison Theater in Ridgewood, where bonds were sold to moviegoers. German Americans, like Italian Americans, Japanese Americans, and African Americans, were vigorous supporters of the bond campaign throughout the war.[25]

African Americans from Queens contributed mightily to the war effort, both abroad and on the home front. In May 1943, it was announced that Belle Calhoun, a twenty-nine-year-old African American woman from Jamaica, had been selected as "Miss Negro War Worker" in a nationwide contest. Calhoun had never missed a day of work as a chief wire machine operator at the Lincoln Wire Company and was a member of the company's labor-management committee. As recognition, Calhoun would receive a $25 war bond at the upcoming Negro Freedom Rally to be held in June at Madison Square Garden.[26]

While unquestionably patriotic, Queens women were not averse to raising a ruckus when they felt it was warranted. Rent control in the borough was a particularly thorny issue. Rather oddly, New York was the only major city in the United States in which the Office of Price Administration (OPA) did not mandate rent control, as federal officials felt it wasn't necessary. In lieu of legislation, there was a "gentleman's agreement" among apartment owners in the borough to keep rents at March 1942 levels for the duration of the war. Voluntary cooperation was in the spirit of rent control, owners agreed, and they were true to their word for a year or so.[27]

By the summer of 1943, however, it was becoming clear that apartment owners in Queens were raising rents or taking steps to make it possible. Reports of rent hikes or lease terminations were coming into the mayor's office by the hundreds from tenants in many neighborhoods, including Rego Park, Jackson Heights, and Forest Hills. With no new construction and family incomes rising due to the robust war economy, demand for medium-priced apartments was extremely high—too much temptation for owners knowing they could make more money in an open market. The vacancy rate of apartments in Queens was just 2 percent—the lowest of all five boroughs—leaving renters with few options.[28]

Not happy that the agreement was not being kept, twenty-five Forest Hills homemakers took direct action, marching into the OPA offices in the Empire State Building in Manhattan in July 1943. (Another twenty-five had stayed home to watch each other's children.) The women held letters from their landlords that announced their new, higher rent or that their lease would not be renewed (allowing the owner to relet the apartment at a higher rate). The letters appeared to be solid proof that the owners were being less than gentlemanly in their agreement, but the OPA simply told the women it would investigate the matter.[29]

A Wonder City

With the war over in September 1945, residents of Queens, like all Americans, turned their attention to a new set of challenges and opportunities. Some believed Queens was ideally positioned for the postwar future, building on the amazing progress it had made over the last quarter century. Frank O'Hara, former president of the Real Estate Association of the State of New York (and a Jackson Heights resident), was especially gung ho on the prospects of the borough. O'Hara foresaw Queens emerging as "a wonder city" and "the talk of the country" in the next twenty-five years due to its impressive assets—land, industry, transportation, airfields, and, most of all, people.[30]

Figure 2.3. A 1945 map of Queens. *Source*: Lionel Pincus and Princess Firyal Map Division, *Hagstrom's Map of Queens N.Y. City*, New York Public Library Digital Collections, https://digitalcollections.nypl.org/items/50baa1a0-2e27-0137-cef4-3bd3d93c39ee.

This was classic boosterism, naturally, but as arguably the most knowledgeable student of Queens real estate, O'Hara recognized how far the borough had come in a relatively short period of time and its great potential. The man got into the business right after serving in World War I, when Queens was primarily rural rather than urban. Dirt roads traveled by wagon were the norm, and demands to City Hall for modern transit were ignored on the basis that there was no need for such a thing in an area dominated by cornfields. That all changed when Edward MacDougall and others laid the foundation for the garden apartment development in Jackson Heights, literally and figuratively putting Queens on the map.[31]

Now, however, with its template in place, Queens was poised to surpass Manhattan as the jewel of New York City, O'Hara predicted. Beautiful apartments and houses, big office buildings, grand hotels, major department stores, and magnificent theaters would all appear in the borough over the next quarter century, he maintained, much of this driven by the continued eastward migration of New Yorkers in search of more space. Queens was still in its youth, O'Hara reminded readers, with much growth and development to take place as it matured.[32]

A wonderful vision, certainly, but builders were more interested in maximizing profits than creating the kind of majestic landscape O'Hara imagined. With a lingering housing shortage in Queens alongside postwar inflation, builders were dividing their lots, knowing there would be buyers for smaller houses with not much of a yard. A 1946 land survey revealed that there were 250,000 vacant lots in the borough, enough space to construct housing for 500,000 additional families. With an active market and rising prices, developers intended to squeeze in as many residents as possible onto the land they owned. Veterans were getting married and starting families in droves, an ideal scenario for the real estate community.[33] The diversity of Queens also continued along an upward trajectory; significant numbers of Germans emigrated to Queens from their devasted country (the borough already had a large German population), and a fair share of the spouses of Chinese American veterans relocated to Queens via the War Brides Act of 1946.[34]

Rather unexpected news in 1946 was that there would be some four thousand new residents of Queens who had interests other than settling down into domestic life. After getting off the ground in San Francisco, the United Nations was moving to Lake Success in Nassau County, which was near the border of Queens. Finding housing for the four thousand UN personnel and their families (some of them people of color) was no easy thing given the shortage and racial segregation. Wanting to avoid an international incident, William O'Dwyer, the new mayor of New York City, took charge of the operation. Through a complex arrangement, a new apartment house development in Jamaica (now considered Briarwood) would be quickly built to accommodate the diverse group, it was announced, and what would be called Parkway Village soon came into existence.[35]

By July 1947, families from a dozen different countries had moved into Parkway Village, which was the first privately financed large-scale housing project in New York City. Many more families from the four corners of the earth were on the way, making the community itself a uniting of nations. (The first brick and concrete building constructed bore the names Albornoz, Cansdale, Duhamel, and Obrdik.) Children from Ecuador, Iran, France, England, the Netherlands, and China could be seen playing happily together, a real-life example of what their parents were trying to achieve on a global level.[36]

However, that kind of harmony could not be found in another part of Queens at the time. In 1946, Sophie Rubin sold her six-room brick house in the Addisleigh Park section of St. Albans for $10,500 to Samuel Richardson, who happened to be African American, but a neighbor filed an injunction against the sale. In 1939, Rubin had signed a covenant with other property owners in the area to not rent, sell, or give her property to anyone who was not White. This was despite the fact that the neighborhood was racially mixed. (Count Basie and Lena Horne were just a couple of the notable African Americans who lived there.) The judge in the case had no choice but to grant the injunction, as courts in New York State and the Supreme Court had previously upheld the legality of such covenants, despite their being clearly discriminatory. An appeal was filed, however, taking the case to a New York appellate court.[37]

While lawyers for each side made their arguments, details about the case surfaced. When Rubin broke the covenant (which was binding until 1975), she was in a hurry to sell her house. She had tried to find a White buyer but was unsuccessful, and she had already bought another property in a different community. There were 472 homes in Addisleigh Park, about half with restrictive covenants. Forty-five African American families had moved into the neighborhood, buying houses from those who had not signed a covenant. Addisleigh became known as an area of Queens that was "going colored," hence Rubin's difficulty in selling her home to a White person. The origins of the covenant had much to do with an adjoining, more affordable neighborhood called Merrick Park, which had already become racially mixed.

Foreseeing spillover of African American families into their neighborhood, thirty residents of Addisleigh Park signed the original covenant, with a second one signed in 1942 by two hundred property owners.[38]

With the war having been fought on the basis of preserving democracy by defeating Nazi racism and fascism, however, it was becoming increasingly difficult to justify residential segregation in Queens County. In fact, the Northern Boulevard Project—a huge development built by the New York City Housing Authority for veterans, located near Idlewild Airport—was integrated by design. Ex-GIs and their families, most of them White but some African American, began moving into the barracks-like buildings in late 1946. Although probably not the dream home they had imagined, the families were happy to leave their crowded apartments until finding a place of their own.[39]

A good number of African Americans in Queens had found their dream home, or at least one they owned, a 1947 survey revealed. According to *Aspects of Negro Life in the Borough of Queens*, a report issued by the Urban League of Greater New York, 31 percent of African Americans in the borough were owners of the homes they occupied. Expectedly, home ownership correlated with areas with the highest African American population, which were East Jamaica, Corona, and Flushing. (The total number of African Americans in the borough was estimated at 33,000.) Home ownership among African Americans in Queens far exceeded that of the four other boroughs of New York City: 21 percent of African Americans in Staten Island owned their homes, 8 percent in Brooklyn, 2 percent in the Bronx, and 0.4 percent in Manhattan (mostly Harlem). Compared with Whites, African Americans tended to purchase older homes, the study also found.[40]

Undoubtedly, few African Americans owned homes in Jackson Heights, which had long been a stronghold of WASPs barring people of color and Jews. Attempts to keep the community restricted continued after World War II, even for those who had helped win the war. The city's Board of Estimate had not expected there to be much objection to the construction of a new medium-income rental housing project for fourteen hundred veterans and their families in Jackson Heights. Mayhem ensued in October 1947, however, when two hundred people showed up at a board meeting, some supporting the project and some strongly against it. The latter consisted of homeowners in the community who complained that the development would lower property values and strain public services. The backstory was that local realtors had apparently warned residents that the project would bring Black and Jewish tenants into WASPy Jackson Heights, advising them to tell the board to put thing in Woodside.[41]

THE COMMON GOOD | 65

A Non-Bias Plan

There were signs, however, that such forms of discrimination were gradually breaking down, in part due to the budding civil rights movement. As well, more progressive thinkers were attempting to advance race relations through interracial events, that is, gatherings at which both Whites and African Americans were welcome. One such event was an interracial art exhibit sponsored by the Queens branch of the Urban League in 1948. Eighteen leading African American artists including Jacob Lawrence and Gordon Parks lent their works to the show that was held at the Jamaica Jewish Center.[42]

More good news came when the case involving the St. Albans property sale was overturned. The injunction against Sophie Rubin's sale of her house to Richardson was upheld by two appellate courts, as neither had the power to ban restrictive covenants. But in 1948 the United States Supreme Court ruled that covenants against minority groups could not be enforced by lower courts, and the New York State Court of Appeals reversed the lower court's decision. Richardson owned the house, in other words, although now he wasn't so sure that he wanted his family to live in Addisleigh Park. "I just want to know that it is possible for Negroes to buy property wherever it is put up for sale," he told a reporter.[43] The two-year court fight ended rather fittingly when the neighbor who had filed the injunction decided to sell her own property in Addisleigh Park and move somewhere else.[44]

However, if the racist neighbor wanted a new house in Queens, she had better move quickly. By the fall of 1950 new curbs on residential construction were put in place as the United States became involved in the Korean War. Many apartment renters in Queens had hoped to become owners of the affordable single-family houses springing up in suburbs across America (notably Levittown in Nassau County), but this latest development dashed their plans. The rental market in the borough was thus a very active one, as it was unclear how long this latest war would last.[45]

The continually rising population of Queens was a major factor in the challenging housing situation in the borough. Roughly seven hundred thousand armed forces personnel had returned to New York City after the war, many of them soon getting married and having children. A wave of migration and immigration, particularly from Puerto Rico, had brought that number to about a million. Since 1940, the largest rate of growth among the five boroughs was in Queens at 14.3 percent, surpassing that of Staten Island (10.3 percent), the Bronx (8.3 percent), Brooklyn (6.2 percent), and

Manhattan (3.4 percent). (The national rate of population growth between 1940 and 1948 was 10 percent.)[46]

The extension of the Eighth Avenue subway, which had been completed in 1933, also literally paved the way for the population growth of Queens. The 1950 census showed that there were 248,678 more residents of the borough than in 1940, with more than 80 percent of that increase within close proximity of the Eighth Avenue line. There remained undeveloped land in Jackson Heights, Forest Hills, Flushing, Jamaica, Bellerose, and Cunningham Park, attracting builders and then families from other boroughs and from older neighborhoods in Queens. The amount of vacant property in Queens far exceeded that in the other boroughs; there was more than three times as much as in Brooklyn and nearly six times as much as in the Bronx. There was no vacant land in Manhattan.[47]

Development opportunities alongside subway service (linked to bus lines) thus made it not surprising that Queens was seen as a desirable place to live. The population of the borough had tripled between 1920 and 1950, adding more than a million residents and more than four hundred thousand dwellings. Some areas of Queens had experienced a decline in population over these three decades, however. Out of a total of 704 census tracts, 222 sections lost people, notably in older areas such as Long Island City or where there was little or no new construction such as Astoria and Sunnyside.[48]

While Queens was becoming more integrated, it was still news when a new housing development accepted people of color. Housing was offered on "a non-bias plan," according to the *New York Times* in 1951, reporting the construction of a new interracial garden apartment complex to be called Parsons Gardens, located smack in the middle of the borough.[49] If there was news to be reported about African Americans and housing, it was more likely to be about "slum clearance," which the city was pursuing on a massive scale throughout the boroughs. Eliminating blight and providing adequate housing for those of low and middle incomes were the goals, the prime example in Queens being Queensview, a 728-family nonprofit cooperative in Long Island City. Queensview, which won a design award from the Queens Chamber of Commerce, was intended for those above public housing level, filling a real need for those who could not pay the high rent being asked by most landlords in the borough.[50]

Public housing was in fact accounting for much of the development of Queens and the other boroughs in the early 1950s. Not coincidently, in what was considered White flight, many city folks were fleeing to the suburbs—Nassau, Suffolk, Westchester, and Rockland Counties. The city's non-White population was noticeably rising (by 62.4 percent through the 1940s) and that, combined with the baby boom, was driving many White families to seek greener pastures. Non-Whites tended to be lower income, making issues of class just as important as those of race in the population shift. With the Korean War winding down by late 1952, however, suburban-like homes were being built and sold in Queens. A brand new three-bedroom, two-bath split-level could be had for $26,900 at The Oaks development in Bayside, for example, complete with a two-car garage and outdoor patio.[51]

Like anywhere else in America, integration of communities often didn't come easy, including in the supposedly progressive North. Even in culturally diverse Queens, sparks sometimes flew when a person of color moved into an all-White or predominantly White neighborhood. That certainly was the case in 1952 when an interracial couple rented a place in the Marine Terrace Apartments in Astoria. Things were initially fine, but soon the married couple received hate calls and letters, some threatening their lives. Klan-like tactics were used, not unlike those found in the Deep South. A meeting was quickly called by the Urban League to address the problem in relation to broader discrimination against marginalized communities in Queens housing.[52]

Meanwhile, what was labeled urban renewal continued at a fast pace, with action being taken in all boroughs save for Staten Island. In 1951, the New York City Housing Authority asked the Board of Estimate to condemn 159 acres of slum property to clear the way for nine low-rent housing projects, three of them in Queens (all in South Jamaica).[53] The following year, it was the Redfern Houses near Far Rockaway that replaced a designated slum area that had been known as Shanty Town. The modern housing project consisted of five six-story buildings with 360 apartments, with first dibs going to war veterans and those who had called Shanty Town home.[54]

Another notable construction project in Queens in 1952 was the restoration of the former New York City Building in Flushing Meadows Park. The building had served as an ice skating and roller rink following the 1939–1940 World's Fair until it became home to the United Nations General Assembly in 1946. (The Security Council remained in Lake Success.) The UN had found a permanent home in Manhattan, and city officials decided to restore the rink. Returning the building back to what it had been took some doing, however, as 175 tons of steel and about one hundred thousand cinderblocks had to be disposed of. The sixty flagpoles that circled the building and bore the flags of member nations were given new homes in playgrounds across the city.[55]

68 | QUEENS

Given the long history of Queens, it wasn't too surprising that artifacts from the past occasionally surfaced in construction projects. Still, excavators working on Horace Harding Boulevard and 225th Street in Little Neck, laying the foundation for a department store, bank, supermarket, and a few other stores, did not expect to uncover four tombstones dating back to the early nineteenth century. It was the burial ground of the Cornell family, who had settled in the area in the early 1700s. One of the tombstones was of Samuel Cornell, who, sadly, died at age twenty in 1841.[56] The inscription on the tombstone read:

Here lies a youth in prime of life
By death was snatched away.
His soul is blest and gone to rest,
Though flesh is gone to clay.
He is gone and forever his life's sun is set,
But its golden beams linger to comfort us yet.
He has gone in the fulness of beauty and youth.
An emblem of virtue, a witness for truth.[57]

Underneath the inscription read the haunting line, "Strangers: remember you must die." Perhaps heeding those words, the developer fenced in the four tombstones and placed a historical marker that can be seen today.[58]

Not for Sale

Working around the occasional forgotten grave marker, developers continued to provide new housing in Queens through the 1950s. Newer houses were in greater demand than older ones, something reflected in prices. By the mid-1960s, it was predicted, there would be little or no suitable land left in the borough to develop, although one could, of course, knock down the old to put up something new (and usually bigger). The outskirts of Queens would be filled in over time, it was expected, as there were still opportunities in areas along Jamaica Bay. The borough's primary appeal—suburban-style living with a short, inexpensive commute to Manhattan—remained unchanged.[59]

What had changed over the decades were the demographics of the borough and of New York City. Between 1950 and 1957, the non-White population of the city had increased by 41 percent while the number of Whites fell 6 percent, a major shift in historical terms. African Americans from southern states were migrating to northern cities, both to seek higher wages and escape social unrest stemming from integration. As well, the number of Puerto Ricans in New York City had doubled over this same time period, although the Census Bureau didn't quite know how to classify them in terms of race. (Some were sorted as "Negroes" and others as Whites.) Queens, because of its lower rents and real estate values, led all boroughs in the increase in non-White population, with a 129 percent jump (compared to just 4 percent in Manhattan).[60] A sizable population of Japanese immigrants first settled in Queens in the late 1950s, further diversifying the borough.[61]

A 1958 survey conducted by the Community Council of Greater New York provided additional reasons why so many people were deciding to call the borough home. Compared to all the other boroughs, according to the survey, which covered seventeen different neighborhoods, residents of Queens had a higher median family income and were less likely to be on welfare. As well, children in Queens were less inclined to get in trouble with the law, the data showed, a point of interest given that juvenile delinquency was a major concern at the time. With such positive findings, was it any surprise that the population of Queens had risen by 375 percent since 1920?[62]

Was all well in Queens in the late 1950s? Hardly. Low-income city projects—the outgrowth of slum clearance—could be hotbeds of racial tension, especially among teenagers connected with gangs. Queens may have ranked low on juvenile delinquency rates, but one might not have guessed that based on an incident in March 1957 at the Queensbridge Houses, where fifteen hundred families lived. A father and his teenage son were clubbed by some youths, followed by a fight between a group of Whites and African Americans. Many arrests were made, and ten New York City police officers were assigned to twenty-four-hour duty at the public housing development until further notice.[63]

Meanwhile, a new group calling itself the Queens Fair Housing Committee formed to try to stop discrimination in private housing. The committee consisted of members of four Queens civic groups: the Urban League, B'nai B'rith, the NAACP, and the American Jewish Congress. The New York State Legislature was considering a fair housing practices bill that would make discrimination in private housing illegal, but loopholes remained. Property owners were still redlining (the discriminatory practice in which certain groups were contained in specified residential areas) and using restrictive covenants, and the committee sought to make those practices an ugly part of the borough's past.[64]

70 | QUEENS

Figure 2.4. The outdoor playground of the nursery school at the Queensbridge housing project in 1942. *Source*: Arthur Rothstein, *Queens, New York. Nursery School at the Queensbridge Housing Project. Outdoor playground*, 1942, photograph, Library of Congress Prints and Photographs Division Washington, DC, https://www.loc.gov/item/2017833284/.

The racial problems in Queens housing were so acute that they made national news. In January 1959, Edward R. Murrow hosted a radio program addressing the issue as part of a CBS series called *The Hidden Revolution*. The piece focused on race relations in Springfield Gardens (once home to a large spring), which had been all-White until African Americans began moving there a few years earlier. White and African American residents were interviewed, after which a panel of experts assessed the situation. While there was some conflict in Springfield Gardens, there were also cases where racial "harmony" could be found. The villains in the story were real estate agents who tried to drive White residents out of the neighborhood through "blockbusting"—a scare campaign warning that homeowners' property values would plummet with the arrival of African Americans. Whites would sell low and African Americans would buy high, turning a tidy profit for the agent.[65]

The radio broadcast lessened the use of such nefarious tactics that fostered segregation in some neighborhoods of Queens. A civic group consisting of community members from Springfield Gardens, Rosedale, and Laurelton asked Caroline Simon, New York's secretary of state, to do what she could to stop blockbusting and panic selling. Her office was responsible for licensing real estate agents, so it was in her power to take disciplinary action against someone who coerced an owner to sell their property in a fraudulent manner. (Beyond blockbusting being unethical, there was no evidence that an influx of African American homeowners lowered property values.) Backed by the secretary of state, the civic group was combating both blockbusting and banks' practice of not offering mortgages to Whites wanting to buy property in integrated neighborhoods. Fifty block captains had been appointed to report any infractions and to distribute signs to residents that read, "Not for sale, we believe in democracy."[66]

Blockbusting continued in the Ridgewood-Glendale area, however, a byproduct of the busing of African American and Puerto Rican students from overcrowded schools in Brooklyn's Bedford-Stuyvesant to underutilized schools in Queens.[67] Persistent discrimination against people of color not just in housing but also employment and education made some wonder whether the 115,000 African Americans in Queens were making progress in the struggle for equal opportunity. There were more African Americans in Queens than in any other borough of New York City except Manhattan, but they remained largely concentrated in the lower-income areas of Jamaica, Corona, St. Albans, Long Island City, and the Rockaways. Integration of other neighborhoods was gradually taking place, but considerable de facto segregation remained, an understandable source of frustration.[68]

The busing of African American and Puerto Rican students from Bedford-Stuyvesant to Ridgewood and Glendale was proving to be an especially thorny issue, with all parties seemingly unhappy with the city's Board of Education.[69] Residents of those two Queens neighborhoods were further upset when they got news of a proposed new zoning regulation. The homes in Glendale and Ridgewood would be "destroyed" by the new zoning code, local leaders fretted, believing it would lead to the construction of big housing projects. Blacks and Jews often came with such projects, they knew, more cause for alarm. James Felt, the chair of the City Planning Commission, calmed an angry mob of residents who swarmed into City Hall, explaining that the new zoning would actually prevent the big apartment buildings and the kind of neighbors they didn't want.[70]

The xenophobia and prejudice being displayed by some Queensites was in opposition to the profound diversity of the borough and city in which they lived. Data from the 1960 census showed that Queens had a larger percentage of first- and second-generation Americans than any other borough, quite a thing given the number of immigrants or children of immigrants in New York City. Except for Staten Island, about half of the people in each of the boroughs had been born abroad or had at least one parent who had been. As a bonus, the 1960 census provided principal countries of origin for first- and second-generation Americans in each borough. For Queens, the order was Italy, Germany, the Soviet Union, Poland, Ireland, Austria, Great Britain, Hungary, Czechoslovakia, Greece, Canada, Romania, and France.[71]

Interestingly, the White flight in New York City (and many other major cities in the United States) through the 1950s barely affected Queens. About 1.3 million Whites moved out of New York City over the course of the decade while 436,000 African Americans and Puerto Ricans moved in, but this swap was almost entirely limited to Manhattan, Brooklyn, and the Bronx. (Staten Island actually gained White residents.)[72] There could be many conclusions made from these numbers, the most sanguine of them being that residents of Queens were more racially tolerant than those of the other boroughs. That Queens was generally a cheaper place to live likely had more to do with White residents staying put, however.

Indeed, glaring inequalities in housing, employment, and education remained in Queens, cause for a greater number of civic organizations to try to do something about them. One was the North-East Queens Fair Housing Committee, a group committed to bringing equality in housing to Bayside, Flushing, Douglaston, Little Neck, and Whitestone (named after a large white rock that had stood near the shore). The organization gathered a list of apartment houses, garden apartments, cooperatives, and one- or two-family houses in those neighborhoods that did not discriminate on the basis of race. Those looking for a place to live could use the list, free of charge.[73]

Despite Murrow's radio broadcast and the efforts of the secretary of state, some residents of Springfield Gardens were determined to keep African

THE COMMON GOOD | 73

Americans from moving in. Since moving into his two-family house in the fall of 1962, Richard Ellis along with his wife and daughter had endured two bombing and numerous rock throwings, fortunate only that nobody had been injured. To make matters worse, local police (the 105th Precinct in Creedmore) were not inclined to do much about the attacks. ("You're a pioneer, what do you expect?" the desk officer had told Ellis when he brought in fragments of the second bomb.) Acting much like a pioneer defending his homestead, Ellis, a forty-eight-year-old mechanic, promptly bought a 20-gauge shotgun, declaring, "I'm not going to quit my home."[74]

I Didn't Want to Get Involved

Race did not appear to be involved in the murder of Catherine Genovese, but it was clearly no ordinary crime. Hundreds of murders were and are committed in New York City every year, but the slaying of Genovese, and even more the circumstances surrounding it, stood out like no other. The basic facts of the story seemed clear. A murder was committed in the early hours of March 13 in Kew Gardens. The victim was Catherine "Kitty" Genovese, a twenty-eight-year-old bar manager (or "nightclub hostess") who was returning to her home at 82-70 Austin Street after working at Ev's Eleventh Hour in Hollis at around 3:20 a.m.[75]

Six days after the slaying, police arrested twenty-nine-year-old Winston Moseley and charged him with homicide. Moseley, a business (or "computing") machine operator from South Ozone Park (also in Queens), had confessed to the crime, explaining his action as simply having "an urge to go out and kill somebody." Six days after that, a judge committed Moseley, who was married and had two children (and occasionally went to church), to Kings County Hospital for psychiatric observation.[76]

It took a couple of weeks for police and reporters to reconstruct (or construct, as it would turn out) the bizarre details of the case. It was believed that Genovese, who shared her apartment with a female friend who was not home at the time, observed a man at the far end of the parking lot when leaving her red Fiat. Nervous, Genovese proceeded down Austin Street toward a police call box, but the man caught up to her on a sidewalk and attacked her with a knife. The sidewalk, in front of a two-story apartment building and a two-story Tudor-style building, was well lit, a fact that would become important to the case. Genovese screamed, waking up neighbors in the two buildings. Lights went on, windows were opened

74 | QUEENS

(it was a very cold night), and voices could be heard. "Oh my God. He stabbed me! Please help me! Please help!" Genovese reportedly shouted, causing one neighbor to yell out of his window, "Let that girl alone." The attacker backed off and turned around, his plan to kill someone that night thwarted, at least for the moment. Genovese made her way to her feet and struggled to get to her apartment. Lights went out and windows were shut, the terrible incident seemingly over.[77]

The man, now wearing a hat to disguise himself, soon returned and stabbed her again. "I'm dying! I'm dying!" Genovese cried, alerting neighbors once more. The assailant fled, driving away in his white car that was parked nearby. Genovese, meanwhile, had crawled to the foyer of the two-story building, seeking safety inside. The inside door was locked, however, and Genovese had nowhere to go. Determined to kill her, the attacker again returned to the scene, stabbing Genovese for a third and fatal time. He then raped and robbed her of the $49 she had in her possession.[78]

Police reportedly received the first call at 3:50 a.m. from Karl Ross, one of Genovese's neighbors, who had apparently heard and perhaps even seen some of what occurred. Why had others not called earlier? "I didn't want to get involved," one man told police, who were said to have responded to the call in just two minutes. It was later disclosed that Ross phoned the police not from his own apartment but from that of a neighbor, and only after he had called a friend and asked her what to do. (He was very drunk, it later was disclosed.) Some reasons the thirty-seven other witnesses did not call included "We thought it was a lovers' quarrel," "I was tired," and repeatedly "I don't know." The term "witness" itself implied a person who saw or heard something, of course, perpetuating the belief that Genovese's neighbors had acted shamefully. New Yorkers were, as a whole, horrified by what had apparently taken place. "Consternation swept the city when it was learned two weeks after the killing that 38 persons had seen or heard the attack on Miss Genovese but had done nothing to summon help until she was dead," wrote David Anderson, one of the reporters who covered the story for the *New York Times*.[79]

That Genovese's neighbors ignored her loud screams, as reported, has since been disputed, but the bystander effect or Genovese syndrome is a legacy of the event, which became a cultural phenomenon. It crystallized latent feelings residing in the consciousness of both the city and nation. New York was out of control, many felt after hearing about what happened in Queens, the city now too big, too impersonal, and too violent. No one could be trusted, not one's neighbors or even the police. The "system" was at fault, our society as a whole suffering from some sort of pathology. The sense that we were a group of individuals, rather than a community in the true sense of the word, was nothing short of devastating, making New Yorkers and many other Americans feel that they were essentially alone in the world.[80]

The Genovese murder, and more so her neighbors' reported lack of response or even interest, fit with the developing view that people no longer cared about each other. The event confirmed what some already believed, making real the depressing notion that our moral and ethical foundation had somehow crumbled. The story would turn out to be largely untrue, a fabrication, yet it was instrumental in advancing the focus on the self that would become a key cultural marker of the late 1960s and 1970s. As well, women were empowered by the event and others like it, with the murder ironically serving as an agent of the budding feminist movement. To this day people maintain their belief in the Genovese syndrome despite the facts proving it as a myth, a clear sign of the power the event held in the public's consciousness.[81]

The Olympics of Progress

Given these events taking place in Queens and in other urban areas, it was fitting that the chosen theme for the 1964–1965 New York World's Fair to be held in Flushing Meadows Park ended up being "peace through understanding." The fair was originally intended to be a tercentenary celebration of New York City, as City Hall had in 1959 begun thinking about a way to celebrate the three hundredth anniversary of the British takeover from the Dutch in 1664, that is, when the city became known as New York. Another world's fair seemed like an ideal way to commemorate the occasion, as 1964 would also be the twenty-fifth anniversary of the beloved 1939 New York World's Fair.[82]

Although "peace through understanding" ultimately became its official theme (a reference to the Cold War), the fair was really mostly about dollars and cents. In fact, from the very first world's fair in 1851, London's Crystal Palace Exhibition of the Works of Industry of All Nations, global expositions celebrated, above all, commerce. World's fairs themselves were business ventures, although they had a rather dismal financial history. Chicago's Century of Progress in 1933 made a little money (about $700,000 on a $47 million investment), but this was a rare exception. New York's

76 | QUEENS

1939–1940 fair lost $22 million, a much more representative financial performance for major expositions. Despite this track record, Robert Moses, who served as president of the event, was confident that this fair would be a profitable one. Moses was, by late 1963, forecasting seventy million in attendance over the course of two six-month seasons, a number that would generate $120 million in profits—a hefty amount, especially considering most fairs finished in the red.[83]

Moses even knew where profits from the fair should go, proposing that $23 million of it be allotted to build a seven-mile chain of parks in Queens as a "gift to the city." Moses consistently and freely admitted that the main attraction would actually come after the fair, when Flushing Meadows Park would be considered the most important park in the city or, as he described it, "a new sort of super Central Park." Moses had tried to achieve this very thing after the last New York fair but failed when all revenues from the event went back to the city to pay off as much of its loans as possible.[84] As Moses told *Reader's Digest* in September 1964, "Parks are the big thing in my life, and I decided to turn this dump into a great park. When they started planning the 1939 World's Fair, I saw my opportunity. Well, I made the fairgrounds all right, but the fine park never materialized, because we didn't have the money."[85]

Just as in 1939, Moses was considering this fair, as Marc H. Miller later wrote, "a high-budget, high-priority enterprise that he could latch onto for advancing his main business: park and roadway construction." Given a second chance, Moses was determined to not let "the fine park" slip out of his hands, planning for the World Fair Corporation (WFC) to build it before the site was turned back over to the city. "With all due respect to City Hall," Moses said, "if we hand over our profits to the city government and ask them to make the park, the park will never be built."[86]

By viewing the fair as one more opportunity to remake New York City and leave another lasting personal legacy, however, Moses was blatantly ignoring the WFC's lease with the city for Flushing Meadows Park, which clearly stated that any profits from the exposition would first go to education. "All net revenue [from the fair] shall be paid to the city and shall be used for the restoration and improvement of Flushing Meadows Park, and the balance of such revenue remaining thereafter shall be used by the City of New York for educational purposes," the lease stated. Moses's "restoration and improvement" encompassed no less than 2,816 acres worth of park stretching for more than seven miles, a mammoth project obviously beyond the parameters of the lease. Moses even kept a color map of the future park

THE COMMON GOOD | 77

in his office, detailing the exact location of its lawns, picnic areas, athletic fields, day camp, zoo, botanical gardens, and archery courts, along with a step-by-step timetable for its completion in 1967.[87]

Knowing that huge profits to build his park relied on realizing the forecasted attendance, Moses and his WFC colleagues quickly became experts at the art of hyperbole. Almost as soon as he was appointed president, Moses announced that the fair would be the first "billion-dollar" exposition in history, a figure that became permanently attached to the event. This was a catchy factoid but actually a bit of a stretch, including $95 million in construction costs for roadways to the fair, $120 million to improve the Throgs Neck Bridge, and millions more to build an adjacent baseball stadium. Moses also repeatedly referred to the event as "the Olympics of progress" or "the Olympics of global industry" but was outdone by his colleague Thomas J. Deegan, who claimed that the fair would be "the greatest single event in history." (Deegan was, not surprisingly, in charge of public relations.)[88]

A big part of fair officials' wild optimism was the response to their advance ticket sales. Discounted tickets for $1.35 (sixty-five cents off the regular two-dollar fare for adults) were sold from April 22, 1963 (exactly one year before opening day) until February 29, 1964. Fair officials reported that one million discounted advance tickets had been sold by September 1963 and two million sold by November. Advance tickets became a very popular Christmas stocking stuffer that year, so much so that another million discounted tickets were reportedly sold over the holidays. Fair officials proudly announced that almost four million tickets had been sold by January 1964—75 percent more than they had expected—and an incredible twenty-eight million advance sale tickets (three times what the WFC had expected) when the discounting program was ended.[89]

Major exhibitors, such as IBM and United Airlines, had bought 100,000 advance tickets each for employees, and AT&T bought a whopping 250,000, helping the advance ticket program considerably. With advance ticket sales almost three times the actual attendance of Seattle's 1962 Century 21 Exposition, critics who had consistently predicted the New York exposition would lay an egg were hushed. Some in the media began talking about the possibility of 100 million people coming to the fair, translating to a population on an average day equal to that of Wichita (230,000), and on a really good day, that of Washington, DC (764,000). Maybe the fair would be the biggest single event in history after all.[90]

If Moses's ultimate purpose for the fair was to build a world-class park, his penultimate objective was to create a lasting infrastructure for

78 | QUEENS

lots of people to get there. Although the jet set would get whisked to the fairgrounds by helicopter from the Pan Am building in Manhattan, many more would be tossing the kids in the back of family sedans and station wagons. The early 1960s was a golden age for the American automobile, of course, as our postwar love of the freedom of the road was fueled by new and better highways.[91]

Moses, already famous (or infamous) for making New York City more vehicle-centric (and, correspondingly, less pedestrian friendly), seized the opportunity presented by the fair, using the forecasted high attendance figures to sell the need for additional and improved highways and bridges (and parking lots). This was the second time Moses was leveraging a world's fair to build or improve bridges, having used funds earmarked for the 1939 fair to construct the Whitestone Bridge (which was completed twenty-four hours before opening day of that exposition).[92]

As soon as Flushing Meadows Park was named the likely site for the fair in 1959, Moses announced that $85 million was needed to upgrade the city's highways and transit system. A huge highway construction program was in the works by the end of 1961 (Robert Caro called it "the biggest, most lucrative schedule in the history of New York or any other metropolis"), with funds allotted for no less than five different highway projects in Queens.[93]

One early project involved a six-lane traffic link in Forest Hills, a decidedly bucolic urban neighborhood, drawing the wrath of many local residents and the Long Island Safety Council. Millions of dollars were soon allocated to extending what was officially called the Clearview Expressway but known to critics as "the road to nowhere" (a nod to another of Moses's herculean projects, the Triborough Bridge, which during the years it took to build was often referred to as "the bridge to nowhere"). Millions more were approved to improve the Grand Central Parkway and the Van Wyck Expressway, the other major arteries near the park. The fair's impact on Queens's transportation grid and relationship to the new Shea Stadium next door closely paralleled the infrastructure changes made for the previous fair, specifically connecting Grand Central Parkway to the new, Moses-built Triborough Bridge and completing what would become LaGuardia Airport.[94]

As commuters faced horrendous traffic snarls for the next three years of construction, Moses's highway expansion plan and the man responsible for it were widely rebuked. New Yorkers remained rather ambivalent about the upcoming fair in large part because the principal roadways of Queens had been turned into "the world's biggest parking lot" (a moniker that stuck for the Long Island Expressway). "For the present at least," *Time* magazine noted in October 1962, "New Yorkers are most aware of their fair in terms of the bumper-to-bumper embolisms the highway expansion program is causing in the borough of Queens."[95]

To add insult to injury, road construction was continually behind schedule and in danger of not being finished by the fair's opening day. The New York Mets could not occupy the new stadium being built next to the fairgrounds in the spring of 1963 as planned because it too remained unfinished and behind schedule. Even worse, parts of the Long Island Expressway were buckling and cracking from the huge vibrations caused by construction associated with the fair, and air pollution in the area had risen considerably because of all the building going on. Local mechanics were busier than ever, repairing the wheels, springs, and other parts of cars damaged by the rough roads, and motorists detoured to areas of Queens they never knew existed and often could not find their way out of. Moses's plans for the city of the future were, as usual, wreaking havoc with the city of the present.[96]

Figure 2.5. A stretch of the LIE in Queens in May 1974. Given the smog surrounding the area, it's understandable that the EPA was concerned about the well-being of local residents. *Source*: Hope Alexander, *The Long Island Expressway in Queens*, National Archives Identifier 555744, Local Identifier 412-DA-13292, National Archives at College Park-Still Pictures (RDSS).

As millions of dollars were poured into New York's private transportation grid, leaders of the city's public transportation network insisted that it too needed upgrading. Moses had successfully argued against a subway extension to Flushing Meadows (even though the city had built one for the previous fair), a clear sign of his passion for roads (and distaste for people who couldn't afford a car). Fearing that the current system would be inadequate to get the millions of visitors to and from the fair, however, the New York City Transit Authority (NYCTA, later the Metropolitan Transit Authority [MTA]) executives lobbied city officials for eighty extra subway cars and various station improvements at a cost of $10 million.[97]

Like the WFC, NYCTA was expecting a windfall from the fair, forecasting $9 million in additional revenue from increased ridership, and it wanted to make sure its financial ship would come in. Subway fares were fifteen cents in the early 1960s, a cheap and efficient way to get to and from the fair, but there would simply not be enough cars to handle the event if the daily attendance forecasts were at all accurate. City officials agreed to NYCTA's request for more cars, although not as many as they wanted. In May 1962, ten brand new Redbirds made a test run from Times Square and were scheduled to be added to the IRT line between Manhattan and Flushing during the run of the fair. The $110,000-apiece Redbirds were not only technically state of the art but, according to the transit authority, had "interior color schemes recommended by psychologists for relaxed riding." Two cars were added to the line in September 1963, complete with twenty "picture windows" so that visitors could enjoy the scenery on the elevated portion of the fifteen-minute trip (complementing the fair's many sit-back-and-enjoy-the-ride activities).[98]

It remained difficult for Brooklynites to get to and from the fair by public transportation, however, as the subway lines between most of the borough and Flushing Meadows were less than direct. After politicians from Brooklyn complained that NYCTA was not making it easier to get to the upcoming fair via mass transit (more than half of its residents and families did not own automobiles at the time), the authority agreed to run two special bus lines from Brooklyn to Flushing Meadows. Brooklyn may have lost their Dodgers, but residents of the country's fourth-largest city would have their day at the fair. Although NYCTA added new subway cars, Moses vetoed proposed new lines leading to the fair because, according to Caro, they would allow low-income people, especially African Americans and Puerto Ricans, to easily get to his future park.[99]

At exactly nine o'clock in the morning on April 22, 1964, Bill Turchyn, an eighteen-year-old student from New Jersey, entered Gate Number 1 at

THE COMMON GOOD | 81

Figure 2.6. An aerial view of the 1964–1965 New York World's Fair in Flushing Meadows. *Source*: Roger Higgins, *Aeriel View of Unisphere and Other Exhibits at New York World's Fair*, between 1964 and 1965, photograph, Library of Congress Prints and Photographs Division, Washington, DC, https://www.loc.gov/item/2011648209/.

Figure 2.7. Happy fairgoers deboarding a Greyhound bus near the grounds in 1965. Greyhound ran special buses like this one during the fair's six-month runs in 1964 and 1965. The undulating Hall of Science is behind and the Space Park (with real rockets!) to the left. *Source*: Thomas J. O'Halloran, *Greyhound Bus Special to World's Fair from NYC New York City*, 1965, photograph, Library of Congress Prints and Photographs Division Washington, DC, https://www.loc.gov/item/2016647281/.

Figure 2.8. The Space Park at night in 1964. Some of the rockets remain at the New York Hall of Science in Flushing Meadows Corona Park (adjacent to the Queens Museum). *Source*: *Space Park at 1964 World's Fair, New York,* National Archives and Records Administration, Wikimedia Commons, public domain.

the fairgrounds in Flushing Meadows Park, becoming the first official visitor of the 1964–1965 New York World's Fair. Right behind Mr. Turchyn was Michael Catan, who claimed he had been the first to enter the last New York world's fair in 1939, and Al Carter, who said he was first in line at the recent Seattle fair. The three men were the first of 92,646 people (63,791 paid) who would enter the grounds on opening day, a chilly, rainy Wednesday morning. Four thousand people marched in the morning parade, which featured not only Montana cowboys, kimono-clad Japanese geishas, Hawaiian hula dancers, and a group of Shriners but such beauties as Miss America, Miss Universe, and actress Donna Reed. Music included Scottish bagpipes, a Caribbean steel drum band, an Israeli accordionist, strolling Spaniards with guitars, and the University of Pennsylvania marching band.[100] The diversity of the parade was an apt foreshadowing of the direction the borough of Queens would take in the coming years.

CHAPTER THREE

The Golden Door

From this day forth those wishing to immigrate to America shall be admitted on the basis of their skills and their close relationship to those already here.

—President Lyndon Johnson, October 1965

On October 3, 1965, President Lyndon Johnson stood at the base of the Statue of Liberty, with much of New York City to be seen behind and around him. It was a blustery day, but the dignitaries in attendance were paying close attention to the president's speech, knowing that history was being made. His words were indeed moving. "Over my shoulders here you can see Ellis Island, whose vacant corridors echo today the joyous sound of long-ago voices," he said, "and today we can all believe that the lamp of this grand old lady is brighter today." It was the president's image of a kind of magical gate swinging open that was most compelling. "The golden door that she guards gleams more brilliantly in the light of an increased liberty for the people from all the countries of the globe," he stated, drawing upon the idea of the nation being a land of unlimited opportunity. After his speech, Johnson sat a desk where he signed the Immigration and Nationality Act of 1965 (or Hart-Celler Act), putting the wheels of the legislation in motion.[1]

Even more than what had been anticipated, the Immigration and Nationality Act of 1965 (which reversed the restrictions of the 1924 National Origins Act and loosened the quotas of the 1952 Immigration and Nationality Act) fundamentally altered the demographics of the United States, and especially those of the borough of Queens.[2] Opening the nation's "golden

85

door" to groups who had for decades faced strict quotas in entering the country allowed hundreds of thousands of Whites from southern and Eastern Europe, Asians, and non-Whites to settle in Queens in the late 1960s and through the 1970s. Queens was already known for being home to many people of different races, ethnicities, and religions, but the borough of New York City was now poised to become the most diverse place on the planet.

Open Queens

President Johnson's stirring speech belied the fact that the passage of the Immigration and Nationality Act of 1965 was hardly a smooth one. As the bill made its way through Congress, politicians and ordinary Americans questioned why it appeared that more—possibly many more—immigrants would be allowed to enter the country. With Cold War anxieties still running high (the Vietnam War was escalating), it was a curious time to open the golden door to possible Communist sympathizers and other "subversives." As in previous times when the federal government was considering expanding the scope of legal immigration, there were concerns that these foreigners would take Americans' jobs. Unemployment in the United States in 1965 was 5 percent, a high enough number to prompt fears that jobs would be lost due to cheaper labor. Automation was already eliminating some factory jobs, making this new threat especially worrying.[3]

African Americans were definitely concerned about the consequences of the new act, thinking that the strides they were making in achieving equal rights could be reversed. The vast majority of European immigrants would be White, after all, possibly giving them an edge in employment, education, and housing opportunities. The Civil Rights Act of 1964 had made it illegal to discriminate on the basis of race, religion, sex, and national origin, but biases against people of color remained common in the United States. There were state laws too that barred discrimination along these same lines, although those often didn't translate to actual practice.

The Congress of Racial Equality (CORE) had planned to stage a protest on opening day of the second season of the New York World's Fair in Flushing Meadows Corona Park to show its discontent with Mayor Wagner's integration program for the city's workforce. However, the African American civil rights organization was, much to the delight of fair officials and politicians, a no-show. On opening day of the first season, President Johnson had been invited to give the dedication speech, but even with

86 | QUEENS

loudspeakers many couldn't hear it because of the louder shouting of "Jim Crow must go!" by hundreds of activists. The group was led by James Farmer, national director of CORE, and Bayard Rustin, the organizer of the March on Washington, which had been held less than a year before opening day of the fair.[4]

After his address at the Singer Bowl, the president was escorted to the Federal (or United States) Pavilion, giving another speech as he dedicated the nation's official building. There too hundreds of protestors in different groups, holding placards and shouting "Freedom now," disrupted the president's speech, often making it unintelligible. Apparently prepared for such a scenario, Johnson deftly referenced the picketing, saying, "We do not try to mask our national problems. We do not try to disguise our imperfections or cover up our failures. No other nation in history has done so much to correct its flaws." When the president envisioned "a world in which all men are equal," however, the protestors laughed derisively, even more cause for police, who had been waiting patiently for the speech to end, to drag the protestors into nearby paddy wagons.[5]

Although there turned out to be no repeat performance in 1965, not much progress had been made over the past year for civil rights in Queens, at least in terms of housing. Redlining was still a staple in local real estate despite concerted efforts to stop the practice. In 1966, for example, complaints against nine brokers in the borough were made by John E. Gaynus, Queens director of Operation Open City (the fair housing program of the New York Urban League) to the secretary of state. African Americans were attempting to purchase houses in Bellerose, a predominantly White neighborhood, but the brokers wouldn't even show them to the prospective buyers, according to the complaints. The charges resulted from a six-week sting operation under the code name Open Queens, in which both African American and White couples went to brokers' offices asking to see houses for sale in Bellerose. The White couples were allowed to see the houses while the African American couples (some of whom were actually interested in becoming homeowners in the area) were turned away, establishing a clear pattern of racial discrimination.[6]

Ironically, Bellerose was one of about thirty Queens neighborhoods said to have a fair housing committee (including Jackson Heights and Springfield Gardens—two areas with particularly ugly histories of racial discrimination in housing). In October 1966, representatives from across the borough took part in a fair housing fair held in St. Albans designed to familiarize African Americans and Puerto Ricans with housing in Queens and Nassau

Counties. Operation Open City was the co-sponsor of the fair, at which information on the cost of houses, community facilities, schools, churches, transportation, shopping, and taxes was distributed.[7]

There was considerable evidence that unfair housing was the norm in many parts of Queens, particularly in the southeast portion of the borough. At the urging of Spencer Steele, a Laurelton lawyer who was running for an Assembly seat in the Democratic primary in 1966, the New York State Commission for Human Rights was investigating why "all-Negro ghettos" were spreading in that part of Queens. Neighborhoods such as Jamaica, Hollis, St. Albans, Laurelton, and Springfield Gardens were remaining as segregated as ever, with little doubt that banks and brokers were responsible for the redlining. Banks were quicker to foreclose on mortgages held by African Americans in those areas as a means to resell the houses at a profit. Brokers would show those and other houses only to Blacks, however, "resegregating" the neighborhoods. Last, it was rare for brokers to show houses to African Americans in predominantly White areas of Queens, this too perpetuating the borough's racial divide.[8]

Discriminatory practices could also be found in rental policies in Queens and other boroughs of New York City. Landlords were refusing to rent apartments to African Americans, making the City Commission on Human Rights take action. Such was the case in Far Rockaway after a couple had advertised their three-room apartment for rent. An African American man answered the ad but was turned away because of his race, a clear violation of the law. After the commission issued a cease and desist order to the landlords, the man promptly got the apartment.[9]

A year later, the secretary of state determined that at least two Queens brokers had discriminated against African Americans by not showing them houses for sale in Bellerose. (The other cases had been dropped.) The brokers' penalty was a light one, however: a thirty-day license suspension or $250 fine. Eugene S. Callendar, executive director of the New York Urban League, was disappointed. "The penalty is only a tap on the wrist," he said in 1967. "It will have no effect on the discriminatory practices of Queens brokers which will continue unabated until the State gives us real enforcement of the fair housing laws." Indeed, the two brokers could take a month's vacation and then be back in business, with little reason to stop engaging in the same kind of practices.[10]

With housing discrimination against African Americans widespread in Queens and the other boroughs (211 cases were reported in 1968), encouraging brokers found guilty of bias to spend a few weeks fishing added

88 | QUEENS

insult to injury. "Black families have been and still are being systematically discriminated against," John Gaynus observed almost two years after the judgment by the secretary of state. Such practices stemmed from residents' fears that property values dropped when people of color moved into a neighborhood, despite there being no evidence to support this belief. Gaynus went further in explaining the basis for redlining, however. "Open housing forms the first step towards social integration and, consequently, towards inter-racial marriages," he told the *New York Amsterdam News*, trading on ideas expressed by Black intellectuals of the past regarding miscegenation.[11]

While that theory may or may not have explained the reasoning behind housing discrimination, efforts were being made in Queens to prevent African Americans from mixing socially with Whites. Two clubs—the Breezy Point Surf Club and the Silver Gull Club, also in Breezy Point—allegedly engaged in "restrictive membership practices," meaning people of color were not welcome. Private clubs could dictate who could and could not be admitted, but Breezy Point, located on the western end of the Rockaway peninsula, was owned by New York City. Enter one Edward Koch, then a city councilmember, who persuaded the City Commission on Human Rights and the City Department of Real Estate to instruct the clubs to drop their race-based restrictions, which they promptly did.[12]

African Americans who had been turned away by the Breezy Point clubs might have made their way over to Jacob Riis Park. Tolerance was the norm in that sandy stretch of Queens, as various groups enjoyed the beach alongside each other. While Coney Island in Brooklyn was more of a melting pot, with beachgoers of different ethnicities and races congregating in a large mass, Riis Park was more of a salad bowl divvied up by its fourteen bays (segments of surf divided by rows of pilings). According to a lifeguard, the divisions were surfers (Bay 1), gays (Bays 2 and 3), young women (Bay 4), African Americans (Bay 5, or "Soul Beach"), families (Bays 6, 7, and 8), young couples (Bay 9), college students (Bays 10 and 11), and the rather odd mix of teenagers and fishermen (Bays 12, 13, and 14). Live and let live was the unofficial motto of Riis Park, a place where folks were free to, in the parlance of the times, do their own thing.[13]

League of Nations

Astoria, meanwhile, was a true melting pot in Queens. The neighborhood was nicknamed a "league of nations," and with good reason. At a quarter of the population, Greeks were a visible presence, but 1970 records at Astoria's Public School (PS) 166 revealed that the students had been born in twenty-eight countries other than the United States. The school's highlight of the year was an international dance festival, where children dressed in clothing and brought food of their homeland. Astoria was a true mash-up of cultures; a Scottish bakery could be found near a bocci court, which was not far from a grassy patch populated by Irish hurlers. Adding some tension to the neighborhood was the recent arrival of well-off Cypriotes, who were driving up the cost of houses in Astoria, quite a different immigrant experience than the older generation of Greeks who arrived with little money.[14]

The Greek influence could not be missed in Astoria, but there were actually more residents of Italian descent. There were almost as many Irish as Greeks in Astoria, but again, Greeks seemed to dominate the neighborhood, especially on Ditmars Avenue. Everybody seemed to know everybody, regardless of ethnic background, and one would be hard-pressed to find any area of New York City with a greater sense of community.[15]

Residents of Corona might have taken on that challenge, however. Although a significant number of African Americans had called that northern Queens neighborhood home for more than a half century, Italians were dominant, especially in the section running from Martense to Christie Avenues and along 101st and 102nd Streets (which was so crime-free that many didn't lock their doors). In 1970, however, it appeared that the way of life for the 138 families in the area's sixty-nine houses was at an end. A new high school and athletic field would be built on the spot, City Hall declared, condemning the houses (some of which had been built by hand by the parents of the current residents) through eminent domain. Signs in the neighborhood reading "Lindsay abolished Italian community" and "Lindsay uproots Italian community" could be seen, suggesting that Mayor John Lindsay was ethnically biased when he approved where the school and field should go.[16] A compromise was eventually reached, with fifty-five of the houses spared and the owners of the remaining ones given a choice: sell them to the city or have them moved to other sites at the city's expense.[17]

While the tight-knit community was understandably distraught to have their homes taken away, the mayor and City Planning Commission were more interested in grabbing land than evicting members of a certain ethnic group. College Point was another section of Queens where some families had lived for generations, but residents there too were worried that their tranquil and stable neighborhood would be upended by the city. College Point, which sat on a peninsula that extended into Flushing Bay and the

East River, was home to twenty-five thousand middle-class and lower-middle-class residents, mostly of German, Irish, and Italian descent. The neighborhood was surrounded by water on three sides, making it feel like an island detached from New York City. Locals called the place "our town," not after the Thornton Wilder play but because of its extreme friendliness.[18]

Always looking to expand, however, City Hall had its eye on College Point, seeing opportunities for high-rise apartment houses, an industrial park, and recreational facilities on land fill surrounding the area. Most of the residents were opposed to such "progress," especially those familiar with the area's history. With its heavy German population, College Point had once been home to wonderful beer gardens such as Witzel's and Donnelly's. Thousands of Manhattanites would come by boat on weekends to enjoy the festivities at what was nicknamed Little Heidelberg, but Prohibition put an end to the merriment.[19]

Although they did not face the same kind of discrimination as Asian Americans or African Americans, White ethnics too longed for a sense of cultural heritage that had been largely contained. "Communities of white Americans of foreign birth or parentage are beginning to attach a new importance to cultural identity that they have apparently never been able to submerge entirely," observed Bill Kovach in the *New York Times* in 1970. The "re-ethnicization" movement that had begun in the early 1960s appeared to be picking up steam. Immigrants had strongly encouraged their children to assimilate to become full Americans, but the children of those immigrants felt something was missing. "The third generation remembers what the second generation would like to forget," explained Paul Mundy, a Loyola University sociologist, the remembered thing being "ethnic identity."[20]

There were many indications that this revival was quite real. In Cleveland, ethnic groups were demanding representation in textbooks used in public schools, and in Pittsburgh, Slavic groups were lobbying for government-sponsored research centers. Across the country, Italian Americans were making it known that they didn't appreciate the stereotypes that the media used when presenting or describing people of their background. Additionally, the Ford Foundation was establishing a program of fellowships to encourage scholarships in the growing field of ethnic studies. A new generation of American students were gravitating to the field to explore the history and culture of minorities, much like how Black studies was being established as a department in many college campuses.[21]

What had triggered this profound interest in cultural pluralism? The social turmoil of the counterculture certainly had something to do with it, as the postwar consensus rooted in Cold War nationalism fell apart. The civil rights movement too was a contributing factor, as White ethnics looked to Black pride as inspiration to celebrate their own cultural identity. The gradual rise of the Black middle class also can be seen as stirring up ethnic loyalties, if only because the former presented a growing threat to the latter in terms of jobs and housing. Much work remained to reestablish urban ethnic communities, as they had largely dissolved during the postwar years as residents fled to the suburbs. Such communities were still "hazy," Kovach had learned, but they were developing into stronger and tighter ones, modern versions of the communities that flourished between the world wars.[22]

In 1972, Alfred Kazin, the social critic, and James T. Farrell, the novelist, were invited by City College in New York to discuss the recent surge in ethnic awareness. As young men in the 1930s, they told a group of students, being an ethnic minority felt like being "powerless," as the myth of the melting pot was employed to "rub out the past." Now, however, ethnic groups were considered "the richest and most interesting," WASPS having lost much of their social currency. The pair traced the revival of ethnic identity back to the postwar years, when popular Jewish writers such as Saul Bellow, Bernard Malamud, and Philip Roth and Black writers like Richard Wright and James Baldwin brought their cultural heritage to American literature. Ethnicity could serve as a creative force, Kazin and Farrell agreed, a powerful means to reexamine national identity.[23]

Michael Novak's *The Rise of the Unmeltable Ethnics: Politics and Culture in the Seventies* framed the ascent of pluralism within the broader concept of cultural disintegration. Many once widely accepted ideas about American history were being exposed as untrue, and the melting pot theory had now joined the revisionist club. Like Peter Schrag's recently published *The Decline of the WASP*, Novak's book was provocative, although it argued that WASP values (e.g., individualism, rationality, self-mastery, and the conquest of nature) were still dominant. However, the rise of pluralism threatened this hegemony, Novak believed, with defining aspects of ethnic culture, such as the working-class neighborhood, to reshape politics in the coming years.[24]

At least one so-called WASP made it clear that he didn't appreciate his ethnic background being so publicly denigrated. Writing for the *Wall Street Journal*, not too surprisingly, Edmund Fuller defended his Anglo-Saxon heritage, thinking the declarations made by Kazin and Farrell and others were hate-filled and even racist. The very term "WASP" was vague, given that people like himself who were labeled as such could be ethnically and religiously diverse (Fuller was part Welsh and Scottish and Episcopalian).

92 | QUEENS

Fuller argued that he was as ethnic as anyone, resentful that his particular brand had been designated as the bad guys. "Everyone is ethnic," he made clear, even those of British descent who spoke English. There had been no WASP-led conspiracy to erase non-Anglo identity, Fuller told Kazin and Farrell, suggesting that the melting pot was about embracing Americans of all backgrounds rather than expunging what made them different or unique.[25]

It was debatable whether the social currency of WASPs was in a state of decline, but the general consensus was that the cracking of the melting pot was a good thing for individuals and the country as a whole. John G. Milner, a professor of social work at the University of Southern California, certainly thought so, stating that identification with one's ethnic, racial, or religious group was "a healthy sign." "Blacks want to be black, Chicanos want to be Chicano, and Jews want to be Jews," he told the *Los Angeles Sentinel* in 1972, seeing such affinities as a vitalizing force rather than as divisive. Conforming to a set pattern of what was considered American was never going to work, Milner believed, happy to see the idea be tossed into the dustbin of history.[26]

Foreign Stock

While some Germans and Italians continued to immigrate to Queens, as well as others from Europe such as Poles and Croats, it was Spanish-speaking Puerto Ricans and Dominicans that were reshaping the ethnic landscape of the borough. These immigrants were Roman Catholics, reason for the Catholic Diocese of Brooklyn to help them adjust to their new surroundings. About eight hundred thousand Roman Catholics had recently arrived in Brooklyn and Queens, doubling the population of those of that faith in the two boroughs. Most of the immigrants settling in Queens had chosen Astoria, Woodside, and Jackson Heights as their new home, and English was not their native language. Having priests learn Spanish was thus a priority for the diocese.[27]

Meanwhile, in Forest Hills and Rego Park, it was Hebrew that could often be spoken and read. Thousands of Israeli citizens had moved into the area along Queens Boulevard, making it feel not unlike a suburb of Tel Aviv. Hebrew newspapers were sold at newsstands and Israeli foods could be found at local supermarkets and restaurants to cater to the new arrivals, some of whom intended to stay permanently and others who did not. Like many migrations, the influx of Israelis came about by word of mouth, the word being that rents were cheaper than in Manhattan and that life was easier too. At the Flame Restaurant at eight o'clock every night, patrons tuned into radio station WEVD to hear five minutes of news about Israel (most of it not good). Arabs, mostly Egyptians, also frequented the Flame for its Middle Eastern delicacies, and while relations with the Israelis were cordial, politics was wisely not discussed.[28]

About a quarter of the Israelis viewed their time in Queens as temporary, planning to move back to their homeland at some point. They were there for economic or family reasons, wanting to make some money or have their children get an American education. The Israelis worked mostly as taxi drivers, salespeople, diamond cutters, waiters, and storekeepers—not exactly occupations worth moving thousands of miles for. As well, there was a certain shame attached to Israelis who moved to another country, a function of the strong emotional attachment associated with the small nation. "You ascend when immigrating to Israel but descend when leaving," explained Yaakov Pachter, director of the Eastern United States Region of the Israel Government Tourist Office, thinking many Israelis would not admit that they planned to stay in Queens for the long term.[29]

By 1972, it was clear that something special and even historically significant was taking place in Queens. "The Maltese, the Japanese and the Indians are quietly thriving in Queens, a borough whose anonymous towers and frame houses have been sheltering an increased number of ethnic minorities," wrote Richard F. Shepard in the *New York Times* in 1972. Those groups too were making their presence known in the borough, part of the huge wave that resulted largely from the 1965 Immigration and Nationality Act. Smaller ethnic groups who had more recently arrived in Queens had yet to assimilate like the Italians, Germans, and Irish had over the course of generations, tending to congregate together in stores, clubs, and houses of worship.[30]

Not surprisingly, given its reputation as a welcoming place for immigrants, Astoria was home to many of the Maltese. (A quarter to half of the Maltese in New York City lived in Astoria.) Two clubs served the community, with Maltese the language of choice. Most New Yorkers, however, couldn't recognize that language (Semitic, primarily Arabic but based in Phoenician) or volunteer anything else about Maltese culture, a source of frustration to the group. ("What are you?" was a question asked of many a Maltese in New York.) A visit to Astoria would make it clear that Maltese were regularly churchgoing Roman Catholics who enjoyed eating *pastizzi*—pockets of dough filled with either ricotta cheese or a kind of corned beef hash.[31]

Sounds delicious, but the Japanese community in Queens opted for foods like bean curd, rice, noodles, ginseng, shrimp, lobster, and salted eggs. There was somewhere between two thousand and three thousand Japanese immigrants in Flushing, a relatively small population but one that could not be missed. Flushing was in fact becoming a hotbed of Asian culture, with people from Japan, China, the Philippines, Korea, and India all part of the street scene. The Japanese community was said to have begun when visitors to the 1964–1965 World's Fair decided to relocate to Queens, staying close to the site of the event because they were familiar with the area (and also didn't want to pay Manhattan rents).[32]

Indians (Gujaratis, from the country's western region) and a smaller group of Pakistanis had also chosen Flushing as a place to live and shop. Indians not just from Queens but from all over the metropolitan area and Long Island flocked to a little shop on Main Street that stocked foods and spices, and Indian movies were shown at PS 20. Hindus held services at the Jewish War Veterans Center on Parsons Boulevard until plans were made to build a temple in Flushing.[33] By 1975, about three thousand Indians were calling Queens home, many of them renting apartments in the huge Lefrak City.[34]

Given the league of nations in Queens, it was not surprising that the borough reported the highest proportion of "foreign stock" in the tristate metropolitan area. Half of Queens residents were either born in a country other than the United States or had at least one foreign-born parent, according the 1970 census. Brooklyn actually had more residents of "foreign stock," but they represented 41 percent of the borough's total population—less than the 50 percent in Queens. Expectedly, those of Italian descent represented the largest group of ethnics in Queens, just as they did across the metropolitan area.[35]

Importantly, however, the census data documented the ethnic heritage of only the two most recent generations, that is, current residents and that of their parents. As third and older generations died off, ethnic representation thus declined unless there was another wave of immigration from their respective native countries. In the case of Queens, Italians still led, but more recent arrivals were catching up fast. Immigrants from the Caribbean—notably Cuba, West Indies, Trinidad, and Jamaica—placed second, with those from the Soviet Union, Germany, Poland, Ireland, Austria, England, Hungary, and Czechoslovakia following, in that order. Another interesting finding from the 1970 census is that 46 percent of the total population of Queens reported that a language other than or in addition to English was spoken in their home during childhood.[36]

THE GOLDEN DOOR | 95

The relative decline in immigration from Europe and increase from other countries in the Western hemisphere was rather remarkable. Between 1960 and 1970, the number of Queens residents from Latin, Central, and South America rose from 34,121 to 114,962, a gain of more than 235 percent. The third-place finish of the Soviet Union was perhaps surprising given the difficulty of emigrating from that country. Most of the ex-Soviets were Jews escaping persecution, however, who were somehow able to leave that country for a better life in Queens (the majority settling in Rochdale Village).[37]

The 1970 census offers a wealth of information regarding the ethnic makeup of Queens, should one decide to dig deeper into the data. The borough had roughly 670 census tracts, with about three thousand people in each of these official counting areas. While the foreign stock averaged 50 percent in Queens, there were quite a few designated tracts in which the proportion of ethnic groups exceeded 60 percent and even 70 percent of the population. These neighborhoods included Astoria, Long Island City, Woodside, Jackson Heights, Rego Park, Elmhurst, sections of Forest Hills, Kew Gardens, and Richmond Hill, as well as parts of Jamaica and Flushing. Neighborhoods in which there was an underrepresentation of ethnics included College Point, Bayside, Little Neck, Bellerose, Queens Village, St. Albans, Rosedale, Howard Beach, Woodhaven, and Glendale.[38]

Also of note in the census figures is the drop in immigrants from Ireland. The Irish remained quite a presence in Queens and the other boroughs, of course, but most of them were third, fourth, and earlier generations of immigrants, and were far greater in number than the first and second generation reflected in the 1970 census. Still, Queens had more first- and second-generation Irish than any other borough, pulling ahead of the Bronx (from the previous census) and significantly ahead of Brooklyn.[39]

A Great Stride Backward

While the Immigration and Nationality Act of 1965 had made it much easier for foreigners to enter the United States legally, some were coming to this country without going through the proper channels. The issue of illegal immigration emerged as a serious problem in the early 1970s on both a national and local basis. In March 1973, for example, agents from the Immigration and Naturalization Service (INS) raided a Jackson Heights hotel, where they arrested fifteen people who could produce no documentation that they were in the United States legally. The "guests," as they were referred to, had come from Columbia, Argentina, Jamaica, and Ecuador, and it was likely that they would be deported.[40]

The raid was part of a nationwide effort to address what federal officials believed was the "alarming and growing" problem of "illegal aliens." Not everyone, however, held that view. The American Civil Liberties Union charged that false arrests had been made in a previous raid in Queens, and Roman Catholic dioceses across the metropolitan area were also opposed to the escalating federal campaign against who the dioceses preferred to call "foreign-born residents." Representative Peter Rodino Jr. (D-NJ) was trying to push through legislation that would penalize employers for hiring what he called "illegals," something that would bring "incredible suffering" to the hundreds of thousands of such residents in the New York City area, according to the dioceses. If passed, the legislation would "encourage subtle discrimination by making employers fearful of hiring or keeping Latin-looking people."[41]

How did the INS find the undocumented immigrants (who were believed to number at least four hundred thousand in Greater New York City)? Tips came in from neighborhood organizations, labor unions, tenant groups, and, once in a while, a disgruntled lover. From there, investigators would scout a particular location and, after a stake out, move in via a "dragnet raid." In Queens, investigators were likely to target toy factories, as those companies often hired undocumented people for menial jobs at below minimum wage. The typical profile was a married man from Latin America or the Caribbean who entered the United States on a tourist visa while intending to earn money to send back to his family.[42]

While immigration officials picked up undocumented "guests" who posed no threat to national security, other organizations made efforts to help recent arrivals ease the transition to their new home in Queens. A prime example of this was the Korean Community Action Center in Flushing, which offered a variety of services ranging from finding housing and employment to marriage counseling. Koreans and other Asians had not made much of an impression in the 1970 census, but it appeared that things would be different when the next census was taken. Koreans were already becoming known for their work ethic and self-determination—attributes that would serve them well as they pursued the American dream. There were about two thousand Korean families in the Flushing area in 1973, with many parents working in factories, sewing shops, and bakeries. According to one source, not a single one accepted welfare.[43]

The biggest challenge for the Koreans in Queens was, not surprisingly, the language barrier. The Korean Community Action Center offered English instruction, with most of the students there to learn basic skills such as how to count change or buy groceries. Many of the Korean immigrants were college educated but had trouble adapting to life in New York City, making it understandable that they were concentrated in a single area. The South Korean government led by Chung Hee Park made it difficult to emigrate, allowing each family to take just $500 out of the country. While adults typically had difficulty picking up English, children became fluent quickly, placing them in two different worlds—East and West—that often proved challenging to negotiate.[44]

While Queens became increasingly diversified by nationality and ethnicity, discrimination against African Americans in housing remained pervasive. The latest charges were against the Trump Management Corporation, which allegedly refused to rent, or negotiate renting apartments, to Blacks based on their race. The corporation owned and operated more than fourteen thousand apartments in Brooklyn, Queens, and Staten Island, including buildings in Jamaica and Forest Hills. In 1973, the US Justice Department ordered the Brooklyn Federal Court to investigate the cases, with Donald Trump, president of the corporation, and his father Fred Trump, chairman of the board, named as defendants.[45]

Charged with ignoring the Fair Housing Act of 1968, Donald Trump was quick to deny the accusations, describing them as "absolutely ridiculous." His corporation had never turned away Black people, he insisted, and had no intent to discriminate against them. "There have been a number of actions against our company, and we succeeded in quashing all of them in court," he told the press, adding that "we were once charged with discrimination, and we proved in court that we were not guilty." The Trumps had up to sixty days to respond to the charges brought by J. Stanley Pottinger, the US assistant general for civil rights.[46] Five years later, Trump Management would again be charged with discriminating against African Americans in apartment rentals in Queens, Brooklyn, and Staten Island. A federal district court and the civil rights division of the US Justice Department filed a motion saying that the company hadn't complied with a 1975 court order by continuing to refuse to rent apartments to Blacks because of their race. Again, all charges were denied by the Trumps.[47]

Those charges were minor compared with the overt racism of a bill put forth by Assemblymember John Esposito the following year. Esposito, a conservative Republican who represented Cambria Heights-Queens Village, proposed that the flow of "minorities" be limited in order to maintain the racial balance of integrated communities. African Americans would be denied access to the local housing market by preventing real estate agents from using the multiple listing service, which Esposito considered responsible for the large number of Blacks moving to Queens from the other boroughs. Two of Esposito's colleagues explained that the underlying reason he proposed bill was that he faced losing his seat as Cambria Heights and Queens Village became more African American. Another assemblymember, Woodrow Lewis (D-Brooklyn), described the bill as "a great stride backwards" and "constitutionally questionable," part of the reason Esposito decided to withdraw the bill.[48]

Also constitutionally questionable were the continuing INS raids in Queens. Columbians were being especially targeted due to alleged drug activity, so much so that the roughly eighty thousand Columbians who lived in Jackson Heights and Woodside nicknamed the service *emilia* (rival). Many Columbians did not go to restaurants or movie theaters for fear that Emilia would take them away for being "indocumentados," and even at home they did not feel safe. The majority of Columbians without papers worked hard, but civic groups complained that they took jobs and housing away from taxpayers. The deputy district director of the INS admitted that his staff targeted Columbians in public places by their accents. "One time we arrested about 100 in one hour at a subway stop in Queens," the man proudly said.[49]

The subject of undocumented immigrants was equally contentious in Corona and Elmhurst. The same complaints were made against these hundreds of Spanish-speaking immigrants, the primary one being that they were willing to work below minimum wage. In November 1974, about three hundred residents of those neighborhoods attended a public hearing at Newton High School to vent their concerns, although it wasn't clear what local officials could or should do about the situation. (The INS estimated that there were a million undocumented people in New York City.) Not just Columbians but people from Ecuador and Venezuela had come to that part of Queens on temporary visas and stayed despite the State Department's screening methods. Suspects who were apprehended could typically be released upon posting $500 bail, with most simply returning to their community and not showing up for their hearing.[50]

Choose Your Own Neighbors

The Soviet Jews who had in recent years settled in Queens didn't face deportation but had a different set of challenges. About six thousand Soviet Jews came to the United States between 1973 and 1975, with about half settling in the New York City area. Many (Georgians, in particular) were clustered in Brighton Beach, Brooklyn, while others were in pockets of Rego Park, Forest Hills, and Kew Gardens. Finding a way to make money represented the biggest obstacle, as even physicians had to be retrained and learn some English before practicing medicine. Still, the freedom to express their ideas and observe Jewish traditions was considered worth having escaped life under Communist rule. (In fact, of those six thousand Soviet Jews who had come to America between 1973 and 1975, just one individual chose to return to Russia, according to the New York Association for New Americans.)[51] Unlike in some other parts of the city (notably the West Bronx), synagogues were filled in Forest Hills, with some of the congregants never having previously attended a Jewish service.[52]

The fall of Saigon in March 1975 brought a wave of about two thousand Vietnamese refugees to New York, many of them putting down new roots in Queens. As with previous groups of immigrants, many Vietnamese people found it difficult to adapt to a much different kind of life. Getting familiar with the streets, subways, money, and language would take months or years, with finding work the number one priority. Although most of the Vietnamese were living in Queens, they were scattered across the borough and had no social clubs or eating and drinking establishments in which to collectively gather like other immigrant groups did. It was thus not unusual for Vietnamese to feel homesick and lonely, having hastily left their country, and often members of their family, behind. One family, the Nghiems, had settled in Jackson Heights, bringing just three items with them from Vietnam: a teapot, a vase, and a Buddha.[53]

While immigrants struggled to make new lives in Queens, attempts to prevent African Americans from moving into certain areas of the borough continued. In November 1975, the federal government had to take action against a group of Rosedale residents who were trying to keep their predominantly White community just that. The group, which was calling itself Return Our American Rights (ROAR), was "threatening, intimidating, or otherwise interfering" with Black home buyers, according to the suit filed by the government. (This was reported to be the first time that the government had pursued a civil rights action per the Federal Fair Housing

Act of 1968.) ROAR was harassing not only African Americans but White residents who showed or sold their homes to Blacks; thus the group facilitated redlining in the community.[54]

Certain members of ROAR already had ugly histories of racism in Rosedale. One had been charged with firebombing the home of the Spencers, natives of the West Indies who had come to the United States after living in London. Fire had also been set to a nearby home into which another Black couple was planning to move. The alleged firebomber admitted that his group also used "psychological warfare" to drive current African American residents out of Rosedale, even showing up at schools to try to prevent Black children from using the playgrounds. ROAR members defended their actions, (mistakenly) believing that as Americans they had the right to control the racial makeup of the neighborhood. "The minorities are taking over our rights," explained one ROAR member, another adding that minorities were "running this country."[55]

Much like how Edward R. Murrow hosted a radio program addressing race relations in Springfield Gardens in 1959, Bill Moyers covered the Rosedale story in a 1976 television documentary. "Rosedale: The Way It Is" was part of *Bill Moyers' Journal*, which aired on PBS stations and examined controversial current affairs issues that typically could not be seen on television. Moyers visited Rosedale, a working-class community of some six thousand families, and met with the Spencers, whose house had been bombed. Viewers learned that a note had been attached to the bomb that read "Nigger be warned. We have time. We will get your first-born" and was signed "Viva Boston KKK." Most ROAR members declined to be interviewed but were identified as ethnic Catholics (Italian, Irish, Slavic) and Jewish. The members that did appear in the show said they feared that Rosedale would become another South Jamaica, the mostly poor, mostly Black crime-ridden neighborhood just three miles away.[56]

Real estate brokers were also capitalizing on such fears in Richmond Hill through classic blockbusting. Realtors distributed flyers under the doors of homeowners advising them to sell before prices dropped precipitously as more people of color moved in. "Choose your own neighbors" was the headline of one such ad that had become so prevalent in Queens and Brooklyn that Secretary of State Mario Cuomo had made those boroughs off-limits for unsolicited housing sales. It was thus illegal for real estate agents to directly ask homeowners if they wanted to list their property, but that wasn't stopping the more unscrupulous from trying to create panic selling.[57]

Figure 3.1. *The Story of Richmond Hill*, a mural in the Richmond Hill Branch Library by artist Philip Evergood, June 1946. *Source*: Philip Evergood, "*The Story of Richmond Hill* [. . .]*,* photograph, Library of Congress Prints and Photographs Division, Washington, DC, https://www.loc.gov/item/2009632212/.

Older residents of Jackson Heights had feared that their neighborhood would be ruined as non-Whites moved in, but that hadn't been the case at all. In fact, businesses were thriving in the section now heavily populated by immigrants from Latin America and the Caribbean, repeating the pattern that had been established by new arrivals from Europe in decades past. Few of the adults who had come from Cuba, Columbia, Peru, Puerto Rico, Argentina, Haiti, the Dominican Republic, Ecuador, and Uruguay were on welfare, and their children were doing well in school. Many Whites had fled Jackson Heights as the Hispanics appeared, but the neighborhood was by all measures a healthy and vibrant one.[58]

Having become more diverse than the other boroughs of New York City, Queens was getting considerable attention for being one of America's foremost melting pots. "The borough may be the most varied mixture in the nation," wrote Murray Schumach in the *New York Times* in 1977, the more remarkable thing being that, for the most part, different groups were getting along. The popular television show *All in the Family*, which ran from January 1971 to April 1979, had made many viewers believe that the bigoted character Archie Bunker was representative of racial and ethnic sentiment in Queens, as the program was set there. But with notable exceptions such as ROAR, the borough was a hospitable place for people of all backgrounds who were bound together by a solid work ethic and the classic American faith in upward mobility.[59]

By 1977, the population of Queens had risen to about two million—more than that of many major cities including Philadelphia, Detroit, Houston, Milwaukee, New Orleans, Atlanta, Kansas City, Denver, and Cincinnati. Visitors to the borough were taking note of the variety of languages one might hear in a single day and in a single place; in the Parker Towers building complex in Forest Hills, for example, Hebrew, Japanese, Hindi, Chinese, Spanish, Russian, French, Hungarian, and Turkish were all spoken. Sunday services at the First Baptist Church in Flushing were given in Chinese, Spanish, and English, and the neighborhood was becoming well-known for its offerings of all kinds of Asian food. Newer immigrants were further diversifying the borough that had already been home to generations of Italian, Irish, Jewish, Polish, and German Americans.[60]

The Chinese in Flushing were of particular interest to sociologists and economists. Many Chinese residents were on a property purchasing spree, and unlike most buyers, often paid cash. (Many Chinese people didn't trust banks.) Taking a cue from the Greeks in Astoria, the Chinese in Flushing would frequently buy a two-family house and rent out one floor to both build equity and generate income. Also like the Greeks, they were making a concerted effort to maintain their heritage while embracing American culture, not always an easy thing to do.[61]

As more Mandarin-speaking Taiwanese immigrants began coming to New York City, Flushing would emerge as one of three major Chinese communities in the five boroughs. (Those settling in Queens didn't feel quite at home in Manhattan's Chinatown, where mostly Cantonese was spoken.) Well-educated, middle-class South Koreans were also attracted to Flushing, as a small number moved to Queens after having worked at the 1964–1965 New York World's Fair. The many bus and subway lines in the area was another reason to opt for Flushing over other parts of the city.[62]

As did many new arrivals before them, many of these Asian immigrants perceived Queens as a place where they could move up the economic ladder. The 1970s was a period of slow economic growth, however, and a good number of Whites were deciding to leave Flushing for other parts of the city, state, or country that offered greater opportunity. Asian entrepreneurs invested in the retail businesses abandoned by White owners who had relocated (or passed away), effectively saving Flushing from becoming a depressed neighborhood. Forty-First Avenue and Main Street emerged as the heart of reinvented Flushing, and over the next decade much of the remaining White population decided to move to other neighborhoods in Queens or to Nassau County. Not only had prices of real estate and rent increased significantly following Asians' investment in Flushing, but the cultural transformation of the neighborhood was too dramatic for many longtime residents.[63]

The Most Densely International Neighborhood

About eight miles west, another neighborhood in Queens was flourishing as a different group of immigrants remade the community. Thousands of Armenian refugees had fled war-torn Lebanon for New York City, many of them settling in Sunnyside. The group's arrival added a strong Middle Eastern ethnic consciousness to the city, something that hadn't previously existed. Armenians had also come to the city from the Soviet Union, Rumania, and other countries in recent years, bringing the population of the group to between eighty and ninety thousand. (Armenians no longer had a national homeland.) Earlier Armenian immigrants had largely been eager to assimilate (e.g., by dropping the "-ian" from the end of their family names), but this new wave was taking full advantage of the ethnic revival taking place across the United States.[64]

Greeks still had a homeland, of course, but that didn't stop sixty to seventy thousand from resettling in Astoria, a neighborhood that had been primarily Italian. Astoria was by the late 1970s the largest Greek city outside Greece, something quite believable with a walk down Ditmars Boulevard (previously Ditmars Avenue) or Broadway and their side streets. The 1960s and 1970s had generally been not good years for American cities, including New York, but one wouldn't know that from Astoria. New homes had been built and older ones refurbished, vacant stores had become lively businesses, and deserted factories were once again humming. Greek culture—notably food, music, and movies—thrived in Astoria, and Greek-language magazines and newspapers could still be found despite the drastic drop in ethnic publications over the course of the twentieth century.[65]

It was in the early years of that century when the first Greeks mixed in with the already established Italians, Germans, and Irish of Astoria. It wasn't precisely known why the Greeks chose Astoria as their new home, the working theory being that the group preferred frame and shingle homes with backyards to apartments. A larger wave arrived in the post–World War II years, with the 1965 Immigration and Nationality Act playing a significant

104 | QUEENS

role in encouraging those Greeks who had emigrated to Australia or Canada to relocate to New York City. At the same time, other areas of the city such as the Lower East Side, West Side, and Washington Heights were in decline, impetus for more prosperous Greeks to move to flourishing Astoria. As in the case of the Chinese in Flushing, older residents of Astoria, in this case mostly Italian Americans and Irish Americans, were prepared to pull up their roots as they witnessed the Greek "invasion."[66]

Living alongside the Chinese and Koreans in Flushing and the Greeks in Astoria were Muslims. Those two neighborhoods, as well as Corona, were home to a fair share of the roughly sixty thousand adherents of the Islamic religion in New York City. (Their racial and ethnic backgrounds were Arabic, Caribbean, African American, and Asian.) Like community leaders of other groups, Muslims aimed to impart their cultural heritage to young people, believing that an elementary school dedicated to teaching the Arabic language and principles of Islam was an ideal way to achieve their goal. Such a school in Queens was in the planning stages in 1977, with financial support pledged by the government of Saudi Arabia.[67]

The Hindu community of Queens was understandably very happy to have its long-sought temple in which to practice Hinduism. With its stone exterior, pyramid-shaped dome, and marble steps, the new building certainly stood out amid the sea of nondescript single-family houses in Flushing. Artisans from India had been brought in to help create what was the first dedicated Hindu temple built in the United States. The Indian community in Queens, centered in Flushing and Elmhurst, had grown significantly since the passage of the 1965 Immigration and Nationality Act, with many more Indians expected to emigrate to New York City. Indian culture—clothing, food, music, dance, and Bollywood movies—already could hardly be missed throughout the city, although there were some reports of vandalism and discrimination against the group.[68]

The multicultural mosaic that was Queens was very much in evidence at the Outdoor Queens Immigrant Ethnic and Music Dance Festival held at Bohemian Hall in Astoria in June 1978. It was the third such event, and Astoria was a fitting place for those of a variety of ethnic backgrounds to celebrate the cultural richness of their community. The highlight of the festival was a six-hour dance party, with traditional Greek, Italian, Macedonian, and Romanian-Serbian orchestras providing the music. It would be hard to find a band anywhere else in the United States composed of musicians playing a *gajda* (a kind of bagpipe), *tapan* (drum), accordion, fiddle, clarinet, lyre (a stringed instrument), mandolin, and guitar.[69]

By the end of the 1970s, Astoria was widely recognized as the most diverse neighborhood in Queens, but it appeared that Elmhurst actually took the prize. Elmhurst (designated by zip code 11373) was in fact "the most densely international neighborhood in New York's most international borough," according to the *New York Times*. More than eighteen thousand registered immigrants lived in that zip code, Postal Service figures show, which was about a quarter of the total population of Elmhurst. That was a significantly higher percentage than any other area of New York City and did not include the many undocumented (estimated to be about the same number as those registered). Nationalities in Elmhurst included Columbian, Chinese, Cuban, Filipino, Ecuadoran, Indian, Korean, Dominican, Argentinian, and Hong Kongese.[70]

Reasonably priced apartments and the short hop to Manhattan on the No. 7 train or the Queens Boulevard buses were the main reasons so many immigrants had settled in Elmhurst. A school classroom in the neighborhood could appear like a mini United Nations, particularly for non-English speakers. At PS 89, for example, that class consisted of thirteen children from Korea, four from Taiwan, three from the Philippines and Hong Kong, and one each from Columbia, Haiti, Vietnam, Ecuador, Bangladesh, Honduras, India, Guyana, and the Dominican Republic. At Elmhurst General Hospital, translators could communicate in Arabic, Armenian, Chinese, Czech, French, German, Greek, Hebrew, Hindi, Hungarian, Italian, Korean, Polish, Spanish, Romanian, Russian, Tagalog, Turkish, Yiddish, Yugoslav, Vietnamese, and sign language. "Jingle Bells" was sung in Korean at the Reformed Church of Newtown, a multiethnic church in Elmhurst.[71]

A fine line was drawn between those who had come to Queens legally and those who had not. As in Elmhurst, Jackson Heights, and Corona, emotions ran strong when it came to the subject of the undocumented in Woodside. Woodside, which had a population of about fifty thousand in 1979, had become mostly Irish beginning in 1917, the result of a wave of transplants who moved there from Manhattan's West Side with the expansion of the IRT "el." Germans and a sprinkling of other ethnics made up the balance until the late 1960s, when a fair number of South Americans began arriving. Now Woodside was believed to be 15 percent Hispanic, and concern was intensifying regarding those who were using the community's resources without having their papers. As always, defenders of undocumented immigrants (Catholic church leaders, notably) pointed out that they are an asset to the community because they take menial jobs for low pay that few American citizens would.[72]

While the circumstances for Soviet Jews were much different, having come to the United States legally, it was not unusual for a Russian immigrant to work for the minimum wage or perhaps less. This was true even for those who held professional jobs in the Soviet Union; in America, starting at the bottom rung of the ladder was typical in many careers regardless of what position one may have held in another country. Concentrated in Forest Hills and Rego Park, the group had begun to arrive in 1968 when the Soviet Union started to release a small number of Jews. About 20,000 Soviet Jews came to the New York City area over the following decade (another 20,000 emigrated to other parts of the United States while 145,000 went to Israel).[73]

Although learning English presented a challenge, most of the Soviet Jews in Queens—Brooklyn also had a sizable community, so much so that Brighton Beach was nicknamed Little Odessa—had quickly embraced a capitalist way of life. Owning one's own business was a common pursuit, something that would have been unlikely for a Jew in Russia. Freedom of all kinds, especially the ability to openly practice Judaism, was the main reason for migrating to America or Israel. (Judaism was recognized as a nationality rather than a religion in the Soviet Union.) The ability to send a child to university was another oft-mentioned motive for starting over in a new, much different country. The Service Center for Russian Immigrants in Forest Hills was helping Soviet Jews adapt to American ways, whether that meant training for a job, finding an apartment, learning English, or locating a tutor for bar mitzvah lessons.[74]

At the same time, many Koreans in Queens appeared to be already realizing their American dream. New York City real estate was "going condo," as it was said, and more well-off Korean Americans who had been renting in Flushing were becoming property owners to take advantage of the deductible interest on income tax. Around $50,000 would fetch a two-bedroom condominium in Flushing, and at that price there were more potential buyers than units for sale. (With thirty-one of the forty-one units in one building on Union Street snapped up by Koreans, the owner decided to call it Seoul Plaza.) Twenty thousand Korean Americans now lived in Flushing (one-third of the total Korean population in the city), although the neighborhood also had a fair share of Japanese, Indians, Columbians, Chinese, and Cubans.[75] Those groups too were trying to realize prosperity through hard work and initiative, with the future to determine whether their pursuit would be a successful one.

THE GOLDEN DOOR | 107

CHAPTER FOUR

The International Express

The crossroads of the world has moved eastward about a half-dozen miles from its traditional intersection at Times Square to central Queens.

—Richard F. Shepard, 1991

On June 4, 1983, tens of thousands of people gathered at Flushing Meadows Corona Park, which had been the site of the 1939–1940 and 1964–1965 New York World's Fairs. The large get-together was a party for the borough of Queens, which was celebrating its three hundredth birthday. More specifically, the Queens Tricentennial festival was in recognition of Britain's 1683 decision to create a county and name it after Queen Catherine of Braganza, the wife of Charles II. Absorbed into New York City in 1898, Queens was, at 126.6 square miles, the city's largest borough and home to some 1.89 million people.[1]

With the festival serving as a showcase for Queens, organizers were sure to include events and exhibits that could be found in the borough. The festival also featured a small portion of the startling range of ethnic culture that existed in Queens, including Ukrainian embroidery and how Greek artisans made a *bouzouki* (a type of mandolin). Most impressive, perhaps, was the 250-pound, 50-foot-long loaf of Italian bread made by the Bellacicco Bakery of Queens Village. To get the gargantuan loaf out of his shop, the owner of the bakery had to knock down one of its walls, but Joseph Bellacicco considered the rather extreme measure well worth the effort and expense. "Queens is my favorite borough," he explained, "and I'd do anything for it, including breaking down my wall."[2]

109

Such was the pride in many of Queens residents who felt that their borough did not get the respect it deserved. Over the last two decades of the twentieth century, however, Queens would gain national attention, much of it due to its unsurpassed diversity. Earlier, real estate agents had discovered the borough for its open spaces on which to build houses and apartments, but now it was something else that was making people take notice. Queens had become, without exaggeration, unlike anywhere else on earth, a story that was as remarkable as that of America itself.

A Sprawling Polyglot

The phenomenal diversification of Queens over the past few decades was notable on many accounts, one of them being that the people of the borough had no discernible unified accent. After all, residents of its immediate neighbor to the west certainly had a distinct way of talking—Brookynites *woiked* rather than worked—and *dose* in *da* Bronx also spoke with a certain flair. Long Islanders liked to say they lived on *Lawn Giland*, and Manhattanites might *pahk* their *cahs*. Why then did Queensites not have an identifiable way of speaking? "Queens developed very rapidly after the Second World War with large numbers of persons coming in from many areas," blurring any idiosyncratic features in dialect, explained Arthur Bronstein of Lehman College. In earlier centuries, the relatively sparse population of Queens did have a recognizable way of speaking, added John B. Newman of Queens College, noting that the area's farmers talked much like other Long Island farmers.[3]

The lack of a particular form of speech in Queens could be seen as a metaphor for the polyglot nature of the borough. While the unique heritage and tradition of different ethnic groups could certainly be detected, it was perhaps inevitable that there would be a combination of customs and ways of life. This was most apparent in food; a gastronomic meetup was taking place in Queens that would eventually lead to innovative cross-pollinations. In 1980, Sylvia Carter, the food editor of *Newsday*, took note of the dozens of restaurants along Roosevelt Avenue (in Woodside) and Jackson Avenue that were serving what was being described as Chinese-Latin (or Chino Latino) cuisine. Customers could begin a meal with egg rolls and end with flan and café con leche, but it was when the two cuisines would be mashed up that things would get really interesting.[4]

110 | QUEENS

A mashup of sorts was already taking placed in some of the churches in Queens. By 1982, the Reformed Church of Newtown was conducting its Protestant services in English and Taiwanese, reflecting the composition of its membership. Immigrants were breathing new life into Queens churches that were facing extinction a decade earlier, especially in Elmhurst, New York City's most ethnically diverse neighborhood. Twenty thousand immigrants from 110 countries now called Elmhurst home, making church leaders in the area ponder the degree to which their institutions should adapt to the interests of a different congregation. The pastor of the First Presbyterian Church of Newtown—just a few blocks from the Reformed Church—was taking a more assimilationist approach, conducting its services only in English despite its parishioners having emigrated from forty different nations.[5]

The national media began to take notice of the remarkable, perhaps unprecedented diversity of Elmhurst. "It may be the most ethnically diverse community in the world," wrote Susan B. Garland for the *Hartford Courant* after walking down Broadway. It was in the late 1960s when the mostly Jewish and Irish neighborhood began to see large numbers of Latin Americans, Caribbeans, and Asians move in. Now, in 1983, the local schools were teaching subjects in about twenty-five languages, and residents had no real need to learn English. People lived and shopped on the same streets but there was little socializing among those of different ethnic backgrounds. Still, it was a peaceful community, a noteworthy thing given the many opportunities for misunderstanding and conflict.[6]

In the summer of 1984, reporters from across the country who had never given much thought to Queens were fervently traipsing across the borough. Walter Mondale, who was running for president as the Democratic candidate, had chosen Geraldine Ferraro, a congressional representative from Queens, as his running mate. That Ferraro "harked from the land of immigrants and Archie Bunker," as the *Christian Science Monitor* put it, was fascinating to journalists and no doubt many readers and viewers. Ferraro was a liberal from a conservative area (she lived in Forest Hills but represented New York's Ninth District, which included neighborhoods such as Richmond Hill and Ozone Park), a sufficient enough puzzle for the press to try to learn more about the apparently strange place that was Queens.[7]

Reporters quickly took note of the fact that while there remained many "traditional" or "old" ethnic groups such as Italians, Jews, Blacks, and Irish, there were a host of new immigrants from all over the world. And unlike the immigrants of the past, who frequently lacked money and education, a good number of the newer immigrants were what could be considered middle class.[8] On July 31, Ferraro took Mondale on a tour of her borough, which Bill Peterson of the *Washington Post* described as "a sprawling polyglot of 2 million people." Politically savvy borough president Donald Manes instead presented Queens as "a microcosm of America," where hardworking middle-class people were pursuing the American dream.[9]

Some journalists acted as if Queens was an undiscovered country, despite the area having been populated by farmers for centuries. "A new sovereign territory has captured the public's imagination," wrote Horace Sutton for the *Chicago Tribune*, thinking that "to the rest of the nation, Queens was about as familiar as Botswana." Sutton felt the need to tell his readers where this foreign land was ("wedged between Brooklyn and Long Island"), as well as its geographic makeup ("many villages connected by a network of streets and byways").[10] Mondale and Ferraro would lose the election in incumbent president Ronald Reagan's landslide victory, but Queens had been put on the map.

Reporters couldn't help but notice that each neighborhood in Queens had its own set of dynamics as the borough became more multicultural. Richmond Hill had long been predominantly German, Irish, and Italian, and longtime residents there were concerned about the arrival of Columbians, Ecuadorans, and Venezuelans. The locals were surprised to learn that the new arrivals were not the rowdy partiers they were often said to be, however, but rather hard workers dedicated to their families. By 1985, Richmond Hill had become 22 percent Hispanic and more South Koreans and Taiwanese were moving in, but there was little ethnic or racial tension in what had been considered by some as "an Archie Bunker neighborhood."[11]

The latest to immigrate to Forest Hills were about two hundred Georgian Jewish families. The hub of that community was the congregation of Georgian Jews of Russia on Yellowstone Boulevard, which was believed to be the only synagogue in New York City where no English at all was spoken. These were Sephardic Jews—descendants of Spanish Jews who had settled in different parts of Europe and the Middle East rather than be forced to convert to Catholicism—who distanced themselves from other Russian immigrants and other Jews. The group was decidedly traditional; women rarely worked outside the home and arranged marriages were common.[12]

The Georgian Jewish community in Queens would grow through the remainder of the 1980s and into the 1990s; there were 450 such families in Forest Hills and Rego Park by 1997. With its growth, however, a common theme within the immigrant experience became apparent. Teenagers found themselves straddling two worlds, one steeped in the rigid traditions of the Old World and the other offering the many freedoms readily available in contemporary America. That this struggle was typical of first-generation Americans did not make it any easier for the Georgian Jews, given the dusk curfews for girls (but not boys), not just arranged marriages but arranged dates, and taboo of mingling with a non-Jew. While insular, the Georgian Jewish community was not "ghettoized" as were the Amish and the Satmar Chasidim (the only groups in America said to be self-isolated). In short, the teens wanted to be American Jews and were less inclined to embrace Georgian culture.[13]

In addition to attracting the national media, the singular diversity of Queens was drawing the attention of academics. Realizing they were in a unique position within the world of academia, leaders of Queens College began to leverage the institution's presence in what appeared to be the most diverse place in America. The college was hiring more international instructors and offering more globally oriented courses to appeal to its very diverse student body. In 1985, it held a symposium called American Ethnic Families in Transition, which focused on how various ethnic groups were, rather than "melting" into one big American pot, retaining their uniqueness, traditions, and customs. Five different groups were included in the symposium: Jewish, Irish, Black, Greek, and Italian. Shared values among the groups were also identified, showing that people had much in common despite having diverse ethnic backgrounds.[14] At the same time, Queens College was developing a multidisciplinary series of courses that were global in focus, leading to what be called world studies.[15]

A City of Immigrants

Scholarly attention to Queens was an indication that what was taking place in the borough was an important and historically significant thing. More broadly, the diversification of the borough was helping to dispel its image as a center of ignorance and bigotry. Publicly displaying its pluralism was a means to present the "new and improved" Queens, something that could certainly be seen at the Queens Festival. The "urban fair," as it was described, was in its eighth year in 1985, and with more than two hundred exhibits and one hundred food vendors, it was bigger and better than ever. Like the 1983 Queens Tricentennial festival, the event was held in Flushing Meadows Corona Park and featured cultural representations from various communities. Visitors could take in a Japanese tea ceremony, Chinese kite making, Korean wedding ceremonies, Indian sari draping, and Spanish dancers, all designed to illustrate how the borough was a crossroads of the world.[16]

Fittingly, nowhere more than in Flushing could one detect the internationality of the borough. The neighborhood had extended its identity as a kind of middle-class, multi-ethnic version of Manhattan's Chinatown in the early 1980s, with more than 70,000 current residents of Asian heritage (about 37,000 Korean Americans, 30,000 Chinese Americans, and 7,000 Indian Americans). Contrary to popular belief, the Flushing Asians were not an insular group resistant to assimilating within the larger fabric of the community. Some were getting involved in local politics and real estate development, adding to their retail presence on Main Street (the city's sixth-largest shopping district).[17]

Immigrants were not the only ones attracted to northern Queens, however. Manhattanites, seeing the excellent value of real estate in the area, were ditching their tiny, expensive apartments for bigger and cheaper homes in many neighborhoods, including Jackson Heights, Astoria, Woodside, Sunnyside, Long Island City, Corona, and Elmhurst. The rush to the area, which was an easy hop by train to and from Manhattan, was driving up prices quickly; not since the "discovery" of Brooklyn Heights and Park Slope in the mid-1960s had there been such a rise in real estate values in a particular part of New York City. Prices of houses in northern Queens had doubled and even tripled through the early 1980s, and commercial real estate was also soaring. Apartment houses were converting to condominiums and cooperatives, making this an attractive option for Manhattanites who preferred apartment living.[18]

While Rego Park in Central Queens was not seeing a spike in real estate values—at least not yet—immigrants from around the world liked the neighborhood just fine. Stephen A. Halsey Junior High School was as polyglot a school as one could imagine; students in one class included Ho Suk Ping He, Yana Katzap, Tikkun Amongsi, Azaria Badebr, Rotcheild Boruhov, and Eduardo Yun (the latter a Portuguese-speaking Korean who had immigrated from Brazil). Complicating matters for teachers was that some students were from countries in which first names were put last; it was not surprising that American names were often used as substitutes (Chin Sheng Chu went by "George"). The neighborhood and school had been primarily Jewish, but the arrival of a Chinese man who opened a luncheonette (serving egg creams) was said to have started the transition. Due to such stories, New York City had once again become "a city of immigrants"; there

Figure 4.1. The Sunnyside Yards, a wide swath of tracks slicing through Long Island City. *Source*: Jack E. Boucher, *Northeast Railroad Corridor, Amtrak Route [. . .]*, photograph, Historic American Engineering Record, Library of Congress Prints and Photographs Division, Washington, DC, https://www.loc.gov/item/ny1317/.

were now more foreign-born residents (one in three) than at any time since 1930.[19]

Also rather complicated was the relationship within certain ethnic groups in Queens. Many outsiders lumped Spanish-speaking people together as "Hispanic," for example, but immigrants from different countries had their own cultural identity. Groups were in some respects competing against each other, something to which residents could attest. "In one way or another, we all want to demonstrate that our nationality is better than the other," said a Cuban man after recalling a debate with an Ecuadorean over which country had the tastier cuisine. One way that Latin Americans showed their separateness was by demanding they each have their own parade and by holding their own celebrations. (Ecuadoreans, Columbians, Uruguayans, and Dominicans sponsored independent festivals in Queens in the summer of 1986.)[20]

Even using "Spanish-speaking" as a common denominator for Hispanics was somewhat misleading, as regional dialects could make the same word mean different things to different groups. History and class understandably played heavily into divisions, yet there were bridges as well, the most significant one being the experience of living in a new country and leaving an old one behind. Shared goals—moving up economically, providing a good education for one's children—also tended to overshadow the variations among Hispanics in Queens.[21]

That was made clear in a remarkable series of articles published between April 1986 and April 1987. Called *Making Their Way in the USA*, the four articles followed the lives of the Almontes, who immigrated to Corona from Santo Domingo in the Dominican Republic. Visa difficulties delayed the arrival of a couple of members of the family, but by the end of the series they were together in Queens. The final piece carried the headline "At Home, at Last" and detailed the struggles in learning to speak and write English, making friends at school, dealing with homesickness, and working in a sweatshop. Just getting through the winter hadn't been easy, as Santo Domingo was a lot warmer during those months than New York City. But the family prevailed and aspired to something that most New Yorkers, immigrants or otherwise, could relate to: a bigger apartment.[22]

The competitiveness within certain ethnic communities in Queens went beyond which homeland had the most delicious food. One could argue that the borough was a remarkably tolerant and inclusive place given the number of different groups interacting on a daily basis, all of them trying to move up the economic ladder. That was not the image of Queens to outsiders, however, especially with regard to race. In quite a few cases, longtime residents of European descent had not welcomed the arrival of people of color to their neighborhoods, to put it mildly, and the fictional character Archie Bunker had come to symbolize the racial sentiment of White working-class men in the borough.[23]

That image was solidified with the racially motivated attack of an African American in Howard Beach in December 1986, which ended tragically with the man's death. Mayor Koch expressed great surprise that such a thing could happen in Queens and called the incident a "lynching."[24] A couple of other racially motivated attacks followed over the next few days, cause for extra police to be assigned to patrol the streets.[25] The following month, more than three thousand people marched in protest against racism (ending at Koch's home in Greenwich Village).[26] Recognizing that Queens was viewed by many across the country and even around the world as not at all inclusive in terms of race, ethnicity, and religion, elected officials and community leaders tried to address the problem. Even before the terrible Howard Beach incident that received considerable media attention, efforts were being made to bridge those divisions, but the attack intensified that initiative.[27]

That initiative was made most apparent at Queens Unity Day in April 1987, at Reception Hall in Flushing, where a cultural mosaic of three hundred people got together to discuss how those of different races, ethnicities, and religions can live in peace. Considerable hugging took place at the event, used as symbolic acts to demonstrate unity between Blacks and Whites, Jews and Arabs, and a host of other groups. Queens Unity Day was actually part of a national and international movement designed to promote harmony among people of diverse backgrounds. Given that 150 languages and dialects were now said to be spoken in Queens, however, striving for unity was seen as a particularly relevant cause. Many positive outcomes could be achieved by diffusing culturally based conflict, participants agreed, and ideally lead to a more level playing field in housing, education, and employment.[28]

A Window on the World

Such a goal was clearly needed given the persistent discrimination being displayed by some landlords in Queens. While the Trumps appeared to be practicing rental bias on a large scale, small-time operators too were refusing to lease apartments to people because of their race or ethnicity. In June 1987, a Hispanic woman was awarded $18,000 for the "severe humiliation and emotional distress" that she suffered after a landlord in Glendale declined her application based on her national origin. That was the largest award ever granted by the New York City Commission on Human Rights for housing discrimination.[29]

Although the heyday of the Ku Klux Klan was in the 1920s, the group still existed, something made quite apparent in Queens in 1987. In December of that year, Hank Erich Schmidt, the "exalted cyclops" of the national KKK, announced that his organization was planning to light a seventy-foot-tall cross in front of the Queensbridge Houses, the predominantly African American public housing development built in Long Island City in 1939. Schmidt's aim was "to provoke a violent racial confrontation," he told reporters, wanting "to show the dark people a thing or two." Schmidt planned to apply for a city permit to allow the Klan to march in front of the Queensbridge Houses (the biggest housing development of its kind in North America) in their full dress, although safety laws required the use of an electric cross rather than the traditional incendiary one.[30]

The KKK was going all out for their latest demonstration, whose ultimate goal was to drive Blacks out of Queens. Members from across the country were invited to attend, and Schmidt had also asked the equally heinous neo-Nazis to participate. "It's going to be wild," he promised, despite the fact that his national organization currently had only forty official members. Schmidt wanted to create an incident similar to one in Greensboro, North Carolina, in 1979, when a shootout between Klansmen and members of the Communist Worker Party left five of the latter group dead. Schmidt, who had grown up in Estonia and Romania, did not reveal the exact date of the event but did say that it would be held on a weekend or holiday so that Klansmen wouldn't have to miss work.[31]

The event never happened, of course, if only because the KKK would have been seriously outnumbered, even if some neo-Nazis showed up. A more representative example of racial and ethnic relationships in Queens could be found in Elmhurst, which remained the most diverse neighborhood of New York City and likely the United States. "Elmhurst is a window on the world," wrote Felicia R. Lee in the *New York Times* in 1989 after observing women in saris pushing baby strollers past Irish pubs and Korean fruit stands. Immigrants had come from about 120 countries to live in the neighborhood, bound together by a determination to "make it" in America. The diversity was indeed striking; church services were given in Tamil, students at PS 89 spoke forty-three languages, and the public library stocked books in both Spanish and Chinese.[32]

Elmhurst was hardly a paradise at the end of the 1980s, however. Crack dealers operated their businesses on sidewalks, schools were at 120 percent capacity, and garbage seemed to be everywhere. Many older residents held that the neighborhood had declined as it grew, and as with other areas of Queens, it was believed that there were as many undocumented immigrants as documented ones. Also, like a good number of places in the borough, Elmhurst had been primarily a blue-collar neighborhood composed of White ethnics until it began to evolve in the post–World War II years.[33]

The demographics of Elmhurst illustrated the vast change in the makeup of the community. The 1990 census numbers would soon be in, but the current figures showed that the neighborhood was 40 percent White, 35 percent Hispanic, 22 percent Asian, and about 2 percent African American. Those of Italian, Irish, or German descent tended to live south of Queens Boulevard, which ran through Elmhurst, while most of the Hispanics and

118 | QUEENS

Asians lived north of it. All groups were concerned about crime in the area, however, as the number of murders, rapes, robberies, and burglaries had risen sharply in recent years.[34]

Adjacent neighborhoods of Elmhurst had experienced a smoother residential transition. Sunnyside Gardens had seemingly recovered from its racial divide; the eight-block enclave was now considered a charming neighborhood, although not completely immune to crime and drugs.[35] The Gardens, as locals referred to it, was a planned community that was included on the National Register of Historic Places. Developed in the 1920s by a team of planners who saw no contradiction between greenery and urbanism, Sunnyside Gardens consisted of six hundred two-story rowhouses nestled within landscaped courtyards. Sunnyside proper was developed in the 1930s and 1940s for working-class families, enveloping the seventy-seven-acre, enclave-like Gardens.[36]

Woodside, also next door to Elmhurst, was a similarly sanguine place where Asian and Latin American immigrants lived peacefully alongside the older Irish population. (It had once been nicknamed Irish-Town.) Almost half of Woodside's current forty thousand residents were immigrants in 1990, and it was considered a model of ethnic and racial integration. Unlike in other neighborhoods in Queens, in which immigrants had largely displaced the White ethnics, most of the Irish in Woodside were staying put. Interestingly, a new wave of Irish had recently settled there (illegally, for the most part), a result of Ireland's troubled economy. In fact, the Irish brogue had returned to Woodside, a happy sound to old-timers who hadn't heard it for decades.[37]

Through the 1990s, Sunnyside too saw a resurgence of its Irish community alongside the existing Korean, Spanish, Rumanian, German, and Greek immigrants. Quite a few pubs opened on or near Queens Boulevard, which served as gathering spots for a younger generation of Irish. The sound of babies crying could be heard in the neighborhood's Catholic churches, another sign that Sunnyside was being remade as Irish returned to the area.[38] The chamber of commerce of Sunnyside was doing what it could to attract traffic, and the owners of the various Irish pubs and restaurants were more collegial than competitive.[39]

Upon hearing the news that a new program (Schumer DV-98) would allot fifty-five thousand visas a year for designated countries, hundreds of Irish who were not in the United States legally rushed to the Emerald Isle Immigration Center in Queens. There was a sense of urgency, as President Clinton had in 1996 signed the Illegal Immigration Reform and Immigrant Responsibility Act, which included a stipulation making it more difficult for undocumented immigrants to meet the steps necessary to obtain a green card. Soon, a movement with the rallying call of "Legalize the Irish" was in the works to make it easier for the undocumented to stay as long as they desired in America without fear of being deported.[40]

It made sense that the Legalize the Irish movement was based in Queens. There were pockets of Irish in most of the other boroughs, but Queens had the deepest and richest Irish history and culture in the city. New Irish residents were heading not just to Sunnyside and Woodside but to Maspeth and Middle Village, and there were older communities of Irish in Rockaway and Bayside (named for its location on Little Neck Bay). The renaissance of Irish culture in New York City was understandably seen as something to celebrated. While the Immigration and Nationality Act of 1965 allowed in groups that had previously not been allowed to enter the United States, it also excluded other groups, including the Irish. Some Irish people who had come to Queens in the 1980s to escape Ireland's troubled economy were by the 1990s returning to their homeland, as times there had improved and formerly Irish neighborhoods in the borough changed with new waves of immigrants.[41]

The revival of Irish culture in Queens, including its brogue, was just one more reason to believe that the place was like no other. Upon hearing what he described as the "babble of tongues," Richard F. Shepard of the *New York Times* labeled Queens "the doorstep to the whole wide world." Roosevelt Avenue, which formed the border of Elmhurst and Jackson Heights, appeared to be the epicenter of globalism in Queens, a not surprising thing given that the No. 7 train ran right above it. Earlier immigrants—Italians, Irish, and Jews—had come to the area when the Roosevelt Avenue elevated subway arrived in 1917. Now Columbians, Uruguayans, Koreans, and Indians all had robust communities in the area, something easily detected by the restaurants and bakeries that ran along the avenue. If one didn't know better, one might mistake Seventy-Forth Street for Bombay; there were no less than twenty-one sari shops. Oddly, however, it was Columbians rather than Indians who lived on Seventy-Forth Street; their nickname for the area was Little Chapinero—a reference to a barrio in Bogota.[42]

It Is America

Those looking for quaintness or charm in the Roosevelt Avenue area of Queens would likely be disappointed, however. There was some aesthetically pleasing architecture in the borough, notably the Jackson Heights garden apartment houses that had been put up north of Roosevelt Avenue between the world wars, but most of Queens could be seen as a string of rather undistinguished buildings. "There are streets and streets of one- and two-family dwellings," Shepard noted, "ranging from modern brick to Archie Bunker wood, stone and shingle." Rather than the collection of imposing turn-of-the-twentieth-century brownstones found in Brooklyn, Bronx, and Manhattan, it was the incredible variety of authentic ethnic cuisine that made a trip on the No. 7 train from Manhattan worthwhile.[43]

Dena Kleiman, also of the *New York Times*, took such a journey to Elmhurst to report on the food in the city's most ethnically diverse neighborhood. (Data from the US Immigration and Naturalization Service showed that there were immigrants from 114 different countries in Elmhurst in 1991.) Kleiman took a tour of the Chinese food markets, Indian spice shops, Korean barbecue restaurants, Argentine butcher shops, Hong Kong bakeries, and Columbian coffeehouses, finding the area to be very much the "melting pot" it was said to be. A prime example of Queens-style cultural mélange was Singa's Famous, a restaurant on Broadway run by a Greek whose pizza was especially popular with Indians. "Food is its own currency in Elmhurst," Kleiman wrote. "It is a means to learn English, a way to feel at home, a chance to experiment, a bridge between vastly different cultures."[44]

To that point, traveling to different areas of Queens for memorable culinary experiences had become somewhat of an adventurous activity among more sophisticated Manhattanites. (The same could be said to be true for Brooklyn, the Bronx, and Staten Island.) Astoria was naturally the place to go for Greek food, but those in search of genuine Korean, Indian, Russian, or Central and South American cuisine could find it somewhere in Queens. Bragging rights were awarded to epicureans who journeyed to a place like La Fusta on Baxter Avenue in Elmhurst to partake of its Argentinian mixed grill. Telling friends about the carnivorous delights—morcilla (blood sausage), chorizo (Spanish sausage), sweetbreads, kidneys, and calf's liver, all garnished with chimichurri sauce—would no doubt elicit envious looks from the most urbane of foodies.[45]

Points could also be scored for exploring Farmers Market Jamaica, which was the only year-round covered farmers' market in New York City. Opened in 1992, the twenty-six-thousand-square-foot space was the only farmers' market in Queens, despite the borough having a population of some two million people. Beyond making fresh produce and other foods accessible, the farmers' market was part of the Greater Jamaica Development

THE INTERNATIONAL EXPRESS | 121

Corporation's effort to revitalize downtown Jamaica, which had declined considerably in the 1960s and 1970 due to White flight to the suburbs. Although new, the market was carrying on a very long tradition in Jamaica; just a block away, there had been in the 1920s a "Jamaica market" where farmers brought their goods to sell. Going much further back, the same kind of trading took place in the area in the early 1700s, although it was unlikely that Caribbean foods such as spicy chicken patties, roti, and oxtail were sold there.[46]

The revival of Jamaica was all the more impressive given the stagnant national economy of the early 1990s. Jamaica's retail district had just a 2 percent vacancy rate, largely the function of it being a major transportation hub. (The LIRR, two subway lines, and around two hundred buses served the area during rush hour.) Hundreds of thousands of students from Queens College, St. John's University, and York College passed through the district every day, good news for the local bars and restaurants. Somewhat like Flushing, immigrants had infused Jamaica's retail area with new life, and business leaders believed further growth was in the neighborhood's future.[47]

The arrival of a new restaurant on Union Hall Street, whose owners had bypassed hipper areas around the city for a seemingly rejuvenated Jamaica, suggested just that. There remained much potential in Jamaica's commercial hub, they and others believed, backed up by positive signs that the neighborhood was indeed coming back from its decades-long slide. Both private ventures and public projects were in the works, and economic data from the 1990 census showed that the Black middle class in southeastern Queens was prospering. Blacks not just in Jamaica but St. Albans, Hollis, Springfield Gardens, and other neighborhoods had reached virtual economic parity with Whites, an important milestone. Immigrants from the Caribbean, who were starting up new businesses in that section of the borough, were credited with having much to do with this revival.[48]

Caribbean culture was thus a big part of the fifteenth annual Queens Festival in Flushing Meadows Corona Park in 1992. The theme of that year's festival was "ethnic pride and cultural diversity," a reflection of the multiculturalism movement that was now in full swing across the United States. An estimated two million people came to the event over the weekend, making it the most attended festival in the nation. Besides being the biggest, it's safe to say that the Queens Festival was different from any other due to its astounding diversity. The huge fete was "the annual coming-out party for a borough that is forever reinventing and reinvigorating itself with flows of immigrants from Asia, India, the Caribbean and Latin America," J. Peder Zane of the *New York Times* observed. Phyllis Shafran, the organizer of the event since its beginning, put it more simply: "It is America."[49]

Also American, regretfully, was racial and ethnic conflict, and Queens had at least its share in the early 1990s. Police denied that race or ethnicity was a factor in the borough's rising crime rate, but residents believed that the changing mix of neighborhoods was responsible. Corona in particular was in flux; immigrants from Ecuador, Columbia, and the Dominican Republic had in recent years moved into the area that had been largely Italian. Laurelton too had morphed considerably, something to which locals attributed the escalation in violent crime. That neighborhood had been middle-class African American, Irish, and Italian but was much transformed by immigrants from Haiti, Trinidad and Tobago, and Jamaica. At the same time, residents of Brooklyn and the Bronx had relocated to Laurelton, and that too put an end to what old-timers described as almost a small-town feeling.[50]

The vast majority of residents of both Corona and Laurelton were staying put, however, hoping that the rise in crime was just a blip. The same was true in Far Rockaway, which had been primarily Jewish but was now mostly African American, Indian, and Hispanic. In Flushing, meanwhile, a number of the White, Black, and Hispanic residents who had lived there before the "Asian invasion" felt that their neighborhood had essentially been taken over. Queensites were proud of their status as the most diverse place in the city and perhaps the entire world, but it appeared to be coming at a cost.[51]

Although certainly disturbing, ethnic and racial tensions in Queens could have been significantly greater given how many people and groups there now were in the borough. Census data from 1990 showed the population of Queens to be exactly 1,951,590, and the New York City Mayor's Office claimed that the borough was now home to 178 ethnic groups. There were no groups in the city that weren't in Queens, according to Frank Vardy, a demographer for the Department of City Planning, which published *The Newest New Yorkers: A Look at Immigration.* (Between 1982 and 1989, people from 112 countries emigrated to Elmhurst alone, according to Vardy.) Immigration to Queens, like that of many places, tended to snowball, with pioneers taking in relatives and friends from their homelands. Helping find homes and jobs for the new arrivals was usually the first order of business, after which they did the same for another wave.[52]

THE INTERNATIONAL EXPRESS | 123

The Community of Homes

Given the cultural mosaic that now was Queens, one might ponder what Archie Bunker of the television show *All in the Family* would have thought about the extreme transformation of his home borough. He was a fictional character, of course, but was representative of a certain archetype—White, Protestant, and conservative—that really existed in Queens (and probably everywhere else in America). Bunker could very well have been in a Florida retirement community by the early 1990s, and based on many of his diatribes, might worry about who was living in his house on the also fictional Hauser Street in an unnamed neighborhood of Queens. (The house shown in the show's opening sequence is on Cooper Avenue in Glendale, but Corona and Astoria were better fits for his blue-collar, labor union–oriented character.)[53]

Bunker's concern would have been justified. Officially America's most diverse county, according to the census, the 112 square miles of Queens was divided in roughly equal proportions of non-Hispanic Whites, African Americans, Hispanics, and Asians. The population was not equally distributed across the borough in terms of race and ethnicity, however, especially with regard to African Americans.[54] Sociologists were particularly intrigued by Queens because they believed it was a fair representation of what the United States as a whole would look like in the twenty-first century. Local politicians, not surprisingly, framed the diversity of Queens in wholly positive terms; David Dinkins, who became mayor of New York in 1990, liked to use the terms "gorgeous mosaic" and "rainbow coalition" to describe the city, with Queens the foremost example of that colorful image.[55]

While Queens was unique in some respects, its residents shared the common concern of how to strike a balance between further development and retaining a high quality of life geared toward home ownership. In fact, the borough was nicknamed "the community of homes" within New York City and with good reason: there were a total of 753,000 housing "units" in Queens, most of them row houses but also duplexes and single-family dwellings. "Queens has always been the place where people moved to from other boroughs," said demographer Frank Vardy, a reference to its perception as a quasi-suburb. There were more than fifty individual communities in Queens, however, each one distinct in some way, exponentially multiplying the borough's diversity.[56] Queens was often seen as a nondescript place, probably because of its bland architecture, but that belied the borough's unsurpassed culture, particularly the food, as well as its fascinating post-colonized history that went back centuries.[57]

124 | QUEENS

Figure 4.2. While most architecture in Queens is less than exceptional, there were and are plenty of beautiful homes. Given the impressiveness of houses like this one on Jamaica Avenue in Queens Village in 1942, one could see how Queens was nicknamed "the community of homes." *Source*: Gottscho-Schleisner Inc., *Frederick C. Stutzmann, Residence at 224-39 Jamaica Ave. [. . .]*, 1942, photograph, Library of Congress Prints and Photographs Division, Washington, DC, https://www.loc.gov/item/2018741242/.

Archie Bunker would no doubt be shocked by the fact that a fresh analysis of the 1990 census data revealed that Blacks in Queens had not just matched but surpassed non-Hispanic Whites in median household income. (He certainly wasn't happy to see his Black next-door neighbor "movin' on up" to the Upper East Side because of a prosperous dry cleaning business.) Working women and immigrants were cited as the key players in the economic progress in what Sam Roberts called "New York City's quintessential middle-class borough." That both spouses in Black families were likely to have jobs was the differentiator, in other words, plus the tendency to work longer hours. Finally, children in Black households often remained at home, adding to household income.[58]

Relative prosperity within the African American community of Queens did not deter less ethical real estate agents from using blockbusting. The

Figure 4.3. A very typical house in Queens, c. 1964, but unusual in its legacy, as this one was the residence of Malcolm X. *Source*: Dick Demarsico, *Exterior View of Home of Malcolm X [. . .]*, 1964, photograph, Library of Congress Prints and Photographs Division, Washington, DC, https://www.loc.gov/item/97503442/.

New York State prohibition against solicitations to homeowners had been overturned, making it legal for agents to try to drum up business. And that they did—with letters, phone calls, and door knocking causing panic in some communities, especially among older residents, as there were cases in which whole neighborhoods turned over after a few residents sold at lower than market value (Laurelton was a good example). Solicitation was one thing, but using high-pressure (and still illegal) tactics was another, particularly when subtly suggesting that a certain ethnic group was moving in—this time agents used South Asians, rather than African Americans. That was the situation in Bellerose, where postcards suggested that homeowners meet their new Indian and Pakistani neighbors.[59]

Stirring up ethnic prejudices went against everything that Queens was about. No one knew that more than Ilana Harlow, a folklorist for the Queens Council on the Arts, who was documenting the myriad ethnic enclaves along the No. 7 train (which she like many others had labeled the International Express). Harlow was putting together a visitor's guide to the borough, which had become the most culturally diverse county in the United States. (Harlow later directed a film on the subject called *The International Express*.) "I can't imagine ever running out of material," she said in 1995, a good point given that Afghans, Chinese, Columbians, Dominicans, Filipinos, Indians, Pakistanis, Bangladeshis, Koreans, Mexicans, Uruguayans, Argentines, Peruvians, Romanians, Thais, and Irish all lived under the seven-mile stretch of the elevated subway line.[60]

Perhaps the most amazing thing about the diversity in Queens was its fluidity. Flushing, for example, had been mostly Jewish, but Asian churches and grocery stores had replaced most of the synagogues and all the kosher delis. But in its place another Jewish community had popped up in Kew Gardens Hills, this one made up of immigrants from Israel and the former Soviet Union. Even Flushing was already in transition: Indians and Pakistanis were heading there from Jackson Heights, which had been dominated by Columbians. Mexicans were now moving into Jackson Heights, however, another example of the revolving door that was Queens. Some neighborhoods were heavily populated by combinations of groups one would not expect or predict; both Guyanese and Poles favored Ozone Park for some reason.[61] (The name Ozone Park originated from its developer, who found the air from the nearby bay and ocean to be particularly invigorating.) Interesting fusions were also being formed; kosher Indian food could be found in Forest Hills to serve the Jewish community that had emigrated from Calcutta.[62]

While New Yorkers took pride in their city being a welcoming place for immigrants, there was still some friction between old-timers and newcomers. That was most apparent in Flushing, which had undergone vast change in a relatively short period of time. Pundits credited the Asian immigrants with revitalizing an area in serious decline, but some locals felt their neighborhood had essentially been stolen from them. This immigration experience was certainly different from the standard one in which foreigners assimilated into the existing social fabric, and the first wave of Asians were not poor, fleeing persecution, or escaping a famine like many émigrés during the late nineteenth and early twentieth centuries. Critics argued that the Koreans, Taiwanese, and Indians had "colonized" Flushing by buying property and raising rents that drove out residents whose families might have been there for generations. The second, less affluent wave was even worse, they held, believing that most had entered the country illegally and were involved in some kind of criminal activity.[63]

Inevitably, perhaps, comparisons were made among the three Chinatowns in New York City. The one on Manhattan's Lower East Side was the most well-known, of course, having been around in some form since the 1870s when Chinese immigrants began to settle around Mott Street south of Canal Street. However, there was growing recognition of the two newer ones, which came to be a century later. Like Flushing's Chinatown, a parallel community had soon developed in Sunset Park, Brooklyn, the latter also resulting from the relaxing of immigration laws beginning in the late 1960s. Interestingly, however, the Queens and Brooklyn communities had little to do with each other; mostly Mandarin-speaking Taiwanese populated the former, while the latter closely mirrored multilingual mainland China. Unlike the Flushing Chinatown, which was generally considered a model, if dominant, community, the Sunset Park Chinatown had earned a bad reputation, said to be heavily populated by undocumented immigrants and criminals from the Fujian province.[64]

Residents of Sunnyside were likely pleased to see that the sizable number of Turks arriving in the neighborhood followed the traditional path of immigration rather than resembling an "invasion." This group was reminiscent of earlier émigrés like the Italians, Jews, and Irish who had come to America around the turn of the twentieth century. Often with little money, no job, and no place to stay, Turks were settling in gradually and had no plans to remake Sunnyside into a Turkish village. Also like previous immigrants, the Turks were striking a balance between assimilation and retention of their cultural heritage. Most were secular Muslims, but a masjid (small mosque) had appeared where Islam was practiced, much like in Turkey itself. Observers were waiting to see what kind of relationship the Turks would have with the Greeks in nearby Astoria and the Armenian community in northern Queens, as both of those nationalities had been traditional enemies of the Turks.[65] Hope was that those groups would live peacefully alongside each other, much like the Indians and Pakistanis in Jackson Heights, as those two nationalities had been staunch enemies since 1947.[66]

Beyond the Melting Pot

Perhaps the biggest problem associated with immigration in Queens, however, was in the borough's school system. There were almost one hundred thousand more students than what the system was designed to hold, the result, in part, of numerous young families arriving from the Dominican

Republic, Mexico, and Asia. Beyond having to find space for so many students, language barriers and the bureaucracy of public schools presented major challenges, particularly in polyglot Jackson Heights. One school in that neighborhood had moved to a department store to accommodate the extra students, while another was using trailers as classrooms. Enrollment instructions were given in English, Chinese, and Spanish, but even that wasn't nearly enough given the number of languages being spoken.[67]

The turnover of some neighborhoods was another downside to the continuing arrival of so many people from so many lands. Many who had immigrated to Queens before or soon after passage of the Immigration and Nationality Act of 1965 now felt like strangers again, as different nationalities or ethnic groups moved in. It had been mostly Cubans who settled along Junction Boulevard and Roosevelt Avenue, for example, but now Elmhurst, Corona, and Jackson Heights were heavily Mexican, Dominican, Columbian, Peruvian, and Ecuadoran. Spanish was still spoken, of course, but the accents varied widely, a source of frustration to older Cubans (who had displaced the Irish and Germans). Quite a number of neighborhoods in Queens had become pan-Hispanic or pan-American, according to sociologists, who were now using the metaphor of a salad bowl rather than a melting pot to describe such areas.[68]

To that point, many Americans believed that immigrants had to give up their ethnic backgrounds to fit into the national quilt, but this simply wasn't true. The metaphor of the "melting pot" was a powerful one, yet there was little evidence to support the idea that the United States had ever been a national "alloy." As Nathan Glazer and Daniel Patrick Moynihan pointed out in their 1963 *Beyond the Melting Pot*, a cultural blending of hyphenated Americans "did not happen"; the pluralistic society we have always had was a direct reflection of the ability for immigrants to retain their ethnic heritage. "People are free to retain as much of their native cultural values as they desire or to deviate from it and still be assimilated," wrote Peter D. Salins in *Reason* (1997), taking note of how many different ethnic groups were flexibly accommodated to form a single nation.[69]

Religion was a prime way to detect the increasingly pluralistic nature of Queens, and the United States, at the end of the twentieth century. The numbers of those belonging to non-Judeo-Christian religions were quickly rising across the nation; statistics showed that more than twelve million Americans were members of various such faiths and that Islam could soon surpass Judaism as the country's second-largest religion. This shift was undermining the popular belief that the United States was essentially a Christian country. "The facts prove that pluralism has become an American way of life however fundamental Christian preachers may rally against it," William B. Williamson observed in *Free Inquiry* (1993), referring to the tendency among certain fundamentalists and ultraconservatives to marginalize other faiths. The Baptist televangelist Pat Robertson had recently called for a "grand plan" for the United States to institutionalize an American Protestant theocracy, for example, while the political commentator Pat Buchanan proposed a Christian "jihad" or holy war. Such appeals were ignorant on a number of levels, including missing the obvious fact that the United States was, more than anything else, a fundamentally multicultural society.[70]

For those who consider freedom of faith a prime symbol of our national identity, a look around New York City would confirm that belief. At dusk, regardless of the weather, Muslim taxi drivers routinely pull their cabs over, spread a rug on the ground, and then kneel and begin praying. Orthodox Jews, meanwhile, can be seen walking home on Friday afternoons, their faith not allowing them to use the subway (or any other mechanical device) after sunset on the Sabbath. More devout Catholics with large families still refuse to use birth control, according to the Pope's wishes (hardly the most practical choice given the price of real estate in New York City). Mormons and Seventh-day Adventists who own grocery stores in one of the boroughs typically choose not to sell cigarettes or beer, not the smartest business decision perhaps but considered necessary because of their religious doctrines.[71]

Whether Queens was a melting pot or salad bowl, the Metropolitan Transit Authority (MTA) was definitely pleased about the ongoing influx of immigrants to the borough. Subway ridership was higher than it had been in a generation, much of it due to the young families going to work or school. Ridership on the F train in 1997 was up by more than 50 percent since 1990, correlating with the Russian and Bukharan Jewish émigrés who were now living near Queens Boulevard in Rego Park and Forest Hills. It was the No. 7 train where one could most easily detect the mark that immigrants had made in Queens, however, as it was on that line where one went through Corona, Elmhurst, Jackson Heights, and Woodside. The MTA was delighted to see its annual revenues increase by tens of millions of dollars, reversing the decades of decline when many urbanites had fled for the suburbs.[72]

By the late 1990s, a different kind of rider was also taking the subways to and from Queens. By 1997, the borough was seen, among a certain subculture, as chic, the ironic result of its residents making no effort to be so. Always on the lookout for The Next Big Thing, trendier urbanites were heading to Astoria to go clubbing, tired of the same old, same old in Chelsea or the Village. "Faster than you can say Archie Bunker, Queens has morphed into what its residents plausibly claim is the hippest and hottest of the five boroughs of New York City," proclaimed Joe Mathews of the *Baltimore Sun* after speaking with a few of the city's avant-garde. Many artists had abandoned Chelsea and SoHo for Long Island City for its bigger spaces, cheaper rents, and grittiness. Queens was seen as "real," edgier young adults explained, a welcome alternative to the cleaned-up, "Giuliani-ized" Manhattan.[73]

A fair number of riders on the International Express in the summer of 1998 had something other than clubbing or gallery-hopping on their minds: the World Cup. There were dozens of bars and restaurants catering to Latin Americans, each one a place to watch *futbol* (soccer) and cheer for one's favorite team. Four South American teams had made it to the World Cup that year (the first time in history), making life under the No. 7 train especially exciting. The police in northern Queens were put on high alert and a special task force assigned to handle any potential clashes among the Brazilians, Argentinians, Columbians, and Chileans. (Mexico had also made it into the competition.) New York's Finest remembered what happened in 1994 when thousands of fans flooded onto Roosevelt Avenue after a successful match, stopping traffic by partying and playing soccer in the busy street. Extra Boys in Blue would also be sent to Broadway in Astoria, where there was a sizable Brazilian community, should there be excessive celebration.[74]

South Americans' habit of going a little crazy every four years during the World Cup likely had little to do with the billboard that went up in Sunnyside in 1999. The sign, made by a Sunnyside resident who had paid $2,250 to rent three billboards for three months, read: "Over 80 percent of Americans support very little or no more immigration. Is anyone listening to us?" Sunnyside was highly populated by immigrants, making it not surprising that many residents and community leaders strongly objected to the message. An identical billboard had gone up in Ridgewood, and a similar one in Brooklyn, paid for by the same man, who defended his position. Most Americans shared the same sentiment about immigration, he told reporters, explaining that he simply wanted to raise attention to the issue.[75]

Claire Shulman, Queens borough president, made it clear that the message on the billboards was not in the spirit of Queens. "Here in Queens, immigrants have revitalized our communities and enriched our culture," she said at a hastily arranged news conference, adding that her borough was "proof that people of every race, nationality and ethnicity can live and work together for the improvement of all our communities." A dozen religious and community leaders stood behind Shulman, literally and figuratively, in agreement that immigration was a positive force in Queens. Immigrants represented 55 percent of the 31,891 residents of Sunnyside, according to the 1990 census, a higher percentage than that of the borough as a whole (36 percent).[76]

Just a few weeks later, however, stickers began to appear on some stop signs and fire alarm boxes around Queens, the work of the West Virginia–based National Alliance, a hate group founded by a former American Nazi Party official. The orange or green stickers carried different messages, one of them being "Earth's most endangered species, the white race, help preserve it." While the recently put up billboards were solely focused on immigration, the stickers were hateful toward anyone who wasn't White, which included the hundreds of thousands of Africans, Asians, and Hispanics who had come to Queens in recent decades.[77]

At the same time, hate-based crimes against Sikhs were a real problem in Ozone Park. Young White men were attacking Sikhs and stealing or breaking into their cars, with police slow to investigate the cases or prevent further ones. Sikh children were also being harassed and beaten up while going to school, the impetus for members of the Sikh community to march down to Precinct 102 and demand that action be taken.[78]

Those responsible for these hateful acts appeared to be ignorant of the fact that the United States is a nation of immigrants, with the exception of Native Americans, and that Queens is a borough of immigrants. Rivaling the diversity of Sunnyside was Woodside, where residents had come from forty-nine countries and spoke thirty-four different languages. The numbers from the 2000 census would soon be in, but the 1990 census figures showed that the percentage of the foreign-born in the neighborhood had risen from 25 percent in 1950 to 55 percent in 1990. The demographics of New York City as a whole had changed dramatically in the past fifteen years; one in three citizens was an immigrant in 1999, with nearly half of them having arrived since 1985. Not since 1910—the peak of immigration in the twentieth century—had the ratio of new arrivals been so high.[79]

Those opposed to immigration also seemed unaware of the dedication shown by new arrivals to move up the social and economic ladder. Immigrants in Queens were taking full advantage of the educational opportunities in order to learn English, become more fluent in American culture, and apply their newfound knowledge in the workplace. One might not have guessed that the Queens Public Library was the most active library in the entire country; it circulated the highest number of books and other materials (15.3 million annually). "The people who use our library are highly motivated," stated Gary Strong, the library's director. "They want jobs and they want to learn how to live in America." Queens Public Library was actually following a long tradition; the busiest libraries in New York City had always been in areas with the highest number of immigrants. Given that, it was perhaps not surprising that the most active of the sixty-two branches in Queens's library system was Flushing, where a brand new library was about to open.[80]

The desire for immigrants to pursue their American dream by becoming more knowledgeable was thus an old story. It had been the Immigration and Nationality Act of 1965, which had opened "the golden door" to people from Latin America, Asia, the Middle East, and Africa, that altered the fundamental landscape of New York and many other parts of the country.[81] Susan Sachs of the *New York Times* presented this idea most eloquently: "Classic old ethnic neighborhoods that had successfully resisted change for half a century now belong to no one and to everyone. They are a clashing, colorful, polyglot, multiethnic collection of micro-communities whose members sometimes come together on neutral ground . . . and sometimes lead parallel lives."[82] As always, however, the future was unknown, making it impossible to predict the direction that New York City and the borough of Queens would take.

THE INTERNATIONAL EXPRESS | 133

CHAPTER FIVE

Tomorrow's America

Queens is the Future

—Jackson Heights mural, 2007, by
Eve Biddle and Joshua Frankel

In February 2002, just a few months after 9/11, an unusual band of fifty elementary school children was formed in Queens. The Music Masters, as the band members called themselves, consisted of students from a number of schools within Community School District 28, which encompassed various neighborhoods running through the middle of the borough. The students' families came from a cross section of socioeconomic, racial, and ethnic groups, making the band as diverse as Queens itself. African Americans, Jews, Ukrainians, Indians, Guyanese, and children of many more cultural backgrounds found themselves happily jamming with each other, a too-rare gathering of international harmony, especially after the recent terrorist attacks.[1]

The multicultural band was an apt symbol of the borough as a whole in the beginning of the twenty-first century. Queens had been radically transformed over the past one hundred years, both in terms of its built environment and the people who populated it. It was becoming apparent that the evolution of the borough, while amazing in itself, served as a beacon for the nation's future as the United States became increasingly diverse. Queens was "tomorrow's America," according to some, with no better place to see what lay ahead for America.

135

A Kind of Archipelago

Since the 1920s, and for some much earlier, Queens has been recognized as an appealing place to call home, and that had not changed despite its demographic upheaval. In the beginning of the twenty-first century, considerable attention was deservedly on Elmhurst, as it was widely seen as the most diverse neighborhood in the most diverse county in the United States. The once heavily Irish, Italian, and German area was now more than three-quarters Asian and Hispanic, with no less than one hundred nationalities and forty languages found among the students at Newtown High School. Elmhurst had become crowded, however, as immigrants flocked to the neighborhood for its affordable housing, international cuisine, and easy hop to and from Manhattan. (Newtown High was designed for 2,000 students but now had 4,600.) The Chinese were buying property in Elmhurst as they had done in Flushing a generation earlier, the result of years of hard work and saving.[2]

There were no parks in Elmhurst, however, making some home hunters choose the Kissena Park section of Flushing to plant their roots. Kissena Park had the actual 235-acre Kissena Park, complete with a spring-fed lake and nature trails that made the neighborhood a bucolic alternative to downtown Flushing. Like Elmhurst, Kissena Park had been mostly Italian, German, and Irish, but now one was more likely to find Chinese, Koreans, Indians, and Filipinos. The neighborhood had retained the suburban-like feeling that had drawn so many to Queens decades earlier, although preserving its older homes and charm was not easy as it gradually became more commercialized.[3]

Middle Village not only had a great park (Juniper Valley) but was as close-knit and community-oriented as any neighborhood in the five boroughs. The mostly Roman Catholic neighborhood was literally a "middle village," surrounded by Glendale, Elmhurst, Rego Park, and Maspeth, and much earlier it served as the halfway stop for farmers traveling from Long Island to markets in Manhattan and Brooklyn. It was not uncommon for two or three generations to live near each other in Middle Village, an increasingly rare thing anywhere. Middle Village had somehow escaped development until the late 1940s, in some part accounting for its small-town vibe. Germans were the first to settle in the area, followed by Jewish immigrants, Italians, and, in recent years, Russians and Poles.[4]

Cambria Heights had been part of the 1920s housing boom in Queens, and its development had progressed from the building of new highways and expanded LIRR train service. The subway never extended that far east, however, protecting the neighborhood from the congestion that affected many others. (Farmland and woods survived into the 1950s.) Cambria Heights remained primarily populated by middle-class and upper-middle-class African Americans (many of them having set out from Harlem in the 1960s and 1970s), but the neighborhood had started to change in the mid-1980s when significant numbers of West Indians began to move in. More recently, Haitians and other Caribbean immigrants were finding Cambria Heights to their liking just as the Jews, Italians, Germans, and Irish had between the 1920s and 1950s.[5]

For all of Queens' wonderful neighborhoods, and for all the immigrants who had chosen the borough as their new home, however, the place still lacked a clear identity, especially among Americans from a different part of the country. Many young adults who had been raised in Queens had moved away for job opportunities and were finding that their new friends had little knowledge of anything about the borough except perhaps JFK and LaGuardia airports. (Saying the Mets played there helped a little.) A horde of famous people had come from Queens, but that hadn't seemed to put the place on the map either, so much so that some were making the case that the borough was simply a collection of neighborhoods rather than a distinct entity itself. Those who had moved away and hadn't visited for decades were stunned by how international it had become when they did return, perhaps for a class reunion, not quite realizing it was the extraordinary diversity of the place that made it unique and special.[6]

That diversity extends into death, as a look around Calvary Cemetery in western Queens suggests. The first occupant of the 365-acre Roman Catholic cemetery arrived in 1848, and since then around three million more people have come there for eternal rest. Most were Irish, Italian, and Polish, but more recently Hispanic immigrants and their descendants have been buried in the cemetery, which stretches from the Brooklyn border into Woodside and Maspeth. (The Mespeatches Indian tribe had occupied the latter area.) Interestingly, those of different ethnic groups tend to have different ways of decorating the graves of their loved ones, experts have learned. Italians are typically far more attentive and elaborate than Irish in their adornment of plots, preferring annual flowers like petunias and marigolds over perennials or bulbs. Mexicans and South Americans, the newest arrivals, prefer *cerquitas* (little fences) as well as rose bushes. There are more than two dozen cemeteries in Queens, each one filled with revelatory stories of immigrants.[7]

The release of the 2000 census provided quantitative evidence that New York City and especially Queens were more diverse than ever. If there was one takeaway, it was that Hispanics were transforming entire neighborhoods such as East Elmhurst, where they had largely displaced African Americans in the 1990s. A similar story had taken place in Richmond Hill, but it was Sikhs and Hindus who had largely supplanted Hispanics (who had earlier supplanted the Irish). It appeared to be Bayside, however, whose demographics had shifted the most over the previous decade in all of New York City; European immigrants, many of them Jewish, had been greatly superseded by Asians, most of them Chinese. Bayside was essentially being annexed by Flushing in demographic terms, as Asians spilled over eastward. (The same was holding true in the Broadway-Flushing neighborhood.)[8] Queens had not only become more diverse but had experienced the greatest population growth of all five boroughs, most of it due to immigration.[9]

Even demographers were surprised to learn how many Native Americans there were in Queens. There were 6,300 Native Americans and Alaskans (the groups were combined in the data) in the borough (of a total of 17,300 in the city), according to the most recent census, although it was not a close-knit community. In fact, it was not uncommon for a Native American in Queens to not know any other, as the group tended to be highly mobile. While scattered about the borough, most lived in Jamaica, Ozone Park, and St. Albans, and they held a wide variety of jobs. The group consisted of members of a number of tribes, including Powhatan, Mohawk, Cherokee, and Shoshone, with many of them retaining cultural traditions such as growing corn and tobacco and burning sage as a cleansing ritual.[10]

It is important to keep in mind that although it was very diverse, New York City was (and remains) highly segregated, even more so than many other, far less multicultural places. After studying the 2000 census, Janny Scott of the *New York Times* nicely described the city as "a kind of archipelago, its enclaves like islands, each with its own distinct racial or ethnic topography." This was particularly true in Queens, with Breezy Point the most extreme example. That neighborhood, which had once been nicknamed the Irish Riviera, was the Whitest of any in New York City; it wasn't unusual for families there to go back three or four generations. (Gates and a toll bridge helped to keep it that way.) More generally, Whites tended to live among other Whites, and Blacks, with other Blacks, a pattern than Hispanic and Asian immigrants were following as they formed their own enclaves.[11]

Because the arts cross all human social divisions, all Queensites could agree that the arrival of a premier artistic institution was a good thing for the borough. The PS 1 Contemporary Arts Center had opened in Long Island City in 1981, the Isamu Noguchi Garden Museum in Long Island City in 1985, the Socrates Sculpture Park in Astoria in 1986, and the

American Museum of the Moving Image in Astoria in 1988. (The Queens Museum of Art in Flushing Meadows Corona Park had been around since 1972.) Some studios and galleries followed but not much else, until news came that the Museum of Modern Art would temporarily occupy a space (a rehabbed staple factory) at Queens Boulevard and Thirty-Third Street while its Manhattan home was expanded. The opening of MoMA QNS was thus welcome news to the artistic community of Queens, as it could go a long way toward "demystifying" the borough among Manhattanites.[12] Was this the beginning of a full-on artistic community in Queens? Perhaps so, given that no less than seventeen thousand people showed up for the museum's opening weekend.[13]

Figure 5.1. The New York City Building in Flushing Meadows Corona Park in January 1953. The building was built for the 1939–1940 New York World's Fair and survived both that fair and the 1964–1965 Fair. The building housed the General Assembly of the newly formed United Nations between 1946 and 1950 and today is home to the Queens Museum. *Source*: Gottscho-Schleisner Inc., *New York City Building, Flushing Meadow Park. Exterior II*, 1953, photograph, Library of Congress Prints and Photographs Division, Washington, DC, https://www.loc.gov/item/2018725693/.

Color Me Confounded

The events of 9/11—the four coordinated Islamic suicide terrorist attacks carried out by Al-Qaeda against the United States on September 11, 2001—had a profound impact on New Yorkers, of course, especially within the Muslim community. The city's largest Afghan mosque was in Flushing, where the five-thousand-member congregation was divided over support for the Taliban and its leader Osama bin Laden. (Ethnic divisions existed within the community.) Many Afghans denounced the terrorist attacks on the World Trade Center yet feared that their homeland would suffer major damage from a retaliation by the United States. Friends and relatives remained in Afghanistan, the source of conflicted feelings about what would become "the war on terror."[14]

Such feelings naturally went far beyond the borough of Queens. Immediately after 9/11, it became clear that Americans' general attitudes toward diversity were in flux. For the previous few decades, Americans had consistently embraced diversity by retiring the assimilation model of national identity for cultural pluralism and then multiculturalism. The tragic event interrupted this historical progression, however, as a palpable sense of xenophobia emerged. "The terrorist attacks in New York and Washington are making Americans more wary of outsiders than they have been in decades and are having profound implications for the debate over what it means to be American," an editor of the *New York Times* observed a dozen days after 9/11. Hate crimes against Arab Americans and Muslins across the country had already spiked, just the beginning perhaps of a wave of intolerance directed toward anyone deemed a potential foreign threat. Would there be a wholesale backlash against the recognition and appreciation of diversity? some wondered, a form of regression that would, as the editor put it, "tilt the nation's ethnic balance back in favor of the American side of the hyphen."[15]

John Leo of *U.S. News & World Report* certainly believed that multiculturalism had gone too far. "Color me confounded," he wrote a few months after the attacks, thinking that "most Americans are sick of the racialization of everything." There was an excessive amount of what Leo called "one-from-each-column" typecasting going on to ensure multicultural (typically White, Black, and Hispanic) representation, even if it falsified reality. Being White and male had become a distinct liability, Leo argued, even if one happened to be both a hero and dead. (Brooklyn borough president Marty Markowitz had just removed a portrait of George Washington in his office as a nod to diversity.) America was moving backward by altering facts to achieve a racial,

140 | QUEENS

ethnic, or gender balance, he believed, likening recent efforts to do so with what repressive regimes did when a new political party came into power.[16]

Leo had a good point, at least in that purposely deviating from the truth in any situation was morally questionable. Where he well may have been wrong was that multiculturalism had gone too far, as a fair argument could be made that given the country's diversity, it is impossible to go too far. America is "probably the most diversity society on earth," Peter Schuck posited in the *Brookings Review* in 2002, no matter how one decided to measure it. As well, the United States is different from other countries in that we view diversity as a positive thing and as an integral part of who we are and how we are different. Michael Walzer, the author of *On Toleration*, agreed, thinking no other country, past or present, could claim to be such an immigrant-based society. There are those on the far right who might not agree with or like that, but America is, perhaps more than anything else, multicultural and getting more so.[17]

Although Americans were deservedly proud of their diversity and the general tolerance shown to people of all cultural backgrounds, there were, at the time, a host of related thorny issues in play. Opinions diverged regarding affirmative action and bilingual education, and even the term "diversity" was impossible to define with any precision.[18] The question of how race should be treated in public universities' admission process went all the way to the United States Supreme Court. In *Grutter v. Bollinger*, 539 US 306 (2003), it was accepted that there is value to diversity because it encourages different points of view. (In 2023, the Court overturned college affirmative action policies.) But is the need for diversity greater than the legal mandate to not use skin color as the basis for either favoritism or discrimination?[19]

Indeed, the impetus to acknowledge diversity because it was judged to be a good thing seemed to go directly against our democratic and political conservatives' call for "colorblindness." Racial or gender-based exclusivity was not the American way, according to public opinion, an interesting thing in itself in that no such judgment was applied to class. Economic diversity was considered to be entirely in the spirit of our capitalist society, making the divisions between the upper, middle, and lower classes appear natural and normal (even though the vast majority of Americans considered themselves middle class). It could be seen how the privileges that came with wealth were deemed deserved—the result of hard work or good luck—while no one could control their cultural background inherited at birth, making any distinctions based on the latter unfair.[20]

While liberals and conservatives fought it out in courts to support their respective views on affirmative action and other controversial issues revolving around race, demographers made it clear that whatever legal decisions were made, America was becoming ever more diverse. Minorities would become the majority by 2040, demographer Harold Hodgkinson forecasted in 2004, with 90 percent of the nation's population growth to come from minorities. The 2000 census showed that the number of Hispanics was increasing particularly rapidly—almost fifteen times the rate of Whites in the country's twenty fastest-growing cities. The implications of this shift were already significant. "It is no longer the case that minorities are assimilating into a culture dominated by whites," Nat Irvin II wrote in *The Futurist*, adding that it was "the white Western majority [who] must learn how to assimilate to a new cultural identity that is more multicultural."[21]

The idea that it was Whites who would have to assimilate to a more multicultural country and world was an intriguing one that many had not considered. Tumbling the numbers was helpful to imagine the nation's demographic future, but one didn't need to be an expert to predict what America's population would look like in a few decades. Just take a look at a typical schoolyard, suggested Roderick Harrison of the Joint Center for Political and Economic Studies, as those children were a fair representation of the kind of diversity that lay ahead. Because of immigration, children were more ethnically and racially diverse than previous generations, more reason why the American melting pot had become more of a salad bowl. It was now clear that a sea change in national identity had occurred when the tight restrictions on immigration were relaxed in 1965, allowing a new and large wave of people from Asian and Latin American countries to reach our shores. The ripple effects of that wave, which rivaled the massive immigration from northern and western Europe that took place prior to the 1920s when quotas were established by Congress, could now be felt.[22]

The contentiousness surrounding diversity was, at the time, all the more unfortunate given the general agreement among scholars that race was a social or cultural construct rather than a biological trait. That was the consensus at a 2004 American Anthropological Association meeting at which a hundred social scientists and geneticists gathered to discuss race. "It doesn't exist biologically, but it does exist socially," said Alan Goodman, the incoming president of the association, that view not making the matter of race any less complicated and fuzzy. Research into the human genome found no evidence of there being a "Caucasian" or any other race, suggesting that

142 | QUEENS

our species was quite genetically homogenous compared to other animals. Americans were especially attuned to racial categorization, however, making an individual's appearance very significant in terms of how he or she would be perceived and treated.[23]

If You Can't Beat 'Em, Join 'Em

That was made quite clear from the tensions that arose with the arrival of a new group of immigrants to Douglaston and Little Neck, each a prosperous neighborhood where the number of Asian immigrants had more than doubled since 1991. While there were sanguine fusions—a Korean offering tango and rumba lessons, a kosher Chinese restaurant run by a Fujian—what made the news was established residents' sentiment that the Koreans were not showing much respect toward them. The signs in Korean shops often did not include English translations of what was being sold, an indication that the Koreans didn't recognize that retail stores in America should serve an entire community rather than a particular shopper.[24]

There had been little friction when the Chinese settled into those two neighborhoods, as with their different languages and origins, they were a less cohesive group. Almost all the Koreans had come from South Korea and spoke the same language, however, making them strongly tied to their own ethnic network.[25] Over in Flushing, meanwhile, some longtime residents who predated the "Asian invasion" of that neighborhood were taking adult education classes in Mandarin, adopting an attitude of "If you can't beat 'em, join 'em."[26]

That kind of intergroup tension, however, was not a new thing, including in multicultural Queens. Immigrants of a century past—Italians, Irish, Jews, and Germans—occasionally mixed it up, and racial conflict was routine (and remained so, to some extent). But now, hundreds of thousands of immigrants from more than a hundred countries speaking more than a hundred languages were occupying the same 178 square miles, making things quite a bit more complicated. Approximately 46 percent of the borough's population of 2.2 million was foreign-born, according to the 2000 census, with about one-fifth of its immigrants arriving in the 1990s. (Some believed the 46 percent figure was low given the many undocumented.) It still wasn't entirely clear whether Queens was a metaphoric melting pot or salad bowl, as there was evidence to make a case for either (or even both, in which case a hearty stew might be more appropriate).[27]

With the arrival of newer immigrant groups in Queens, it was becoming increasingly clear that older ones, notably Germans, were fading. Ridgewood had been a vigorous German community, but the sauerbraten and polkas were disappearing as the ethnic group fully assimilated into the American mainstream. Two world wars had advanced that process, some believed, particularly given the large Jewish population of New York City. It was estimated that Ridgewood had been more than 70 percent German from the 1880s through the 1960s, but by 2000 it was just 6 percent; Italians, Poles, Romanians, and Albanians now dominated the neighborhood. Yorkville in Manhattan had also been a German enclave until it waned in the post–World War II years, and a similar thing appeared to taking place in Ridgewood.[28]

While not good news for certain ethnic groups, the constant fluidity of Queens's population was certainly helping New York City tour guides. Some tourists wanted to bypass the usual destinations such as the Empire State Building and Statue of Liberty to see the "real" New York, which usually meant venturing into the "outer boroughs." Taking a tour group for lunch at a Malaysian restaurant and then sari shopping in Elmhurst was just the thing for visitors who had already seen the iconic sites. (Seeing live eels, frogs, and turtles for sale in a market not as pets but as culinary delights served as good fodder for storytelling back home in Indiana.) Even some New Yorkers were signing up for such tours, never really having explored the borough. Riding the No. 7 train was a must to get the full sense of the internationality of Queens. Besides that, getting a really good view of the Manhattan skyline meant getting off the island, in which case Gantry Plaza State Park in the Hunters Point section of Long Island City made an ideal spot.[29]

Should one of those tourists fall off a curb while in Elmhurst, perhaps after having one too many Kingfisher lagers, they might see another side of the real New York. Elmhurst Hospital Center was a far cry from the hospitals depicted in television shows like *Grey's Anatomy* or *ER*, reflecting the diversity of the borough and the neighborhood. More than half a million patients came into the hospital every year, half of them not fluent in English. Doctors and staff in turbans and saris could be seen caring for Mexican laborers, Sikh cab drivers, and covered up Muslim women, making the place a kind of United Nations for the sick or injured.[30]

The Queens General Assembly had a much different purpose but was equally multicultural. The twenty-eight-member group, which was made up of community leaders of a wide assortment of nationalities, religions,

144 | QUEENS

and races, met once a month at Borough Hall in Kew Gardens to discuss quality-of-life matters in Queens. The gathering was a brainchild of borough president Helen Marshall, who had a special interest in improving relations among the borough's diverse population. Many of the representatives were immigrants themselves and thus could personally relate to incidents involving racial, ethnic, or religious clashes, which were a common theme at the meetings. Issues related to education and housing were also regularly discussed.[31]

Given the range of ethnic groups that had settled in the borough, one could see that the Queens General Assembly had no shortage of topics to discuss. The dissolution of the Soviet Union on Christmas Day 1991 had had a ripple effect around the world, including in Queens. Tens of thousands of residents of Uzbekistan, Tajikistan, and Kyrgyzstan immigrated to Rego Park and brought their culture with them, including their cuisine. As well, some forty thousand Bukharan Jews from Central Asia came to New York City after the collapse, many of them also choosing Rego Park as a good place to open restaurants featuring their gastronomic fare. Diners might hear Russian, Hebrew, Uzbek, Farsi, and Tajik spoken as they ate their *kebabs*, *plov*, and *chebureks*—foods indigenous to the Silk Road, the ancient Eurasian trade route.[32]

Such delicacies served as a means to bring Manhattanites to "the hinterlands," as some called it. Residents of Queens were used to having to make the trek into Manhattan to see relatives and friends, but what would motivate the latter to cross the East River? Manhattanites had an array of flimsy excuses to avoid making the journey to the borough: the geography is confusing, the traffic is bad; there is nothing to do there; we've already been there; there is too much pollen; and it (somehow) takes longer to go to Queens from Manhattan than the other way around.[33]

Growing Pains

Manhattanites might have been happy to hear the news that community leaders in Flushing had plans to transform its Chinatown into a major shopping district. Nearly 1.3 million square feet of retail space—about the same as your average mall—was in the works in 2006, something that, if completed, would turn the pan-Asian enclave into a shopping destination with national chain stores and upscale retailers. More office space, condominiums, and a hotel were also on the way, according to developers who saw much opportunity in gentrifying Flushing.[34] Local Chinese immigrants supported what was planned to be called Flushing Commons, as their stores weren't likely to be much affected, but Koreans opposed the development, thinking its construction would put their shops out of business.[35]

The planned overhaul of Flushing was an anomaly, however, as the dozens of other neighborhoods in Queens developed on a more gradual basis. Elmhurst had thankfully gotten rid of its huge white-and-red natural-gas tanks; the eyesore was transformed into Gas Tank Park, a six-acre oasis of ball fields and a playground.[36] Cambria Heights, as well as other neighborhoods in southeast Queens such as Rosedale and Laurelton, continued to thrive as the more well-off immigrants from the West Indies who arrived in the late 1980s and early 1990s moved further up the economic ladder. That group was primarily responsible for making the median income of Black households higher than that of Whites in Queens, helping to dispel the stereotype that Blacks necessarily lived in poor, crime-ridden neighborhoods.[37]

Fresh Meadows remained a haven for Reform, Conservative, and Orthodox Jews in the 2000s, although high home prices were preventing young adults who grew up there from staying in the community. There was little friction between the Jews and the Chinese and Indian families who had settled in the neighborhood over the previous few decades, and the latest arrivals—Jews from Russia and Uzbekistan—were fitting in nicely.[38] Jews from Russia and Uzbekistan, as well as from Georgia, the Ukraine, and Iran, had also immigrated to Forest Hills, which was the hub for Queens Jews. There were more than one hundred thousand Jews in Forest Hills, making it one of the largest Jewish communities in the world outside Israel. The Bukharan Jewish presence could be very much felt, as they founded their own temples and schools.[39]

Astoria had undergone a major transformation since the 1980s, when it was primarily Greek and Italian. Many of those ethnicities had moved on, although excellent feta cheese, homemade yogurt, baklava, and a seemingly infinite variety of olives could still be found in the local delis. But in the early 2000s, Bangladeshis, Columbians, Brazilians, and Mexicans were just as likely as Greeks to call Astoria home, and saris, Bollywood movies, and chorizo quesadillas could be found in the shops. North Africans—Egyptians, Tunisians, Libyans, Moroccans, and Algerians—had also come to the area, evidenced by the string of hookah cafes on Steinway Street.[40]

In Flushing, it was the multiplicity of religions that was perhaps the most outstanding feature of that neighborhood. There remained mainline Protestants, Catholics, and Jews, complemented by Asian immigrants who attended Korean churches, Muslim mosques, and Sikh and Hindu temples.

(Flushing had a long history of religious tolerance; in the late seventeenth century, early settlers rebelled against Peter Stuyvesant's ban on Quakerism.) In fact, priests, ministers, and professors came to Flushing to learn more world religions, as the neighborhood served as a kind of one-stop shop for global theology.[41]

Douglas Manor—a section of Douglaston—was a little-known neighborhood, even among Queensites, in part because it is surrounded by water on three sides. The turnover of houses there was so low that it could take years for neighbors to award full residency to a new arrival, considering the home still belonging to the previous owner. (Designated as a historic district, exterior renovations were prohibited unless approved by the city's Landmark Preservation Commission.) Still mostly Irish and Italian (despite being named after a Scottish ship builder), Douglas Manor was gradually diversifying; the population within the neighborhood's zip code, which included parts of Douglaston and Little Neck, was about three-quarters White and a quarter minority.[42]

For staying put, however, it was East Elmhurst that took the grand prize. Residents of that neighborhood remained in their houses for an average of thirty-six years—the longest in the entire city, according to Census Bureau surveys taken between 2005 and 2009. (Cambria Heights finished second.) According to the survey, 47 percent of East Elmhurst residents were African American, and the neighborhood had been home to Malcolm X and other Black notables. Some longtime residents remember looking at houses on Long Island, but upon seeing "No blacks allowed" signs, chose prejudice-free East Elmhurst. Older residents were retiring and often moving to warmer climes, however, with many of their homes being bought by Hispanics.[43]

Floral Park, right near the Nassau County line (but with about half the property taxes of that county), was an ideal place for people who wanted to remain in Queens but escape more crowded areas. (Its name came from the area's many flower farms in the early twentieth century; the farms were gone, but streets named Tulip, Clover, and Geranium could still be found.) One-third of that neighborhood's population was foreign-born, about half of them identifying themselves as Indian in the 2000 census. Many more Indians had moved to Floral Park since the taking of that census, however, finding considerably more elbow room there after living in places like Richmond Hill and Jackson Heights.[44]

In 2008, Jackson Heights was the site of some ethnic conflict due to events in Columbia, Ecuador, and Venezuela. There were 278,000 Columbians, Ecuadorans, and Venezuelans living in New York City, many of them in

Jackson Heights, where they usually got along well. Complex goings-on in those countries involving national sovereignty, drug trafficking, and guerilla war upset that delicate balance in Queens, however, making passionate political debates unavoidable. Still, most of the Columbians, Ecuadorans, and Venezuelans found they had more in common than they had differences, treating the diplomatic kerfuffle a couple thousand miles away not unlike a brotherly squabble that would be soon resolved one way or another.[45]

Some ethnic conflict would also soon take place on Hillside Avenue, which ran through Bellerose and Floral Park. Hillside Avenue was, as Kavita Mokha of the *Wall Street Journal* described it in 2011, experiencing "growing pains" as immigrants from India, Pakistan, Bangladesh, and Afghanistan competed for retail business. That section of the street, which was often called Little India, was highly commercial, and differences regarding how businesses were being run could arise. Issues related to permits, parking, and garbage were increasingly popping up, with longtimers feeling that inner-city kinds of problems had come to their suburban-like neighborhood.[46]

No ethnic tensions could be detected in Jamaica Hills despite its ever increasing diversification. Indians, Pakistanis, Bangladeshis, and African Americans all attended the two-thousand-congregant Jamaica Muslim Center, which began operating out of a basement and was now housed in a large building complete with a minaret. Cricket was a popular sport in India, Pakistan, and Bangladesh, and enthusiasts could be found in the neighborhood. In fact, if you were having trouble finding cricket equipment in the city, a trip to Jamaica Hills would be well worth your while.[47]

Time Bombs

Tensions of a different sort were about to confront residents of Queens and those across the country. It had been mostly clear sailing for aspiring homeowners in Queens in the early 2000s, a function of a robust economy. There was, however, a growing market for subprime loans, that is, loans in which banks and other lenders charged higher initial fees and higher interest rates to reflect a greater risk of default.[48]

At the time, not much was being made of the transformation of the mortgage business. The traditional method was for local bankers to issue mortgages based on that market's conditions, with the loan then held by that bank. But increasingly, for the sake of stability and efficiency, a full two-thirds of mortgages were farmed out to secondary markets on a national basis, taking locality out of the mix. The more mortgages that were issued, the greater the profit, an equation being expressed by the increasing number of houses that were being bought despite the ever-rising prices. More housing units were being sold and purchased than ever before in history, and rising home value was functioning as a buffer against inflation.[49]

Soon, however, owning even a small house might be more of a liability than an asset. Signs of the much-feared housing bubble pop appeared in 2005 with the news that the thirty-day past-due rate for subprime mortgages rose from 5.4 percent to 7.1 percent over the course of that year. That may not have sounded like much, but just a 1 percent increase in defaults triggered a cascade of financial problems through not just the mortgage market but the national economy. The lure to buy property, by certain lenders, was a powerful one; some didn't even ask for proof of income. The pendulum appeared to have swung the other way—banks and other financial institutions had for decades been criticized for being too cautious in making loans, but the appearance of the subprime mortgage market had incentivized them to be too eager.[50]

If the bad news was the jump in subprime past dues, the worse news was the rise in foreclosures. The foreclosure rate for subprime loans was nine times that of primes in 2005, a clear sign of where the problem was. Neighborhoods with a predominantly minority and low-income population were suffering most, as it was those groups who shadier lenders tended to target with subprime loans. Rather than discriminating against African Americans and Hispanics, as in the past, less-than-ethical lenders were now exploiting them with low-down-payment, high-ratio, and interest-only mortgages. Such lenders knew full well that there would likely be trouble ahead for borrowers who may have had "impaired credit," but that wasn't their problem.[51]

By 2011, the foreclosure crisis and the recession it had triggered were still major problems across the United States, including in New York City. Queens homeowners had suffered the most, compared to other boroughs, particularly African Americans in middle-class neighborhoods such as Far Rockaway, South Ozone Park, Jamaica, and St. Albans. Over the previous few years, these neighborhoods had declined as residents lost their houses; litter and drugs were pervasive, reversing much of the progress that had been made. "Abandoned homes in Southeast Queens have become a growing quality of life crisis," said City Councilmember Leroy Comrie, terming the empty houses "time bombs." Comrie urged landlords to maintain the houses to prevent further urban decay and potential health hazards for existing residents.[52]

TOMORROW'S AMERICA | 149

Sunnyside was not a likely destination for African Americans displaced from their houses. The neighborhood had a long history of intolerance toward Blacks regarding housing, and problems remained. The Fair Housing Justice Center (FHJC) had to step in after the superintendent of one large building on Forty-Sixth Street told three African Americans that no apartments were for rent, even though there were, refusing to show them the units because of their race. Whites were shown the apartments, however, with the super saying, "You look like nice people, that's why I show you." The case was hardly an anomaly; just 2 percent of the apartments in that section of Sunnyside were rented by African Americans, while African Americans accounted for 18 percent of all renter households in Queens (and 27 percent in all of New York City). The FHJC was taking active steps to end segregation in Queens, a full four decades after the landmark 1968 Fair Housing Act.[53]

Given how diverse Queens had become, it was discouraging and perhaps a bit surprising that discrimination based on race, ethnicity, or religion still existed in the borough. Multiculturalism was, after all, everywhere by 2012, making such differences seem normal. The sixty-two branches of the Queens Public Library continued to add to their holdings in their patrons' native languages. At the Astoria branch, for example, children's books in Arabic, Bengali, Chinese, Russian, Portuguese, and Gujarati could be found, a small sample of the materials that were available in fifty-two languages across the borough's library system. (That was twice the number it had been a decade earlier.)[54]

Political life too was becoming increasingly multicultural in Queens. It had taken some time, but both Hispanics and Asians were being elected to the Queens City Council and then to the New York State Assembly, a clear sign of those groups' ascending political power. Voting regulations reflected how many immigrants had not become American citizens, at least yet. In 2005, a bill had been introduced in the City Council to grant voting rights to noncitizens in municipal elections. And in the fall of 2011, the United States Census Bureau required Queens County (as well as Los Angeles County) to provide language assistance to Indian American voters under the Voting Rights Act. Months later, the New York City Board of Elections chose the specific languages for which assistance would be provided: Bengali, Hindi, and Punjabi. Voters who spoke one or more of those languages were asked to volunteer as poll workers.[55]

One might think that by now Queens would have reached a kind of saturation point in terms of accommodating immigrants from around the

150 | QUEENS

world, but that was not the case. In 2013, a new group arrived: Orthodox Christians from Egypt, known as Copts. The rise of the Muslim Brotherhood in that country following the overthrow of President Hosni Mubarak was sufficient cause for Orthodox Christians to flee the country, with thousands of the refugees choosing Brooklyn, Queens, and Jersey City as their new home. In Queens, it was Ridgewood where most of the group (who were seeking asylum) settled, doubling the number of members of the St. Mary and St. Antonios Coptic Orthodox Church. Services there had been delivered in English, Arabic, and Coptic (the Egyptian language written with Greek letters and some other symbols), but then the latter two languages became the most spoken.[56]

The year 2014 marked fifty years since the 1964–1965 New York World's Fair in Flushing Meadows Corona Park, an ideal occasion upon which to reflect on the changes that Queens had experienced since then. Joseph Tirella, author of *Tomorrow-Land: The 1964–65 World's Fair and the Transformation of America*, astutely recognized that the fair portended things to come not just in the borough but across the country. "The World's Fair laid the groundwork for the demographic revolution that would transform America in subsequent decades," he wrote in the *New York Times* exactly a half century after the fair's opening day, noting that the event really was a "world's fair."[57]

It is difficult today to fully appreciate the impact that the fair made on visitors (including myself), particularly with regard to its internationality in these pre-internet days. "Africa and Asia, the Middle East and the Caribbean, and Central and South America all came to Queens," Tirella wrote, "bringing with them their peoples, their languages and their cultures." Many people from those parts of the world would, over the next few decades, relocate to America, especially Queens, a migration enabled by President Johnson's signing of the Immigration and Nationality Act of 1965 (which took place the very same month that the fair closed). No one knew it at the time, but the fair was a vision of "tomorrow's America," as Tirella nicely put it, a glimpse into the demographic future of the nation and borough.[58]

Policies of Hate

Immigrants were not the only ones who thought Queens would make a good place to live. Brooklyn had been discovered by Manhattanites looking for more affordable property or rent, making it inevitable that a similar story would take place in Queens. Young professionals and families wanting more space yet proximity to the city were moving to traditional working-class neighborhoods in the borough such as Long Island City, Astoria, and Jackson Heights—each a short subway ride to and from Manhattan. Developers, noticing the trend, recognized the opportunity and built more housing in such areas, repeating what had taken place in Brooklyn a decade or so earlier. Williamsburg and Cobble Hill proved to be popular with hipper urbanites, and now Crown Heights and Bushwick were coming on strong.[59]

In Queens, Rego Park was another neighborhood that real estate people believed could go upscale, thinking there was a sizable market there for luxury apartments. Such developers were using Long Island City as a model. Development or redevelopment in that neighborhood (closest to Manhattan, not coincidentally) had gone well, justification to branch out into other parts of the borough. If Crown Heights and Bushwick could go upmarket, why not Queens neighborhoods like Elmhurst or Sunnyside? Naysayers said Queens was no Brooklyn and would never be, however, as Queens simply lacked that cool factor.[60]

Janet Silver Ghent was one such naysayer. Ghent, who had grown up in Rego Park (whose name came from its developer, the Real Good Construction Company), took the time to respond to a *New York Times* article that claimed Queens had become chic. "It is hard to think of a locality that has rivaled the borough as popular culture's image of white, urban American working-class life," Gina Belafonte of the *Times* had written, citing the TV shows *All in the Family* and *The King of Queens* as having cemented that image. Those programs were now in syndication, inscribing that same proletarian image of the borough among current viewers.[61]

But with luxury condos in Long Island City selling for millions of dollars, the televisual interpretation of Queens was no longer an accurate one (if it ever was). Real estate in Queens was hot and prices were soaring—more so than in hipster Brooklyn, in fact. Rents in Astoria were escalating, a sign that the Queens neighborhood had become "the new Williamsburg." The phenomenon could be seen beyond real estate; a popular TriBeCa-based medical clinic had set up a branch in Long Island City, and Tom Finkelpearl, the executive director of the Queens Museum, had been named New York City's cultural commissioner.[62]

Ghent, however, who was now living in Palo Alto, took issue with Belafonte's view. Rego Park was decidedly unchic in her day (her family wrote Forest Hills as their return address on envelopes, embarrassed to be associated with Rego Park), and had no hope of ever being chic, she believed.

152 | QUEENS

Queens Boulevard had nothing in common with Rodeo Drive, and the idea of Queens becoming a fashionable neighborhood was pure hype, even if some rich folks were buying apartments there.[63]

Soon, however, Queens was infused with a considerable dose of coolness when Marvel Comics announced the protagonist of its newest comic book. It was Cindy Moon (a.k.a. Silk), an Asian American from Queens who had earlier appeared in the *Spider-Man* series. Comic book fans liked the character (whose ethnicity was not specified but was likely Korean based on her name), hence Marvel's decision to create a spin-off (no pun intended) with her own series. Having been bitten by the same radioactive spider as Peter Parker, Cindy Moon had similar superpowers as Spider-Man but also some additional ones, something likely to especially appeal to female fans. This was actually not Marvel's first protagonist of Asian heritage; Ms. Marvel had been reintroduced as a Pakistani (and Muslim) teenager from Jersey City.[64]

Definitely not cool, however, was some continuing anti-immigrant sentiment in South Ozone Park. Some graffiti reading "Hindu gang!!!" was sprayed in red paint on a window of a Knights of Columbus building in that neighborhood, alarming local residents. That the fraternal group allowed the graffiti to remain there for a month was also disturbing, reportedly because of bad weather conditions. There was a sizable Hindu community in South Ozone Park and nearby Richmond Hill, including many Hindu temples built by Indo-Caribbeans who migrated to Queens and other parts of New York City from Guyana, Trinidad, and Suriname. Even though it was a silly thing to write (there was no such thing as a Hindu gang, at least not in Queens), the act was troubling, especially given the fact that two Hindu temples in Seattle had recently been vandalized.[65]

Such hate crimes may have been fueled by anti-immigrant rhetoric coming from Donald Trump, who was at the time on the presidential campaign trail. Trump's language was "infected with an Archie Bunker-era nativism," wrote Jason Horowitz of the *New York Times*; the Republican candidate had spoken of "rapist" immigrants who were in the United States illegally, trying to exploit fears of xenophobic White voters. The irony was that Trump had grown up in Queens, a fact not lost on current residents, who held that the man had no understanding of the immigrant experience.[66]

That should not have come as a surprise given that Trump had, a half century earlier, been raised in Jamaica Estates, a secluded neighborhood almost wholly populated by wealthy Whites. (Trump's father, Fred, had been one of its developers.) The younger Trump claimed the area had been a "microcosm" of New York City and made him understand "what it was all about," but locals had a different opinion. Hillside Avenue was a stone's throw from what had been Trump's house (a twenty-three-room mansion with nine bathrooms), and residents of the area—mostly Hispanics, Trinidadians, Haitians, and South Asians—were not reticent to express their thoughts about the candidate. Yet more irony was that Fred Trump was the son of impoverished German immigrants who lived in the working-class neighborhood of Woodside, but, sadly, he did not teach his own son the vital role that immigrants have played in America throughout its history.[67]

Donald Trump would get elected, of course, something that caused much concern throughout the borough of Queens, given the man's stance toward immigrants and people of color. In December 2016, a month before Trump's inauguration as president, more than a thousand people gathered at the aptly named Diversity Plaza in Jackson Heights to discuss how to address what was described as the "policies of hate" expected to be part of the Trump administration. Those who were undocumented were especially anxious, thinking that they faced a greater chance of being forced to leave the country under the new administration. It was quite an eclectic group; Latinos, Muslims, Jews, LGBTQ members, and representatives from South Asian, Asian, and Black organizations showed up. Speakers said they would create "hate-free zones" in Queens and make their communities ones in which people "loved and protected each other." After holding a news conference, leaders of the rally marched through Jackson Heights, Woodside, Elmhurst, and Corona to show their solidarity.[68]

The groups' concerns were justified. A few months later, workers at the Tom Cat Bakery in Long Island City were threatened with mass termination following an immigration audit. Company executives had informed the workers that the Department of Homeland Security was investigating the bakery; thirty-one of the employees, many of whom had been there for a decade or more, would be fired within ten business days if they couldn't provide legal employment documents. In response, Tom Cat workers, along with community leaders and elected officials, soon led a protest at Trump Tower in Manhattan to demand that the Trump administration cease its ongoing crackdown on immigrants that would break up families and communities.[69]

Reaction was strong to Trump's continued attack on undocumented immigrants, which would assuredly have a devastating effect on life in Queens. One person coming to those residents' defense was Laura Raicovich, the president and director of the Queens Museum. There had been talk that the Trump administration would cancel the Deferred Action for Childhood Arrivals (DACA) policy, which protected the young undocumented from deportation. Raicovich took to Twitter, a rare instance in which a museum director expressed a political opinion. "Defending DACA is the right thing to do," she tweeted, urging her followers to "prevent its dissolution and pass legislation to make it permanent." There were estimated to be 91,000 undocumented immigrants (or Dreamers, as they were known) in Queens who were eligible for DACA (the most of any of the city's boroughs), making it understandable why Raicovich spoke out on the issue. As well, 5 percent of her staff members were DACA recipients, giving her a professional and perhaps personal stake in the matter.[70]

A New Day

While Dreamers wondered whether their American dream would be put to an abrupt end, the cultural currency of Queens continued to ascend. Writing for the *New York Times* in 2019, Barbara Brotman defined the borough as an "ultra-happening multicultural mecca" and "the darling of artists, creatives, and foodies." But much like Janet Silver Ghent five years earlier, Brotman, who grew up in Bayside in the 1960s and 1970s, questioned the hype surrounding the borough. Back then, Queens was considered by Manhattanites as pure "bridge and tunnel," meaning provincial and thoroughly uncool. "When I was a kid there, the thought that Queens could become cool was so ridiculous that no one ever thought it," she wrote, stunned at the transformation of the borough over the last half century.[71]

Brotman's recollections offered keen insight into how Queens had been essentially reinvented as it became a prime destination for immigrants. "Back then, it was the home of Archie Bunker," she continued, primarily White with the various ethnic groups generally siloed in their own enclaves. Neighborhoods she frequented—Flushing, Astoria, and Long Island City—had no culture to speak of, and Bayside then was truly suburban and, amazingly, still forested. The arrival of things like co-working spaces in Sunnyside, craft breweries in Ditmars, and yoga in Hunters Point South Park served as proof that "a new day has dawned over the Throgs Neck Bridge," Brotman concluded, happy that she could now "claim my now-honorable heritage."[72]

A little more than a year later, however, yet another new day was dawning in Queens and everywhere else around the globe. COVID-19, the contagious disease caused by a coronavirus, was spreading, with few places as hard-hit as Queens. The borough was of course densely packed and homes were often overcrowded, making it not surprising that hospitalizations and deaths were climbing fast. Many residents were poor immigrants who could not afford healthcare or adequate food, making the bad situation worse. Central Queens—Corona, Elmhurst, East Elmhurst, and Jackson Heights—was the epicenter of the pandemic in New York City, with thousands of cases reported and many more unreported. COVID-19 had severely affected day laborers, restaurant workers, and cleaners—occupations held by many residents of those neighborhoods.[73]

Data was generally not being recorded by race or ethnicity, although it was known that so far Latinos comprised a full third of deaths from COVID-19 in New York City. It was also known that neighborhoods highly populated by Indian, Bangladeshi, Chinese, Filipino, and Nepalese residents were severely affected. Already crowded Elmhurst Hospital was a disaster area, with dozens of patients jammed into hallways until a bed was made available. Dozens of New York City taxi drivers, the vast majority of whom were immigrants who lived in Queens, had already died. Normally hectic Roosevelt Avenue was silent except for the occasional siren, and churches and mosques throughout the borough were closed.[74]

Although it would be some more months before the availability of vaccines for COVID-19, things had improved in Queens by August of 2020. People were venturing outside in masks, even in high-risk neighborhoods like Jackson Heights. The population of Jackson Heights was now 180,000, and some 167 languages were spoken there. The neighborhood would be unrecognizable to its early twentieth-century developers who had created it for a White middle class, as it was now Latinos and South Asians who mostly called it home. In fact, Jackson Heights had surpassed Elmhurst as the most diverse part of New York City and was arguably the most diverse place on earth.[75]

Woodside, meanwhile, had become the preferred location for New York City's Filipino community, with signs often written in Tagalog. Roosevelt Avenue between Sixty-First and Seventieth Streets was the heart of the neighborhood, so much so that many residents signed an online petition to co-name that stretch Little Manila. There was no Little Manila yet in New York City, and business leaders wanted to brand the area along the lines of commercially successful Little Italy and Chinatown.[76]

Not to be outdone, the Indian community of Queens soon named a street in Richmond Hill in order to acknowledge the contributions made by South Asian residents. The intersection of 101st Avenue and Lefferts Boulevard would now be named Punjab Avenue, it was announced in 2020, with a ceremony held in the area to celebrate the decision. "Today is a celebration meant to unite and we must have unity in our entire community," said City

Councilmember Adrienne Adams, who attended the ceremony, a reference perhaps to the attacks made against Sikhs in South Ozone Park, which was just a few blocks away.[77]

A trend apparently having begun, next up were the Bangladeshi of Queens, who led the way for the intersection of Homelawn Street and Hillside Avenue in Jamaica to be known as Little Bangladesh Avenue. It was believed that about two-thirds of New York City's Bangladeshi population resided in Queens, with most of them in Jamaica. The choice of the name Little Bangladesh for the new avenue might have seemed obvious given the pattern, but there was some debate. Some made the case that the street should be named after significant figures from Bangladesh's history, while others were in favor of a simpler, apolitical name such as "Bangladesh." The area was ultimately named Little Bangladesh Avenue as a compromise for all groups involved.[78]

The claiming of neighborhoods through such street signs illustrated different ethnic groups' strong attachment to Queens. Carving out a section of the borough was important given the continually ascending value of real estate in New York City. Many New Yorkers used StreetEasy, an online listing site, to search for homes, and industry professionals kept a close watch on what were the "hottest" neighborhoods. Four neighborhoods in Queens—Elmhurst, Woodside, Sunnyside, and Middle Village—finished in the top ten for 2023, the most of any borough. Both buyers and renters were attracted to the relative affordability of Queens, as well its easy access to and from Manhattan. These factors were precisely the same as the ones that had brought people to the borough from Manhattan a century earlier; Queens had undergone immeasurable change since the 1920s, but its original appeal apparently remained.[79]

Astoria didn't make the 2023 list, having peaked a decade or two earlier, but it remains a highly desirable place for New Yorkers to call home. Both renters and property owners in Manhattan continue to flock there, finding much more bang for their buck, that is, greater square footage for the same money. Couples starting families (or just wanting a dog) are especially attracted to Astoria, also finding a stronger sense of community there compared to other neighborhoods. While trendy and having undergone much new development in recent years, Astoria also somehow retains its working-class feel and friendliness. Greek restaurants can still be found there, of course, but now there is world-class Mexican, Egyptian, and Moroccan food as well. Incredibly, Bohemian Hall, the social club and beer garden frequented by Czech and Slovak immigrants in 1910, has survived, and I go there whenever possible to enjoy the goulash or schnitzel along with a Pilsner Urquell or, if in season, a Spaten Octoberfest.[80]

Willets Point was also not named one of the hottest neighborhoods in New York City, according to StreetEasy's list, but it was considerably "warmer" than in the past. In *The Great Gatsby*, F. Scott Fitzgerald described Willets Point as a "valley of ashes," it being home to the Brooklyn Ash Removal Company, which dumped tons of ashes from the period's coal furnaces. The place was, he wrote in 1925, "a fantastic farm where ashes grow like wheat into ridges and hills and grotesque gardens; where ashes take the form of houses and chimneys and rising smoke and, finally, with a transcendent effort, of men who move dimly and already crumbling through the powdery air."[81]

Now, however, nearly a century later, the ashes are long gone, as are many of the auto repair shops that had come to the area in subsequent decades. An environmental cleanup is underway, and infrastructure improvements for sewage, storm lines, and water mains are being made for a new affordable housing project and K–8 school. Not only that, but a Major League Soccer stadium is planned for Willets Point, nicely complementing nearby Citi Field, home of the New York Mets, and the USTA Billie Jean King National Tennis Center, where the US Open was played every fall. "Willets Point gives us an opportunity to create a new neighborhood with homes, schools and economic possibilities," wrote Eric Adams, the mayor of New York City, believing that the redevelopment of the area offered the chance to "re-envision how our city can meet the challenges of the twenty-first century."[82] If what's past is prologue, there is no more fitting a place than the borough of Queens to share such a positive and inclusive vision.

What lies ahead for the uniquely diverse neighborhoods of Queens? In 2024, a handful of initiatives spearheaded by the New York Department of City Planning are in the works, each of them promising to make the borough a better place to live. The Long Island City Neighborhood Plan and the Jamaica Neighborhood Plan are designed to bring together community members and organizations to provide more housing and jobs, as well as to make improvements to public space and investments in local infrastructure. Environmentally, the Flushing Creek Study will explore ways to support the ecological health of that body of water, and design guidelines have been set to preserve the beauty of the Long Island City waterfront. Finally, zoning and land use regulations are being put in place to protect the "resilient neighborhoods" of Old Howard Beach, Hamilton Beach, Broad Channel, Rockaway Park, and Rockaway Beach, ensuring that the history of those beloved places is passed down to future generations.[83]

Notes

Introduction

1. Lawrence R. Samuel, *The End of the Innocence: The 1964–1965 New York World's Fair* (Syracuse, NY: Syracuse University Press, 2007).

2. Thomas J. Campanella, *Brooklyn: The Once and Future City* (Princeton, NJ: Princeton University Press, 2019); Evelyn Gonzalez, *The Bronx* (New York: Columbia University Press, 2004).

3. Steven Gregory, *Black Corona: Race and the Politics of Place in an Urban Community* (Princeton, NJ: Princeton University Press, 1998).

4. Warren and Judith Sloan, *Crossing the BLVD: Strangers, Neighbors, Aliens in a New World* (New York: Norton, 2003); Claudia Gryvatz, *The Neighborhoods of Queens* (New Haven, CT: Yale University Press, 2007).

5. R. Scott Hanson, *City of Gods: Religious Freedom, Immigration, and Pluralism in Flushing, Queens* (New York: Fordham University Press, 2016).

6. Rob Mackay, *Famous People of Queens* (Mt. Pleasant, SC: Arcadia, 2023; Rob Mackay, *Historic Houses of Queens* (Mt. Pleasant, SC: Arcadia, 2021); Richard Panchyk, *Queens through Time* (Mt. Pleasant, SC: Arcadia, 2022); Richard Panchyk, *Abandoned Queens* (Mt. Pleasant, SC: Arcadia, 2019); Richard Panchyk, *Hidden History of Queens* (Mt. Pleasant, SC: Arcadia, 2018); Richard Panchyk and Lizz Panchyk, *Dead Queens* (Mt. Pleasant, SC: Arcadia, 2021); Kevin Walsh and the Greater Astoria Historical Society, *Forgotten Queens* (Mt. Pleasant, SC: Arcadia, 2013); Christina Rozeas, *Greeks in Queens* (Mt. Pleasant, SC: Arcadia, 2012); Jason Antos, *Queens (Then and Now)* (Mt. Pleasant, SC: Arcadia, 2009); and the Greater Astoria Historical Society and Roosevelt Island Historical Society, *The Queensboro Bridge* (Mt. Pleasant, SC: Arcadia, 2008).

7. Panchyk, *Hidden History of Queens*, 9.

8. "The First Residents," *A Walk Through Queens*, Thirteen PBS, https://www.thirteen.org/queens/history.html.

9. *Queens Borough New York City 1910–1920* (New York: Chamber of Commerce of the Borough of Queens, New York City, 1920), 6.

10. "A Patchwork of Cultures," *Queens Tribune*, Nov. 9, 2007.

11. "93 Families in Township of Queens 248 Years Ago," *New York Herald Tribune*, Aug. 20, 1931, 34.

12. "A Patchwork of Cultures."

13. "A Patchwork of Cultures."

14. Vincent F. Seyfried and Jon A. Peterson, "A Brief History of Queens, Historical Essay: A Thumbnail View," Official History Page of the Queens Borough President's Office, New York City Local Government, http://www.queensbp.org/content_web/tourism/tourism_history.shtml.

15. Seyfried and Peterson, "A Brief History of Queens."

16. "The First Residents."

17. "A Patchwork of Cultures."

18. "A Patchwork of Cultures."

19. Seyfried and Peterson, "A Brief History of Queens."

20. "A Patchwork of Cultures."

21. Seyfried and Peterson, "A Brief History of Queens."

22. Janet E. Lieberman and Richard K. Leiberman, *City Limits: A Social History of Queens* (Dubuque, IA: Kendall/Hunt, 1983), 132.

23. "A Patchwork of Cultures."

24. Seyfried and Peterson, "A Brief History of Queens."

25. Gryvatz, *The Neighborhoods of Queens*, xxiv.

26. Hsiang-shui Chen, *Chinatown No More: Taiwan Immigrants in Contemporary New York* (Ithaca, NY: Cornell University Press, 1992), 34.

27. "Flushing/Whitestone QN07," NYU Furman Center, https://furmancenter.org/neighborhoods/view/flushing-whitestone.

28. Ines M. Miyares, "From Exclusionary Covenant to Ethnic Hyperdiversity in Jackson Heights, Queens," *Geographical Review* 94, no. 4 (2004): 462.

29. J. M. Tyree, "The United Nations of Queens: The Undiscovered Borough," *Antioch Review* 63, no. 4 (Autumn 2005): 648.

30. "Study: Blacks Among Early Queens Settlers," *New York Amsterdam News*, Nov. 12, 1983, 11; Lieberman and Lieberman, *City Limits*.

31. "A Patchwork of Cultures."

32. Lawrence R. Samuel, *Making Long Island: A History of Growth and the American Dream* (Mt. Pleasant, SC: The History Press, 2023).

33. "A Patchwork of Cultures."

34. "A Patchwork of Cultures."

35. "A Patchwork of Cultures."

36. "A Patchwork of Cultures."

37. Hsiang-shui Chen, *Chinatown No More*, 38.

38. Roger Sanjek, "Color-Full before Color Blind: The Emergence of Multiracial Neighborhood Politics in Queens, New York City," *American Anthropologist* 102, no. 4 (Dec. 2000): 762.

39. Miyares, "From Exclusionary Covenant," 462.

40. Tyree, "The United Nations of Queens," 646.

41. Gus Lubin, "Queens Has More Languages Than Anywhere in the World—and Here's Where They're Found," *Business Insider*, Feb. 15, 2017, https://www.businessinsider.com/queens-languages-map-2017-2.

Chapter One

1. "2,000 Home Sites in Queens Big City to be Auctioned," *New York Herald Tribune*, May 30, 1920, A7.

2. "Small Home Builders Active in Queens," *New York Herald Tribune*, June 13, 1920, A12.

3. "First Loan on Queens Realty by Prudential," *New York Herald Tribune*, Aug. 22, 1920, A8.

4. Ines M. Miyares, "From Exclusionary Covenant to Ethnic Hyperdiversity in Jackson Heights, Queens," *Geographical Review*, Oct. 2004, 462–83.

5. "New Queens Apartments for Eighty Families," *New York Herald Tribune*, Apr. 23, 1922, A14.

6. "From Exclusionary Covenant to Ethnic Hyperdiversity in Jackson Heights, Queens."

7. "Well Known Brokers Extend Activities to Jackson Heights," *New York Herald Tribune*, Sept. 3, 1922, B1.

8. "Two-Family House Period in Queens History Nearly Over," *New York Herald Tribune*, Feb. 13, 1921, A8.

9. "$1,000,000 a Week Goes into New Houses in Queens," *New York Herald Tribune*, Aug. 21, 1921, B10. There were more than 150 companies erecting homes in Queens in 1922.

10. Stephen Yates, "Low Land Cost Large Factor in Queens Activity," *New York Herald Tribune*, Dec. 18, 1921, A14.

11. "Forest Hills West, in Queens, Put on Map This Morning," *New York Herald Tribune*, June 25, 1922, B2; Woodhaven Avenue was widened to one hundred feet.

12. "News and Comment of City and Suburban Real Estate Market," *New York Herald Tribune*, Apr. 13, 1924, B2.

13. "Population May Be Diverted to Right by New Subway," *New York Herald Tribune*, June 24, 1923, C1.

14. "Demand Parkway Planned Ten Years Ago Be Built Now," *New York Herald Tribune*, July 29, 1923, C2.

15. "News and Comment of City and Suburban Real Estate Market," *New York Herald Tribune*, July 13, 1924, B2.

16. Frank Ray Howe, "62 Buyers Pay $1,182,422 for Queens Suites," *New York Herald Tribune*, Jan. 3, 1926, B2.

17. "Jamaica Beckons Home Seekers," *New York Amsterdam News*, Aug. 12, 1925, 8.

18. "Race Realty Brokers Making Good," *New York Amsterdam News*, Aug. 19, 1925, 8.

19. "John Hill Another Successful L.I. Realtor Who Grasped His Opportunity," *New York Amsterdam News*, Sept. 9, 1925, 8.

20. "John Hill Another Successful L.I. Realtor Who Grasped His Opportunity."

21. James H. Hubert, "James H. Hubert Writes Interestingly on Long Island Town Now Holding Attention of the Entire Countryside," *New York Amsterdam News*, Oct. 7, 1925, 8.

22. "James H. Hubert Writes Interestingly."

23. "L.I. Lumber Merchant to Build Homes for Colored People in Jamaica," *New York Amsterdam News*, Nov. 25, 1925, 8.

24. "Fifty-Two Plots Secured by Milla-Cohn Company to Erect Homes for Negroes," *New York Amsterdam News*, Nov. 25, 1925, 8.

25. "Jamaica a Miniature 'Land of Promise' Amsterdam News Representative Sees," *New York Amsterdam News*, May 25, 1927, 9.

26. "Corona, L.I., Also Making Bid to Better Class of Race Home Seekers," *New York Amsterdam News*, Sept. 23, 1925, 8.

27. "Corona Homes," *New York Amsterdam News*, Oct. 7, 1925, 14.

28. "Some Facts About Corona," *New York Amsterdam News*, Feb. 23, 1927, 16.

29. "The Klan and the Police in Queens," *Chicago Defender*, June 18, 1927, A2. For an insightful overview of the KKK's activities in Queens in the 1920s, see Paul D. Colford, "An Inside Look at the Klan," *Newsday*, Feb. 18, 1987, A1.

30. "Klan Startled Jamaica, L.I., When Fiery Cross Was Burned Saturday," *New York Amsterdam News*, June 1, 1927, 15.

31. "Klan Will Again Attempt to Stage Parade on Fourth of July," *New York Amsterdam News*, June 29, 1927, 16.

32. "Klan Spent Their Fourth in an Open Lot," *New York Amsterdam News*, July 6, 1927, 10.

33. George S. Horton, "Put Your Money in Real Estate and Reap Profit," *New York Herald Tribune*, Jan. 31, 1926, B10.

34. E. A. MacDougall, "Queens Will Push on Faster in 1926 Than It Did in 1925," *New York Herald Tribune*, Jan. 31, 1926, B12.

35. "Busses Are Hastening Queens Development," *New York Herald Tribune*, Mar. 21, 1926, B2.

36. "Housing Crisis Here Over, Say Albany Chiefs," *New York Herald Tribune*, Mar. 28, 1926, 16.

37. "Harbinger of Big Buying in Queens," *New York Herald Tribune*, Dec. 5, 1926, C2.

38. Edward A. MacDougall, "East River Is No Longer Barrier to Queens' Growth," *New York Herald Tribune*, Apr. 3, 1927, C2.

39. "Ribbons of Steel Have Made Queensborough," *New York Herald Tribune*, Apr. 3, 1927, C3.

40. "Queens Is Destined to Be New York's Greatest Borough," *New York Herald Tribune*, Apr. 3, 1927, C3.

41. "45 Families at Jackson Heights Complete Purchases," *New York Herald Tribune*, July 17, 1927, C2.

42. "Queens Home Owners Protest 'Paper Houses,'" *New York Herald Tribune*, Mar. 19, 1926, 13.

43. "Firetrap Homes in Queens to be Viewed To-Day," *New York Herald Tribune*, July 18, 1927, 5.

44. H. F. Carden, "Rapid Growth," *New York Herald Tribune*, Nov. 2, 1927, 12.

45. "Over-Production of Houses Among Whites Benefiting Colored Purchasers," *New York Herald Tribune*, Jan. 25, 1928, 11.

46. "Queens Families Threaten Riot," *New York Herald Tribune*, Oct. 17, 1928, 2.

47. "72 Per Cent Realty Gain in Queens Values," *New York Herald Tribune*, Aug. 7, 1927, C2.

48. "Queens Real Estate Story a Fairy Tale," *New York Herald Tribune*, May 6, 1928, D1.

49. Major William Kennelly, "Great Push Is Expected in Queens," *New York Herald Tribune*, May 6, 1928, D2.

50. "Tri-Borough Bridge Marks Start of New Era," *New York Herald Tribune*, Oct. 27, 1929, E1.

51. "Tri-Borough Bridge Marks Start of New Era."

52. "Queens Will Lose Forest, for Home Builders Want Site," *New York Herald Tribune*, Jan. 26, 1930, E15.

53. "Queens Will Lose Forest."

54. "Queens Realty Stronger Than Ever Before," *New York Herald Tribune*, Jan. 26, 1930, E24.

55. "$773,982,662 Spent in Queens for Buildings," *New York Herald Tribune*, May 18, 1930, E2.

56. "Queens Has Lost Most of Its Old Village Lines," *New York Herald Tribune*, Aug. 2, 1931, E2.

57. "Multiple Dwellings Law Threat Worries Queens Owners," *New York Herald Tribune*, Dec. 28, 1930, E2.

58. "Queens Has Many 'Bootleg Suites,' Survey Discloses," *New York Herald Tribune*, Dec. 31, 1930, 30.

59. "Remarkable Growth Shown in Population," *New York Herald Tribune*, July 29, 1931, 15.

60. "Queens Needs Better Plants for Its Negro Churches, Federation Reports," *New York Herald Tribune*, Nov. 25, 1931, 15.

61. "Queens Needs Better Plants for Its Negro Churches."

62. "Ku Kluxers Riding Again in Queens," *New York Herald Tribune*, Nov. 23, 1932, 3.

63. "Probers Discover No Discrimination," *New York Herald Tribune*, Mar. 1, 1933, 2.

64. "Denies Race Ban by Jury System," *New York Herald Tribune*, Mar. 22, 1933, 11.

65. "Equality in Relief Urged for Jamaica," *New York Herald Tribune*, May 24, 1933, 11.

66. See Paul Moreno, "An Ambivalent Legacy: Black Americans and the Political Economy of the New Deal," *Independent Review*, Spring 2002, 513–39.

67. "Hitlerites Clash with Hecklers at Queens Rally," *New York Herald Tribune*, Apr. 9, 1934, 1.

68. "Hitlerites Clash with Hecklers at Queens Rally."

69. "Hitlerites Clash with Hecklers at Queens Rally."

70. "Hitlerites Clash with Hecklers at Queens Rally."

71. Joachim Remak, " 'Friends of the New Germany': The Bund and German-American Relations," *Journal of Modern History*, Mar. 1957, 41; See also Leland V. Bell, "The Failure of Nazism in America: The German American Bund, 1936–1941," *Political Science Quarterly* 29, no. 1 (Dec. 1970): 585–99; Sander A. Diamond, *The Nazi Movement in America* (Ithaca, NY: Cornell University Press, 1974); and David M. Esposito and Jackie R. Esposito, "LaGuardia and the Nazis, 1933–1938," *American Jewish History*, Sept. 1988, 38–53.

72. "Great World's Fair for City in 1939 on Site in Queens," *New York Times*, Sept. 23, 1935, 1,

73. "Great World's Fair for City in 1939 on Site in Queens."

74. "Great World's Fair for City in 1939 on Site in Queens."

75. "Real Estate Aided by Plans for Fair," *New York Times*, Sept. 24, 1935, 2.

76. "Big Building Year Seen for Queens," *New York Times*, Jan. 31, 1937, 186.

77. "Queens Builders Open New Units," *New York Times*, Sept. 13, 1936, RE6.

78. "Sounds Warning to Queens Builders," *New York Times*, May 2, 1937, RE6.

79. John H. Morris, "Queens Transit Improvements Assure Upturn," *New York Herald Tribune*, Jan. 30, 1938, C1.

80. "Queens Leads Nation in Home Construction," *New York Herald Tribune*, Nov. 7, 1938, 28.

81. Edward A. MacDougall, "Queens Boom Predicted in '39 by MacDougall," *New York Herald Tribune*, Jan. 29, 1939, C3.

82. "Jamaica Housing Project Is Approved," *New York Amsterdam News*, Mar. 11, 1939, 11.

83. "Jamaica Housing Project Is Approved."

84. "Selects Site for Slum Project in Jamaica," *New York Amsterdam News*, Apr. 29, 1939, 13.

85. "Welfare Group Votes to Battle Problems," *New York Amsterdam News*, June 17, 1939, 8.

86. "South Jamaica Project," *New York Amsterdam News*, June 24, 1939, 6.

87. "Seek Work on Building Jobs," *New York Amsterdam News*, Sept. 23, 1939, 13.

88. "Ready to Select Project Tenants," *New York Amsterdam News*, Dec. 23, 1939, 7.

89. "Many H.O.L.C. Properties Sold in Queens Area," *New York Herald Tribune*, Sept. 24, 1939, C4.

Chapter Two

1. Dennis Duggan, "New Co-Op Draws Host of Queries," *New York Herald Tribune*, Feb. 21, 1960, 1C.

2. "Property History," rochdalevillage.com.

3. "Queens Tunnel Hailed as Spur to Realty Value," *New York Herald Tribune*, Sept. 8, 1940, C11.

4. "City Population Moving Eastward," *New York Times*, Sept. 29, 1940, 141.

5. "A Patchwork of Cultures," *Queens Tribune*, Nov. 9, 2007.

6. "Midtown Tunnel Called Spur to Queens Growth," *New York Herald Tribune*, Nov. 17, 1940, C1.

7. "Queens County Leads Nation in Home Building," *New York Herald Tribune*, Mar. 16, 1941, C2.

8. "Queens Among U.S. Leaders in Apartment Development," *New York Herald Tribune*, May 4, 1941, C2.

9. "Queens Among U.S. Leaders in Apartment Development."

10. "Queens Dwelling Sales Jump 50 Percent over 1940," *New York Herald Tribune*, June 1, 1941, C1.

11. "Buying Queens Homes," *New York Times*, Aug. 3, 1941, RE2.

12. "Expect More Homes in Brooklyn, Queens," *New York Times*, Oct. 19, 1941, RE5.

13. "Italians Carry 86-Foot Tower in St. Paolina Parade in Queens," *New York Herald Tribune*, June 24, 1940, 15.

14. "Easter Is Observed by Greeks in Queens," *New York Times*, Apr. 21, 1941, 13.

15. "Queens Block Goes All Out for Army," *New York Times*, June 23, 1941, 19.

16. "Queens Tenants Arriving from All Over Nation," *New York Herald Tribune*, Dec. 21, 1941, C2.

17. "Girl Describes Nazi Recruiting of Spies Here," *New York Herald Tribune*, Feb. 4, 1942, 9.

18. "High School Girl Gets Five Years as German Spy," *New York Herald Tribune*, Mar. 21, 1942, 24.

19. "FBI Seizes Aliens Here and in Jersey," *New York Times*, June 7, 1942, 35; "Aliens' Homes in Queens and Jersey Raided," *New York Herald Tribune*, June 7, 1942, 15.

20. "42 Aliens Held; One Says She Is Cousin of Hess," *New York Herald Tribune*, Oct. 3, 1943, 31.

21. "Church Site Transferred," *New York Times*, Dec. 15, 1942, 24.

22. Rosamond Clark, "The Japanese in New York City," *The Call*, May 8, 1942, 4.

23. "American-Born Japanese Hangs Herself in Queens," *New York Herald Tribune*, May 24, 1944, 3A.

24. " 'Patriotic' Fraud Is Bared in Queens," *New York Times*, Sept. 11, 1942, 23.

25. "German-American Rally in Bond Drive Friday," *New York Herald Tribune*, June 11, 1944, 29; See Lawrence R. Samuel, *The World War II Bond Campaign* (New York: Fordham University Press, 2025).

26. "Miss Negro War Worker," *New York Times*, May 26, 1943, 25.

27. "Queens Owners Pledge Aid on Rent Control," *New York Heald Tribune*, July 13, 1943, 31.

28. "Efforts to Raise Rents in Queens Stir Complaints," *New York Herald Tribune*, July 10, 1943, 8.

29. "Women Demand Rent Control Now," *New York Times*, July 24, 1943, 16.

30. "Queens Will Rise as 'Wonder City,' " *New York Herald Tribune*, Sept. 23, 1945, F6.

31. "Queens Will Rise as 'Wonder City.' "

32. "Queens Will Rival Manhattan as 'Wonder City,' Says O'Hara," *New York Herald Tribune*, Sept. 23, 1945, F6.

33. "Platzker Finds 250,000 House Site in Queens," *New York Herald Tribune*, Feb. 22, 1946, 26.

34. "A Patchwork of Cultures."

35. Jack Werkley, "U.N. Housing in Queens for 4,000 Planned," *New York Herald Tribune*, Apr. 12, 1946, 1A; "U.N. Housing Unit in Queens to Start at Once," *New York Herald Tribune*, May 24, 1946, 12; "Our History," https://www.parkwayvillage.us.

36. "Families of United Nations Personnel Occupying Parkway Village," *New York Herald Tribune*, July 30, 1947, 12.

37. "Queens Woman Enjoined on House Sale to Negro," *New York Herald Tribune*, June 15, 1946, 3; "Court Forbids Sale of Queens Home to Negro," *New York Herald Tribune*, Feb. 14, 1947, 19.

38. Edgar T. Rouzeau, "Queens Leader in Fight to Bar Negroes Yield," *New York Herald Tribune*, Aug. 15, 1948, 30.

39. Kay Kerby, "Veteran Housing in New York City is Interracial," *New York Amsterdam News*, Nov. 16, 1946, 11.

40. "Negro Home Ownership Highest in Queens, 31 percent," *New York Herald Tribune*, June 13, 1947, 15.

41. "Queens House Site Approval Deferred," *New York Herald Tribune*, Oct. 24, 1947, 36.

42. "18 Negro Artists Join Queens Show," *New York Herald Tribune*, June 20, 1948, 45.

43. "Home Owners Lose Fight to Bar Negro," *New York Herald Tribune*, July 21, 1948, 16.

44. Edgar T. Rouzeau, "Queens Leader in Fight to Bar Negroes Yield," *New York Herald Tribune*, Aug. 15, 1948, 30.

45. "Curbs Spur Rush for Apartments," *New York Times*, Oct. 22, 1950, R7.

46. "City's Population Is Set at 8,005,000," *New York Times*, June 5, 1948, 17.

47. "Queens Population Grew with Subway," *New York Times*, July 1, 1951, 143.

48. "Queens Population Grew with Subway."

49. "Housing Offered on Non-Bias Plan," *New York Times*, Sept. 23, 1951, 236.

50. "Queens Project Sets Pattern for Clearing Slums," *New York Herald Tribune*, Dec. 14, 1952, 2C.

51. Richard B. Lyman, "Felt Expects Present Trends to Continue," *New York Herald Tribune*, Dec. 31, 1952, 22.

52. Richard Lincoln, "Threaten Inter-Racial Pair," *New York Amsterdam News*, Aug. 2, 1952, 17.

53. "159 Slum Acres to Be Condemned," *New York Times*, Jan. 7, 1951, 61.

54. "Redfern Houses Open, Replace Queens Slum," *New York Amsterdam News*, Sept. 20, 1952, 20.

55. "U.N. Hall in Queens Will Be Rink Again," *New York Times*, Mar. 30, 1952, 33.

56. "Queens Builder Finds 100-Year-Old Tombstones on Lot—He'll Spare Them," *New York Herald Tribune*, Dec. 29, 1952, 3.

57. "Queens Builder Finds 100-Year-Old Tombstones on Lot."

58. "Queens Builder Finds 100-Year-Old Tombstones on Lot"; the tombstones were discovered in 1923 by the Queens Topographical Bureau but had apparently been forgotten. Mary French, "Cornell Cemetery, Little Neck," June 22, 2014, https://nycemetery.wordpress.com/2014/06/22/cornell-cemetery-little-neck/.

59. "Good Home Market Seen in Queens," *New York Herald Tribune*, Jan. 30, 1954, 22.

60. A. H. Raskin, "Nonwhites Up 41 percent in City, Whites Down 6 percent Since '50," *New York Times*, Nov. 19, 1957, 1.

61. "A Patchwork of Cultures."

62. "Population Found Soaring in Queens, *New York Times*, Aug. 7, 1958, 23.

63. "Fear Grips Queens Project," *New York Amsterdam News*, Mar. 30, 1957, 17.

64. "Queens Group Plots Assault on Private Housing Prejudice," *New York Amsterdam News*, May 4, 1957, 17.

65. "Race Issue in Queens Studied on Radio," *New York Times*, Jan. 22, 1959, 63.

66. Peter Kihss, "Racial Balance Plea in Queens Assails Panic Selling of Realty," *New York Times*, July 26, 1959, 58.

67. John Wicklein, "Realty Scare Hit by Queens Clergy," *New York Times*, Aug. 6, 1959, 16.

68. "Queens Negroes Losing Ground?," *New York Amsterdam News*, Aug. 1, 1959, 17.

69. James J. Morisseau, "Board Backs Transfer for Negro Pupils," *New York Herald Tribune*, Aug. 15, 1959, 4.

70. Robert A. Poteete, "Felt Averts Stormy Row Over Zoning," *New York Herald Tribune*, Sept. 4, 1960, 24.

71. Will Lissner, "National Origins in City Surveyed," *New York Times*, July 6, 1962, 27.

72. Charles G. Bennett, "City Shows Loss in White People," *New York Times*, Sept. 30, 1961, 27.

73. "Begins Queens Drive for Equal Housing," *New York Amsterdam News*, Feb. 24, 1962, 24.

74. "Bombed Queens Resident Won't Quit His Home," *New York Amsterdam News*, Feb. 2, 1963, 21.

75. Lawrence R. Samuel, *New York City 1964: A Cultural History* (Jefferson, NC: McFarland, 2014), 50.

76. Samuel, 50.

77. Samuel, 50–51.

78. Samuel, 51.

79. Samuel, 51.

80. Samuel, 9.

81. Samuel, 9.

82. Lawrence R. Samuel, *The End of Innocence: The 1964–1965 New York World's Fair* (Syracuse, NY: Syracuse University Press, 2007), 4.

83. Samuel, 11.

84. Samuel, 11.

85. Samuel, 11.

86. Samuel, 11–12.
87. Samuel, 12.
88. Samuel, 12.
89. Samuel, 12.
90. Samuel, 12–13.
91. Samuel, 13.
92. Samuel, 13.
93. Samuel, 13.
94. Samuel, 13.
95. Samuel, 13.
96. Samuel, 13–14.
97. Samuel, 14.
98. Samuel, 14.
99. Samuel, 14.
100. Samuel, 32.

Chapter Three

1. "Immigration and Nationality Act," https://www.lbjlibrary.org; see Daniel Tichenor, "The Historical Presidency: Lyndon Johnson's Ambivalent Reform: The Immigration and Nationality Act of 1965," *Presidential Studies Quarterly* 46, no. 3 (Sept. 2016): 691–705.

2. See Maddalena Marinari, "Divided and Conquered: Immigration Reform Advocates and the Passage of the 1952 Immigration and Nationality Act," *Journal of American Ethnic History* 35, no. 3 (Spring 2016): 9–40.

3. David K. Willis, "Who Will Immigrate?," *Christian Science Monitor*, June 2, 1965, 4.

4. Lawrence R. Samuel, *The End of Innocence: The 1964–1965 New York World's Fair* (Syracuse, NY: Syracuse University Press, 2007), 33.

5. Samuel, 33–34.

6. "Charge 9 Queens Brokers with Bias to Negroes," *New York Amsterdam News*, June 11, 1966, 27.

7. "Fair Housing 'Fair' Saturday in Queens," *New York Amsterdam News*, Oct. 1, 1966, 27.

8. "SCHR Starts Probe on Spread of All-Negro Ghetto in SE Queens," *New York Amsterdam News*, June 4, 1966, 23.

9. "Rights Agency Tells Landlords They Must Rent to Nonwhites," *New York Amsterdam News*, June 18, 1966, 10.

10. "State Rapped for Light Bias Penalty on Brokers," *New York Amsterdam News*, July 15, 1967, 23.

11. "Black Myths Curb Queens House Sales," *New York Amsterdam News*, Mar. 8, 1969, 28.

12. "CCHR, Realty Dept. KO Queens Bias," *New York Amsterdam News*, Jan. 20, 1968, 21.

13. Paul L. Montgomery, "'Bays' are Enclaves for Thousands at Riis Park," *New York Times*, Aug. 25, 1969, 37.

14. Murray Schumach, "Neighborhoods: Astoria's Relaxed Melting Pot," *New York Times*, May 16, 1970, 37.

15. Schumach, "Neighborhoods: Astoria's Relaxed Melting Pot."

16. Murray Schumach, "Neighborhoods: 69 Homes in Corona at Stake," *New York Times*, Aug. 11, 1970, 35.

17. Murray Schumach, "Doubt Lingers in Corona on Housing Compromise," *New York Times*, July 16, 1974, 37.

18. Murray Schumach, "Neighborhoods: College Point Enjoys Life on an 'Island,'" *New York Times*, Feb. 1, 1971, 33.

19. "Neighborhoods: College Point Enjoys Life on an 'Island.'"

20. Bill Kovach, "Struggle for Identity: White Minorities Revive Heritage," *New York Times*, Nov. 27, 1970, 41.

21. Kovach, "Struggle for Identity."

22. Kovach, "Struggle for Identity."

23. Laurie Johnston, "Ethnic Awareness Praised as a Creative Force," *New York Times*, Apr. 13, 1972, 45.

24. Bernard A. Weisberger, "Hard Hats, Blue Collars, Troubled Spirits," *Washington Post*, May 14, 1972, BW6; Michael Novak, *The Rise of the Unmeltable Ethnics: Politics and Culture in the Seventies* (New York: Macmillan, 1972); Peter Schrag, *The Decline of the WASP* (New York: Simon and Schuster, 1970).

25. Edmund Fuller, ". . . A 'Wasp' Defends His 'Ethnicity' . . . ," *Wall Street Journal*, June 12, 1972, 16.

26. "Melting Pot Prediction Has Not Come True," *Los Angeles Sentinel*, Aug. 17, 1972, A11.

27. George Dugan, "Catholic Diocese of Brooklyn to Help New Immigrants Adjust to City," *New York Times*, Mar. 14, 1971, BQ86.

28. Raphael Rothstein, "Little Bit of Israel Thrives in Queens," *New York Times*, Oct. 10, 1971, A8.

29. Rothstein, "Little Bit of Israel Thrives in Queens."

30. Richard F. Shepard, "The Ethnic Crackerbarrels of Queens," *New York Times*, Feb. 20, 1972, A81.

31. Shepard, "The Ethnic Crackerbarrels of Queens."

32. Shepard, "The Ethnic Crackerbarrels of Queens."

33. Shepard, "The Ethnic Crackerbarrels of Queens."

34. Kim Lem, "Indians in Queens Reviving Heritage," *New York Times*, Jan. 5, 1975, BQLI79.

35. Edward C. Burks, "Foreign Stock High in Queens," *New York Times*, Nov. 26, 1972, BGLI58.

36. Burks, "Foreign Stock High in Queens." See Basil Wilson, "Caribbean Immigrants in New York City and the Rise of a Black Middle Class in Southeast Queens," *Wadabagei*, Winter 2009, 33–45.

37. Edward C. Burks, "Queens Leads City in 'Foreign Stock,'" *New York Times*, Apr. 8, 1973, 144.

38. Burks, "Foreign Stock High in Queens."

39. Edward C. Burks, "Irish Eyes Smiling Mostly in Queens," *New York Times*, May 27, 1973, 77.

40. Pranay Gupte, "Is the 'Dragnet' Necessary?," *New York Times*, Mar. 25, 1973, 221.

41. Gupte, "Is the 'Dragnet' Necessary?"

42. Gupte, "Is the 'Dragnet' Necessary?"

43. Kenneth P. Nolan, "Queens Center Helps Koreans to Adapt," *New York Times*, Aug. 26, 1973, 102.

44. Nolan, "Queens Center Helps Koreans to Adapt."

45. "The U.S. Hits Firm on Bias in Bkl'yn, Queens, Staten Island," *New York Amsterdam News*, Oct. 20, 1973, C1.

46. "The U.S. Hits Firm on Bias in Bkl'yn, Queens, Staten Island."

47. "Trump Charged with Rental Bias," *New York Times*, Mar. 7, 1978, 39.

48. Amy Plumer, "Integration—Queens Style Great Strides Backward," *New York Amsterdam News*, May 11, 1974, A5.

49. John L. Hess, "Columbia Looks to Queens for a Key to Her Election," *New York Times*, Feb. 13, 1974, 41.

50. Ari L. Goldman, "Illegal Aliens Living in Queens Assailed," *New York Times*, Nov. 24, 1974, 106.

51. Michael T. Kaufman, "Soviet Jews Are Discovering Difficulties in Adjusting to Life Here," *New York Times*, Mar. 9, 1975, 45.

52. Eleanor Blau, "Population Shifts Beset Jewish Community Here," *New York Times*, Aug. 21, 1975, 1.

53. Ari L. Goldman, "Vietnam Refugees Here Find Plain Task is Getting Jobs," *New York Times*, Aug. 26, 1975, 33.

54. Max H. Seigel, "U.S. Suit Charges Realty Bias Here," *New York Times*, Nov. 6, 1975, 45.

55. Seigel, "U.S. Suit Charges Realty Bias Here."

56. John J. O'Connor, "Taking a Balanced Look at Bias," *New York Times*, Feb. 1, 1976, X27.

57. Francis X. Clines, "About New York: A Blockbuster of a Fight," *New York Times*, Sept. 20, 1976, 39.

58. Murray Schumach, "Enterprising Hispanic Merchants Revive a Block in Jackson Heights," *New York Times*, May 6, 1976, 39.

59. Murray Schumach, "If It Really Takes All Kinds, Queens Certainly Has What It Takes," *New York Times*, Mar. 2, 1977, 19.

60. Schumach, "If It Really Takes All Kinds."

61. Schumach, "If It Really Takes All Kinds."

62. "Flushing's Chinatown, 2003," https://www.mocanyc.org/collections/stories/flushings-chinatown-2003/; Kenny Zhou, "Flushing: Transit Connectivity, Immigration, and Development," Aug. 3, 2021, https://storymaps.arcgis.com/stories/4b827a95ba3346c7956ae4f4b86e9b48.

63. Kenny Zhou, "Flushing: Transit Connectivity, Immigration, and Development," Aug. 3, 2021, https://storymaps.arcgis.com/stories/4b827a95ba3346c7956ae4f4b86e9b48.

64. Eric Pace, "New York's Armenian Neighborhoods Feel a Surge of Ethnic Pride as New Immigrant Wave Arrives," *New York Times*, July 11, 1977, 23; See Michael J. Arlen's *Passage to Ararat* for a stirring account of the author's search for his Armenian identity. (Michael J. Arlen, *Passage to Ararat* (New York: Farrar, Straus and Giroux, 1975).

65. Murray Schumach, "Astoria, the Largest Greek City Outside Greece," *New York Times*, Oct. 7, 1977, 81.

66. "Astoria, the Largest Greek City Outside Greece."

67. Judith Cummings, "Islamic Community in Queens Plans a School with Saudi Financing," *New York Times*, Nov. 25, 1977, 29.

68. Pranay Gupte, "Stamp of India Heavier in City," *New York Times*, June 4, 1978, R1.

69. Jennifer Dunning, "Dancing to an Ethnic Beat." *New York Times*, June 9, 1978, C1.

70. Robin Herman, "Elmhurst Flourished as Melting Pot," *New York Times*, Apr. 4, 1979, D1.

71. "Elmhurst Flourished as Melting Pot."

72. David Bird, "Woodside Rages Over Influx of Illegal Aliens," *New York Times*, June 14, 1979, B1.

73. Laurie Johnston, "Soviet Jews Find Old Woes, New Joys in New World," *New York Times*, Aug. 21, 1979, B1.

74. "Soviet Jews Find Old Woes, New Joys in New World."

75. James Barron, "Apartments in Flushing Snapped Up by Koreans," *New York Times*, Aug. 19, 1979, R1.

Chapter Four

1. Philip Shenon, "At 300th Birthday Celebration, Queens Feels It's One of a Kind," *New York Times*, June 5, 1983, 30.

2. Shenon, "At 300th Birthday Celebration."

3. Joseph Berger, "Linguists: Queens Lacks Its Own Accent," *Newsday*, Mar. 2, 1980, 23.

4. Sylvia Carter, "A Tale of Two Cuisines that Blend in Cuisines," *Newsday*, Aug. 27, 1980, B1.

5. Dena Kleiman, "Immigrants Spur Renaissance for Queens Churches," *New York Times*, Nov. 15, 1982, B1.

6. Susan B. Garland, "New Immigrants Create Babel in Queens," *Hartford Courant*, Aug. 15, 1983, B9.

7. Victoria Irwin, "The Liberal from Conservative Queens," *Christian Science Monitor*, July 13, 1984, 3.

8. Victoria Irwin, "Ms. Ferraro's Diverse District in Queens," *Christian Science Monitor*, Aug. 1, 1984, 3.

9. Bill Peterson, "Ferraro Introduces Mondale to Queens," *Washington Post*, Aug. 1, 1984, A8.

10. Horace Sutton, "Queens: 118 Square Miles of Villages Called Home By 2 Million People," *Chicago Tribune*, Sept. 9, 1984, J17.

11. Jane Gross, "In Richmond Hill, Latins Are Latest in Melting Pot," *New York Times*, Apr. 17, 1985, B1.

12. Adriel Bettelheim, "Life in Queens Enclave of Georgian Jews Centers on Synagogue," *New York Jewish Week*, Dec. 21, 1984, 16.

13. Elicia Brown, "More Than Georgia on Their Mind," *New York Jewish Week*, Aug. 7, 1998, 1.

14. "Ethnic Families in Transition Is Title of Queens Scholars Conference," *Italian Voice*, Oct. 3, 1985, 6.

15. Ronald Waterbury, "World Studies at Queens College, CUNY," *Social Studies*, Mar. 1993, 54.

16. Jerry Morgan, "Queens Is Host to an Urban Festival," *Newsday*, June 28, 1985, C19.

17. Martin Gottlieb, "Asian-Americans Compete to Build Queens Complex," *New York Times*, Aug. 10, 1985, 25.

18. Gene Rondinaro, "House Values Surge in the Older Areas of Northern Queens," *New York Times*, Dec. 1, 1985, R7.

19. William E. Geist, "About New York: The Melting Pot Bubbles in Rego Park," *New York Times*, Apr. 24, 1986, B1.

20. Lydia Chavez, "Life in Hispanic Queens: Together, Yet Separate," *New York Times*, Aug. 15, 1986, B1.

21. Chavez, "Life in Hispanic Queens."

22. Barbara Fischkin, "At Home, At Last," *Newsday*, Apr. 4, 1987, A1.

23. George James, "Queens Groups Strive to Bridge Ethnic Gaps," *New York Times*, Apr. 12, 1987, 44.

24. "Bulletin! There's Racism in Queens," *Chicago Tribune*, Dec. 29, 1986, 12.

25. "Patrols Beefed-Up in Racially Tense Streets of Queens," *Washington* Post, Dec. 25, 1986, A20.

26. "3,000 Blacks March to Protest Queens Attack," *Boston Globe*, Jan. 22, 1987, 6.

27. James, "Queens Groups Strive to Bridge Ethnic Gaps."

28. James, "Queens Groups Strive to Bridge Ethnic Gaps."

29. "Queens Landlord Fined $18000 For Rent Bias," *New York Amsterdam News*, June 13, 1987, 6.

30. Ned Zeman, "Klans Planning Queens Big Cross-Burning Rally," *New York Amsterdam News*, Dec. 19, 1987, 1.

31. Zeman, "Klans Planning Queens Big Cross-Burning Rally."

32. Felicia R. Lee, "Melting Pot, Harmony and Problems Mix," *New York Times*, Aug. 31, 1989, B1.

33. Lee, "Melting Pot."

34. Lee, "Melting Pot."

35. Barbara W. Selvin, "Living In: Sunnyside Gardens," *Newsday*, Nov. 4, 1989, B11.

36. Maggie Garb, "Suburbia Minutes from Midtown," *New York Times*, June 26, 1994, G5.

37. Joseph P. Fried, "New Accents and Old Brogue Quietly Reshape Woodside," *New York Times*, Aug. 13, 1990, B1.

38. Darina Molloy, "The Sunnyside of the Street," *Irish Voice*, Aug. 27, 1996, 20.

39. Darina Molloy, "A Queens Irish Tale," *Irish Voice*, Dec. 10, 1996, 24.

40. Emer Mullins, "'Legalize the Irish' Heard Again," *Irish Voice*, Feb. 11, 1997, 8.

41. Jack Flynn, "Irish Make Their Own Unique History in Queens," *Irish Voice*, Sept. 29, 1998, 28.

42. Richard F. Shepard, "Queens, Doorstep to the Whole Wide World," *New York Times*, May 3, 1991, C1.

43. Shepard, "Queens, Doorstep to the Whole Wide World."

44. Dena Kleiman, "Queens 'Mosaic,' Proof of the Melting Pot is in the Eating," *New York Times*, Oct. 16, 1991, C1.

45. "Ethnic Treats Abound in Restaurants of Queens," *New York Times*, Feb. 9, 1992, 54.

46. Cara De Silva, "To Market, to Market," *Newsday*, June 17, 1992, 74.

47. Therese Fitzgerald, "Jamaica Retail Market: Shining Star in Dim Times," *Real Estate Weekly*, May 20, 1992.

48. Raymond Hernandez, "Jamaica: Prosperous Isle in Queens," *New York Times*, June 27, 1993, 25.

49. J. Peder Zane, "Celebration of Queens and Diversity," *New York Times*, June 29, 1992, 19.

50. Melinda Henneberger, "Crime and Ethnic Tensions Rise as Queens Neighbors Change," *New York Times*, Aug. 17, 1992, B1.

51. Henneberger, "Crime and Ethnic Tensions Rise."

174 | NOTES TO CHAPTER FOUR

52. Elaine Louie, "No Roast Aardvark, No Grilled Zebra, Still, Queens Has an Alphabet Soup," *New York Times*, Feb. 24, 1993, C1.

53. Sam Roberts, "The Cranky Spirit of Archie Bunker Haunts This House," *New York Times*, Dec. 19, 1993, H33.

54. Roberts, "The Cranky Spirit of Archie Bunker."

55. Guy Halverson, "Queens, N.Y.," *Christian Science Monitor*, July 28, 1993, 10.

56. G. H., "Preserving Queens's Diverse and Thriving Neighborhoods," *Christian Science Monitor*, July 28, 1993, 11.

57. G. H., "Queens's Nondescript Image Hides Long History, Culture," *Christian Science Monitor*, July 28, 1993, 11.

58. Sam Roberts, "In Middle-Class Queens, Blacks Pass Whites in Household Income," *New York Times* June 6, 1994, A1.

59. Lynette Holloway, "Brokers Said to Exploit Fear to Stir Queens Home Sales," *New York Times*, May 5, 1995, A1.

60. Michael T. Kaufman, "A Folklorist Finds the Melting Pot Brimming in Queens," *New York Times*, July 26, 1995, B1.

61. Tony Marcano, "Turns of the Ethnic Kaleidoscope in Queens," *New York Times*, Dec. 31, 1995, CY8.

62. Florence Fabricant, "Nothing Says Kosher Like Chicken Livers in the Tandoor," *New York Times*, Sept. 11, 1996, C3.

63. Celia W. Dugger, "Queens Old-Timers Uneasy as Asian Influence Grows," *New York Times*, Mar. 31, 1996, 1.

64. Joe Mathews, "The 3 Chinatowns," *Baltimore Sun*, May 7, 1997, 1E.

65. Pam Belluck, "In the Queens Mosaic, a Turkish Inlay," *New York Times*, Apr. 2, 1996, B1.

66. Celia W. Dugger, "Golden Anniversary in Queens," *New York Times*, Aug. 15, 1997, B1.

67. Norimitsu Onishi, "In Polyglot Queens, Overflowing Melting Pot Adds to Pupils' Obstacles," *New York Times*, Sept. 6, 1996, B3.

68. Mirta Ojito, "More Spanish Accents, but Fewer Are Cubans," *New York Times*, Jan. 29, 1997, B1.

69. Peter D. Salins, "Assimilation, American Style," *Reason*, Feb. 1997, 20.

70. William B. Williamson, "Is the U.S.A. a Christian Nation?," *Free Inquiry*, Spring 1993, 32.

71. Janny Scott, "In the Urban Maelstrom, the Faithful Persevere," *New York Times*, Mar. 5, 1995.

72. Norimitsu Onishi, "On the No. 7 Subway Line in Queens, It's an Underground United Nations," *New York Times*, Feb. 16, 1997, 45.

73. Joe Mathews, "Big Apple's New Gloss," *Baltimore Sun*, Oct. 20, 1997, 1D.

74. Vivian S. Toy, "For a Month, Soccer Is Life," *New York Times*, June 10, 1998, B1.

75. Winnie Hu, "Some Immigrants Have Angry Words for Queens Billboard," *New York Times*, Aug. 5, 1999, B3.

76. Hu, "Some Immigrants Have Angry Words."

77. "Hate Group Stickers Anger Queens Activist," *New Voice of New York*, Sept. 1, 1999, 2.

78. "Anti-Sikh Bias Persists in Ozone Park Area of Queens," *News-India Times*, Sept. 10, 1999, 8.

79. Susan Sachs, "From a Babel of Tongues, a Neighborhood," *New York Times*, Dec. 26, 1999, 1.

80. Blaine Harden, "America as a Brand-New Book, Waiting to Be Cracked Open," *Los Angeles Times*, May 3, 1998, E5.

81. Sachs, "From a Babel of Tongues."

82. Sachs, "From a Babel of Tongues."

Chapter Five

1. Sarah Kershaw, "New Tune in Queens School District," *New York Times*, Feb. 16, 2002, B1.

2. Robert P. Walzer, "A Rich Ethnic Mix in a Crowded Enclave," *New York Times*, Jan. 23, 2000, RE5.

3. Diana Shaman, "Near Flushing's Bustle, a Quiet Enclave," *New York Times*, Mar. 5, 2000, RE5.

4. Diana Shaman, "Where Generation Follows Generation," *New York Times*, Apr. 23, 2000, RE7.

5. Diana Shaman, "An Uncongested, People-Oriented Enclave," *New York Times*, Mar. 25, 2001, RE7.

6. David Snyder, "The Queens Diaspora," *New York Times*, May 21, 2000, CY1.

7. Sarah Kershaw, "Home Decoration: Last Chapter," *New York Times*, Nov. 2, 2000, B1.

8. Diana Shaman, "Gracious and Diverse, With Good Schools," *New York Times*, June 17, 2001, RE7.

9. Dean E. Murphy, "City's Population Changes are on Vivid Display in Queens," *New York Times*, Mar. 19, 2001, B1.

10. Andrew Friedman, "It's Home to Shea, LaGuardia . . . and U.S. Indians," *New York Times*, Apr. 8, 2001, CY4.

11. Janny Scott, "Amid a Sea of Faces, Islands of Segregation," *New York Times*, June 18, 2001, A1.

12. Celestine Bohlen, "For Art: Destination, Queens," *New York Times*, Oct. 3, 2002, E1.

13. Ambrose Clancy, "Queens for a Day," *Washington Post*, Nov. 3, 2002, E1.

14. Dexter Filkins, "A New York Mosque," *New York Times*, Sept. 19, 2001, B10.

15. "Aftermath: Melting Pot; Identify Yourself," *New York Times*, Sept. 23, 2001.

16. John Leo, "Color Me Confounded," *U.S. News & World Report*, Jan. 28, 2002.

17. Jonathan Rauch, "Diversity in a New America," *Brookings Review*, Winter 2002, 4.

18. Rauch, "Diversity in a New America."

19. "The Nation: Diversity's Precarious Moorings," *New York Times*, Dec. 8, 2002.

20. Alan Wolf, "The One and the Many," *New Republic*, June 9, 2003, 26.

21. Nat Irvin II, "America's Increasing Diversity," *The Futurist*, Mar. 4, 2004, 21.

22. Katie Sweeney, "What Growing Diversity Will Mean for America," *Tactics*, Aug. 2004, 16.

23. Joel Achenbach, "Taking Off the Color Blinders," *Washington Post*, Sept. 15, 2004.

24. Joseph Berger, "Korean? Spoken Here?," *New York Times*, Mar. 25, 2003, D1.

25. Berger, "Korean? Spoken Here?"

26. Ellen Barry, "In Queens, Classes in Mandarin Are Also Lessons in Adaptation," *New York Times*, May 28, 2007, A1.

27. Barbara D. Phillips, "A New, Improved United Nations? It's in Queens," *Wall Street Journal*, Aug. 15, 2003, W17.

28. Joseph Berger, "The Germans Came; Now They are Us," *New York Times*, Oct. 25, 2003, B1.

29. Kim Campbell, "Welcome to Queens, Where Diversity Rules," *Christian Science Monitor*, Sept. 8, 2004, 12.

30. Corey Kilgannon, "Queens Hospitals Learn Many Ways to Say 'Ah,'" *New York Times*, Apr. 15, 2005, B1.

31. Joseph Berger, "A Group as Diverse as the Borough Itself," *New York Times*, Aug. 1, 2005, B1.

32. Julia Moskin, "The Silk Road Leads to Queens," *New York Times*, Jan. 18, 2006, F1.

33. Barbra Williams Cosentino, "You Got a Problem with Queens?," *New York Times*, Mar. 12, 2006, CY11.

34. Alison Gregor, "Changing Face of Queens," *New York Times*, June 28, 2006, C11.

35. Fernanda Santos, "A Development in Queens Bares Asian Ethnic Tensions," *New York Times*, July 15, 2010, A29.

36. C.J. Hughes, "For Polyglot Haven, a Park on a Gas-Tank Site," *New York Times*, Sept. 3, 2006, J9.

37. Sam Roberts, "In Queens, Blacks are the Have-Nots No More," *New York Times*, Oct. 1, 2006, 29.

38. Hilary Larson, "Suburban Hamlet in Queens," *The Jewish Week*, Nov. 17, 2006, 57.

39. Hilary Larson, "Nexus for Queens Jewish Life," *The Jewish Week*, Oct. 12, 2007, 47.

40. William Grimes, "Queens Now Has Less Feta, More Jellyfish," *New York Times*, Jan. 26, 2007, E37.

41. David Gonzalez, "For a Master Class on Global Worship, It's Destination Queens," *New York Times*, July 2, 2007, B1.

42. Jeff Vandam, "Where People Stay, and 'Play Musical Houses,'" *New York Times*, Jan. 10, 2010, RE7.

43. Joseph Berger, "A Slice of Queens Where People Who Arrived in 1977 Are Newcomers," *New York Times*, Jan. 8, 2011, A15.

44. C. J. Hughes, "A Town Center at City's Edge," *New York Times*, Dec. 16, 2007, 17.

45. Manny Fernandez and Annie Correal, "In Queens, No Breach of an Ecuadorean-Columbian Border," *New York Times*, Mar. 8, 2008, 35.

46. Kavita Mokha, "Growing Pains on Hillside Avenue in Queens," *Wall Street Journal*, Jan. 7, 2011, A18.

47. Gregory Beyer, "A Singular Place with Plural Ethnicities," *New York Times*, Aug. 29, 2010, RE7.

48. Alexandra Marks, "To Extend Housing Boom, a Push for Minority Buyers," *Christian Science Monitor*, Jan. 28, 2002, 2. For more on the wealth gap based on race, see Kerwin Kofi Charles and Erik Hurst, "The Transition to Home Ownership and the Black-White Wealth Gap," *Review of Economics and Statistics* 84, no. 2 (May 2002): 281.

49. David R. Francis, "Up, Up, and . . . Then What?," *Christian Science Monitor*, May 6, 2002, 15.

50. Sara Miller Llana, "Loans to Minorities Rise, But at a Price," *Christian Science Monitor*, Mar. 24, 2006, 2.

51. Miller Llana, "Loans to Minorities Rise"; Anne B. Shlay, "Low-Income Home Ownership: American Home or Delusion?," *Urban Studies*, Mar. 2006, 511; Sabrina W. Tyuse and Julie Birkenmaier, "Promoting Home Ownership for the Poor: Proceed with Caution," *Race, Gender & Class*, 2006, 295; Donald R. Haurin, Christopher E. Herbert, and Stuart S. Rosenthal, "Home Ownership Gaps Among Low-Income and Minority Households," *Cityscape*, 2007, 5.

52. Cyril Josh Barker, "Foreclosure Crisis Becoming Health Hazard in Queens," *New York Amsterdam News*, Sept. 29, 2011, 14.

53. "Queens Landlord Hit with Renting Bias Against African Americans," *New York Beacon*, Dec. 13–19, 2012, 6.

54. Joseph Berger, "Libraries Speak the Mother Tongue," *New York Times*, Jan. 3, 2012, A18.

55. "LA, Queens to Provide Voting Materials in Indian Languages," *India West*, May 11, 2012, A26.

56. Monique El-Faizy, "Refuge from Unrest in Egypt," *New York Times*, Apr. 21, 2013, CT1.

178 | NOTES TO CHAPTER FIVE

57. Joseph Tirella, "Tomorrow's America, in Queens," *New York Times*, Apr. 22, 2014, A25; Joseph Tirella, *Tomorrow-Land: The 1964–65 World's Fair and the Transformation of America* (Essex, CT: Lyons Press, 2014); see also my own *The End of the Innocence*.

58. Tirella, "Tomorrow's America, in Queens."

59. Michelle Higgins, "The Tilt Toward Queens," *New York Times*, Nov. 3, 2013, RE1.

60. Higgins, "The Tilt Toward Queens."

61. Gina Belafonte, "The King Can No Longer Afford Queens," *New York Times*, Apr. 20, 2014, L17.

62. Belafonte, "The King Can No Longer Afford Queens."

63. Janet Silver Ghent, "Queens Is Chic, Says the New York Times, But Not My Old 'Hood,' " *Jewish News Weekly of Northern California*, May 2, 2014, 2014, 1A.

64. Shirley L. Ng, "Daily News: Asian American Spider Woman Spins from Queens, NY," *AsAmNews*, Oct. 12, 2014.

65. George Joseph, "Graffiti in Queens Alarms Community," *India Abroad*, Mar. 20, 2015, A9.

66. Jason Horowitz, "Trump's Queens Neighborhood Contrasts with the Diverse Area Around It," *New York Times*, Sept. 23, 2015, A15. For more on Trump's early years in Queens, see Maggie Haberman, *The Making of Donald Trump and the Breaking of America* (New York: Penguin Press, 2022).

67. Horowitz, "Trump's Queens Neighborhood Contrasts."

68. Saeed Shabazz, "Creating a 'Hate-Free Zone' in Queens," *New York Amsterdam News*, Dec. 8, 2016, 3.

69. "Queens Immigrants Lead Rally at Trump Tower in Protest of ICE Clampdown," *New York Beacon*, Apr. 13–19, 2017, 2.

70. Robin Pogrebin, "A Director Is as Political as the Art," *New York Times*, Oct. 9, 2017, C1.

71. Barbara Brotman, "I Remember When Queens Was Lame," *New York Times*, Feb. 17, 2019, SR2.

72. Brotman, "I Remember When Queens was Lame."

73. Annie Correal and Andrew Jacobs, "Losses Sweeping Immigrant Enclaves in Queens," *New York Times*, Apr. 10, 2020, A15.

74. Correal and Jacobs, "Losses Sweeping Immigrant Enclaves in Queens."

75. Michael Kimmelman, "This Neighborhood Contains Multitudes," *New York Times*, Aug. 30, 2020, AR7.

76. Randall, "Drive to Install Little Manila Avenue Street Sign in Queens," *AsAmNews*, July 28, 2020.

77. "Queens, New York Street Renamed in Honor of Indian American Residents," *India West*, Nov. 6, 2020, B9.

78. Julia Tong, "Streets in Queens Renamed in Honor of Little Bangladesh," *AsAmNews*, Feb. 25, 2022.

79. Anna Kode, "Queens May Be the Next Hot Spot," *New York Times*, Jan. 1, 2023, RE2.

80. Kathleen Lynn, "Astoria, Queens: A Mix of Traditional and Trendy," *New York Times*, Aug. 30, 2023.

81. F. Scott Fitzgerald, *The Great Gatsby* (New York: Charles Scribner and Sons, 1925).

82. Eric Adams, "Willets Point—A Vibrant New Neighborhood in Queens," *New York Beacon*, Dec. 1–7, 2022, 8.

83. "NYC Planning: Queens," https://www.nyc.gov/site/planning/plans/queens.page.

Selected Bibliography

Antos, Jason D. *Queens (Then and Now)*. Charleston, SC: Arcadia, 2009.

Arlen, Michael J. *Passage to Ararat*. New York: Farrar, Straus and Giroux, 1975.

Bayor, Ronald H. *Neighbors in Conflict: The Irish, Germans, Jews, and Italians of New York City, 1929–1941*. Champaign: University of Illinois Press, 1988.

Campanella, Thomas J. *Brooklyn: The Once and Future City*. Princeton, NJ: Princeton University Press, 2019.

Chen, Hsiang-shui. *Chinatown No More: Taiwan Immigrants in Contemporary New York*. Ithaca, NY: Cornell University Press, 1992.

Ehrig, Stephan, Britta C. Jung, and Gad Schaffer, eds. *Exploring the Transnational Neighbourhood: Perspectives on Community-Building, Identity and Belonging*. Leuven, Belgium: Leuvan University Press, 2022.

Fitzgerald, F. Scott. *The Great Gatsby*. New York: Charles Scribner and Sons, 1925.

Glazer, Nathan, and Daniel Patrick Moynihan. *Beyond the Melting Pot: The Negroes, Puerto Ricans, Jews, Italians, and Irish of New York City*. Cambridge, MA: MIT Press and Harvard University Press, 1963.

Gonzalez, Evelyn. *The Bronx*. New York: Columbia University Press, 2004.

Greater Astoria Historical Society and Roosevelt Island Historical Society. *The Queensboro Bridge*. Mt. Pleasant, SC: Arcadia, 2008.

Gregory, Steven. *Black Corona: Race and the Politics of Place in an Urban Community*. Princeton, NJ: Princeton University Press, 1998.

Gryvatz, Claudia. *The Neighborhoods of Queens*. New Haven, CT: Yale University Press, 2007.

Haberman, Maggie. *The Making of Donald Trump and the Breaking of America*. New York: Penguin Press, 2022.

Hanson, R. Scott. *City of Gods: Religious Freedom, Immigration, and Pluralism in Flushing, Queens*. New York: Fordham University Press, 2016.

Lehrer, Warren, and Judith Sloan. *Crossing the BLVD: Strangers, Neighbors, Aliens in a New World*. New York: Norton, 2003.

Lieberman, Janet E., and Richard K. Leiberman. *City Limits: A Social History of Queens*. Dubuque, IA: Kendall/Hunt, 1983.

Mackay, Rob. *Famous People of Queens*. Mt. Pleasant, SC: Arcadia, 2023.

———. *Historic Houses of Queens*. Mt. Pleasant, SC: Arcadia, 2021.

Miles, Ann. *From Cuenca to Queens: An Anthropological Story of Transnational Migration*. Austin: University of Texas Press, 2004.

Murray, Sylvie. *The Progressive Housewife: Community Activism in Suburban Queens, 1945–1965*. Philadelphia: University of Pennsylvania Press, 2003.

Novak, Michael. *The Rise of the Unmeltable Ethnics: Politics and Culture in the Seventies*. New York: Macmillan, 1972.

Panchyk, Richard. *Abandoned Queens*. Mt. Pleasant, SC: Arcadia, 2019.

———. *Hidden History of Queens*. Charleston, SC: History Press, 2018.

Panchyk, Richard, and Lizz Panchyk. *Dead Queens*. Mt. Pleasant, SC: Arcadia, 2021.

Queens Borough New York City 1910–1920. New York: Chamber of Commerce of the Borough of Queens, New York City, 1920.

Ricourt, Milagros, and Ruby Danta. *Hispanas de Queens: Latino Panethnicity in a New York City Neighborhood*. Ithaca, NY: Cornell University Press, 2002.

Rozeas, Christina. *Greeks in Queens*. Mt. Pleasant, SC: Arcadia, 2012.

Samuel, Lawrence R. *The End of the Innocence: The 1964–1965 New York World's Fair*. Syracuse, NY: Syracuse University Press, 2007.

———. *Making Long Island: A History of Growth and the American Dream*. Mt. Pleasant, SC: History Press, 2023.

———. *New York City 1964: A Cultural History*. Jefferson, NC: McFarland, 2014.

———. *The World War II Bond Campaign*. New York: Fordham University Press, 2025.

Schrag, Peter. *The Decline of the WASP*. New York: Simon and Schuster, 1970.

Tirella, Joseph. *Tomorrow-Land: The 1964–65 World's Fair and the Transformation of America* Essex, CT: Lyons Press, 2014.

Walsh, Kevin, and the Greater Astoria Historical Society. *Forgotten Queens*. Charleston, SC: Arcadia, 2013.

Walzer, Michael. *On Toleration*. New Haven, CT: Yale University Press, 1997.

Index

Addisleigh Park, 5, 64, 66
Afghans, 127, 140, 148
African Americans (Blacks): in
    Addisleigh Park, 6, 64–65; Black
    studies, 91; in Cambria Heights,
    137; and club membership, 89;
    CORE, 86; in Corona, 30, 90;
    and cultural pluralism, 92–93;
    in East Elmhurst, 138, 147; in
    Elmhurst, 118; in Far Rockaway,
    123; first settlement in Queens, 12;
    in Flushing, 123; and foreclosures,
    149; Gregory on, 3; homeownership
    of, 27–28, 34, 65, 87–88, 101;
    and housing 67, 73, 87–89,
    98–101, 125–126; in Howard
    Beach, 116; and the Immigration
    and Nationality Act of 1965, 86;
    interracial events, 66; in Jackson
    Heights, 25, 65; and Jacob Riis
    Park, 89; in Jamaica, 29; in Jamaica
    Hills, 148; and the Ku Klux Klan,
    42, 117–118; in Laurelton, 123; Leo
    on, 140; Lieberman and Lieberman
    on, 17–18; and the LIRR, 28;
    median income, 146; middle class,
    122; migration of, 27, 69–70; and
    Moses, 81; and the Music Masters,
    135; as Muslims, 105; and the New

Deal, 44; and 1990 census, 122,
    124–125; in the 1930s, 41–44,
    49–51; in the 1920s, 22–23, 27–30,
    34–35; population in 1980, 20;
    and Queens General Hospital, 42;
    in Ridgewood-Glendale, 72; in
    Rosedale, 101; and segregation,
    138; in South Jamaica, 43–44; in
    Springfield Gardens, 71–72, 73–74;
    in Sunnyside, 150; and Trump, 98,
    154; and White flight, 73; during
    World War II, 60; between the
    world wars, 18
Albanians, 144
Algerians, 146
Aqueduct Racetrack, 6, 9
Arabs, 94, 117, 140
Argentinians, 97, 102, 106, 127, 131
Armenians, 104, 128
Astoria: American Museum of the
    Moving Image, 139; Bohemian Hall,
    105; Brotman on, 155; and Bunker,
    124; and Catholic immigrants, 93;
    and clubbing, 131; Greater Astoria
    Historical Society, 5; and Greeks,
    56, 90, 103, 104–105, 121; and
    integration, 68; and Irish, 12; and
    Maltese, 94; and Manhattanites,
    114, 152, 157; as melting pot,

183

Astoria *(continued)*
89–90, 106; and 1970 census, 96; population decline, 67; population growth, 26, 55; Public School (PS) 166, 90; Queens Public Library, 150; rents, 155; settlement of, 11; Socrates Sculpture Park, 138; Steinway & Sons, 5; transformation of, 146; and Triborough Bridge, 37; and Turks, 128; and World Cup, 131
Austrians, 73, 95

Bangladeshis, 106, 127, 146, 148, 156, 157
Bayside: demographic transformation of, 138; and Ghent, 155; and Irish, 120; North-East Fair Housing Committee, 73; The Oaks, 68; settlement of, 11; underrepresentation of ethnics, 96
Bayside Hills, 48
Bellerose, 14, 69, 87–88, 96, 126, 148
Brazilians, 114, 131, 146
Breezy Point, 138
Briarwood, 31, 64
British (English): flags, 56; in Flushing, 16–17; Fuller on, 93; and 1970 census, 95; and 1960
census, 73; occupation of Queens, 12; in Parkway Village, 64; takeover of New York City, 76

Cambria Heights, 99, 136–137, 146, 147
Canadians, 73
Catholics: and birth control, 130; Calvary Cemetery, 137; as defenders of undocumented, 106; dioceses, 97; in Flushing, 146; in Jackson Heights, 25, 34; and Ku Klux Klan, 42; Maltese, 94; in Middle Village, 136; parishes, 55; ROAR members,

101; Spanish-speaking immigrants, 93; Sunnyside churches, 119
cemeteries, 6, 12, 13, 137
Chicanos, 93
Chileans, 131
Chinese: in Bayside, 138; Chinatowns, 128; Chinese Exclusion Act, 19, 54; and COVID-19, 156; in Douglaston and Little Neck, 143; in Elmhurst, 106, 136; in Flushing, 19, 95, 103, 105, 107, 114, 145; in Fresh Meadows, 146; kite making, 113; and No. 7 train, 127; in Parker Towers, 103; in Parkway Village, 64; in Rego Park, 114; and War Brides Act of 1946, 19, 63
Citi Field, 8
Civil War, 14
Clinton, Bill, 119
College Point, 5, 90, 96
Columbians: in Astoria, 146; in Corona, 123; in Elmhurst, 106; emigration, 20; festivals, 115; in Flushing, 107; in Jackson Heights, 102, 127, 147–148; and No. 7 train, 127; at PS 89, 106; in Richmond Hill, 112; and Roosevelt Avenue, 120, 129; as undocumented, 97, 99; and World Cup, 131
Corona: and African Americans, 27, 29–30, 41, 65, 72; the Almontes, 116; Black churches, 41; and Bunker, 124; Congregation Tifereth Israel, 14; COVID-19, 156; crime, 123; demographic transformation of, 20, 123, 129; development of, 14; Dump, 46; Gregory on, 3; home ownership, 65; as integrated, 35; and Manhattanites, 114; Muslims, 105; NAACP branch, 42; No. 7 train, 130; sense of community, 90;

184 | INDEX

2016 rally, 154; undocumented, 99, 106

COVID-19, 155–156

Croats, 93

Cubans, 95, 102, 106, 107, 115, 129

Cunningham Park, 69

Cypriots, 90

Czechs, 73, 95, 157

Dinkins, David, 124

Ditmars, 155

Dominicans, 93, 102, 106, 115–116, 123, 127–129

Douglaston, 5, 12, 73, 143, 147

Dutch (Netherlands), 16–17, 64, 76

East Elmhurst, 5, 138, 147, 156

East Jamaica, 65

Ecuadorans: in Corona, 123, 129; in Elmhurst, 106, 129; festivals, 115; in Jackson Heights, 102, 129, 147–148; at Parkway Village, 64; as undocumented, 97, 99; in Richmond Hill, 112

Edgemere, 14

Egyptians, 17, 94, 146, 151

Elmhurst: and African Americans, 22; cemeteries, 6; and Chinese, 136; COVID-19, 156; crime, 118–119; demographic transformation of, 20, 118, 123, 129, 136; diversity of, 106, 111, 118, 120, 136, 156; Elmhurst Hospital, 106, 144, 156; First Presbyterian Church of Newtown, 111; Gas Tank Park, 146; German Second Reformed Protestant Dutch Church, 59; as "hot" real estate market, 157; and Indians, 105; Kleiman on, 121; La Fusta, 121; and Manhattanites, 114; and 1970 census, 96; No. 7 train, 130; population growth, 26; PS 89, 106;

Reformed Church of Newtown, 106, 111; sari shopping, 144; as segregated, 18, 35; 2016 rally, 154; undocumented, 99, 106

F train, 130

Far Rockaway *See* Rockaways

Ferraro, Geraldine, 111–112

Filipinos, 95, 106, 127, 136, 156

Floral Park, 25, 147, 148

Flushing: adult education in Mandarin, 143; and African Americans, 34, 41, 65; Afghan mosque, 140; annexation of Bayside, 138; Black churches, 41; Brotman on, 155; Chinatown, 128; development of 25, 31, 33, 38, 67; First Baptist Church, 103; and Chinese, 103, 105, 114, 136; condominiums, 107; demographic transformation of, 127; diversity of, 114, 127; Flushing Commons, 145–146; Flushing High School, 58; "the Flushing plan," 46–47; Flushing Remonstrance of 1627, 17; friction, 127; Hanson on, 4; and Hindus, 105; home building, 47–48; immigration, 19, 123; incorporation into New York City, 14; and Indians, 105, 114; and Irish, 14; IRT line, 81; and Japanese, 95; and Jews, 127; Kissena Park, 136; and Koreans, 97–98, 103, 105, 107, 114; and Muslims, 105; and 1970 census, 96; No. 7 train, 8; North-East Queens Fair Housing Committee, 73; Queens Public Library, 133; Reception Hall, 117; religions, 146–147; retail, 103, 122; settlement of, 16, 17; and South Asian and Indians, 95; and Taiwanese, 103; and White flight, 103–104

Flushing Meadows, 1–2, 8, 19, 46, 81–82

Forest Hills: development of, 14; and Ferraro, 111; Forest Hills High School, 55; Ghent on, 152; home building, 47; Indians, 127; and Israelis, 93; 1941 survey, 57; and 1970 census, 96; Parker Towers, 103; and Queens-Midtown Tunnel, 54; rent hikes and lease terminations, 61; and Soviet Jews, 100, 107, 112, 130, 146; traffic link, 79; and Trump, 98; undeveloped land, 67; victory garden, 59; West Side Tennis Club, 8, 10

Forest Hills Gardens, 18, 24, 30

Forest Hills West, 26

French, 64, 73, 103

Fresh Meadows, 5, 146

Fujians, 143

Germans: assimilation of, 94; in Astoria, 104; in Cambria Heights, 137; in College Point, 91; and Cubans, 129; in Elmhurst, 118, 136; and Elmhurst Hospital, 106; emigration in early 1850s, 14; emigration in 1970s, 93; emigration after World War II, 19, 63; "enemy aliens," 58; in Flushing, 103; friction with others, 143; Friends of the New Germany, 45; German Second Reformed Protestant Dutch Church, 59; in Kissena Park, 136; Ludwig, 57; in Middle Village, 136; and 1970 census, 95; and 1960 census, 73; patriotism of, 58, 60; in Richmond Hill, 112; in Ridgewood, 144; in Sunnyside, 119; and war bonds, 60; in Woodside, 106; and World War II, 59; Zimms, 56

Giuliani, Rudy, 131

Glendale: and *All in the Family*, 124; blockbusting, 72; busing to, 72; development of, 14; landlord, 117; and Middle Village, 136; Ridgewood Grove Sporting Club, 44; underrepresentation of ethnics, 96; zoning code, 72–73

Glen Oaks Village, 19

Great Depression, 38, 41–43, 45, 47

Greeks: artisans, 109; in Astoria, 56, 90, 103–105, 121, 146, 157; in Elmhurst, 121; at 1985 symposium, 113; and 1960 census, 73; at PS 166; Rozea on, 5; in Sunnyside, 119; and Turks, 128; during World War II, 56

Guyanese, 106, 127, 135, 153

Haitians, 102, 106, 123, 137, 154

Hindus, 95, 103, 105, 138, 146, 153

Hollis, 14, 23, 31, 74, 88, 122

Hondurans, 106

Hong Kongese, 106

Howard Beach, 14, 96, 116, 158

Hungarians, 60, 73, 95, 103

Hunters Point, 11

Idlewild Airport, 6–7, 65

Indians: in Bellerose, 126; and COVD-19, 156; and demographic transformation, 19, 54, 137; in Elmhurst, 105, 106, 121; in Far Rockaway, 123; in Floral Park, 147; in Flushing, 95, 105, 107, 114, 127, 136; in Forest Hills, 127; in Fresh Meadows, 146; in Jackson Heights, 127–128; in Jamaica Hills, 148; and 1965 Immigration and Nationality Act, 105; in Music Masters, 135; and No. 7 train, 127; and Pakistanis, 128; saris, 114; Shephard on, 94, 120; voters, 150

Iranians, 64, 146

Irish: in Astoria, 90, 104–105; in Breezy Point, 138; and Calvary Cemetery, 137; in Cambria Heights, 137; in College Point, 91; in Corona, 123; as displaced by Cubans, 129; as displacing British, 12; in Douglas Manor, 147; in Elmhurst, 111, 118, 136; friction with others, 143; generations of, 103; hurlers, 90; in Kissena Park, 136; "Legalize the Irish," 119–120; and 1985 symposium, 113; and 1970 census, 95–96; and 1960 census, 73; and No. 7 train, 127; pubs, 118; in Richmond Hill, 112, 138; and ROAR, 101; Shepard on, 94, 120; in South Jamaica, 49; in Sunnyside, 119; in Woodside, 106, 119

Israelis, 93–94, 127

Italians: assimilation of, 94; in Astoria, 90, 104–105, 146; and Bellacicco, 109; and Calvary Cemetery, 137; in Cambria Heights, 137; in College Point, 91; in Corona, 90, 123; and demographic transformation, 93, 111, 128; in Douglas Manor, 147; in Elmhurst, 118, 136; and Elmhurst Hospital, 106; friction with others, 143; generations of, 103; in Jamaica, 29; in Kissena Park, 136; in Laurelton, 123; in Middle Village, 136; and 1985 symposium, 113; and 1970 census, 95; and 1960 census, 73; as patriotic, 60; in Richmond Hill, 112; in Ridgewood, 144; and ROAR, 101; Shephard on, 120; and stereotypes, 91; and war bonds, 60; during World War II, 56–57, 59–60

Jackson Heights: bus service, 32; and Columbians, 99; commuters, 54; and COVID-19, 156; demographic transformation of, 102, 129; development of, 24–26, 55, 63; Diversity Plaza rally, 154; fair housing committee, 87; friction with others, 147–148; and "garden city" concept, 18, 121; growth of, 32; and Indians, 127–128, 147; INS raids, 96, 99; and Manhattanites, 114, 152; and Mexicans, 127; Miyares on, 20; mural, 135; the Nghiems, 100; and 1970 census, 96; and No. 7 train, 120, 130; and O'Hara, 51, 61; and Pakistanis, 127–128; public schools, 129; rent hikes or lease terminations, 61; as restrictive, 25–26, 65; Roman Catholic immigrants, 93; tenant ownership plan, 33–34; undeveloped land, 67; undocumented, 96, 99, 106

Jamaica: and African Americans, 27–31, 35, 41–43, 60, 72, 98, 122, 149; and Bangladeshis, 157; Black churches, 41; Calhoun, 60; "el" train, 22, 23; farmers market, 121–122; foreclosures, 149; as fourth ward, 23; incorporation, 12; incorporation into New York City, 14; as integrated, 35; and Irish, 12; and Jamaica Estates, 21; Jewish Center, 66; JFK Airport, 5; and Ku Klux Klan, 31, 42; and LIRR, 12; NAACP branch, 42–43, 50; and Native Americans, 138; Neighborhood Plan, 158; and 1970 census, 95–96; origin of name, 10; Parkway Village, 64; racetrack, 53; real estate, 34–35, 48; as rejuvenated, 122; as segregated, 88; and Trump, 98; undeveloped land, 38, 67; undocumented, 97

Jamaicans, 95, 97, 123

INDEX | 187

Jamaica Estates, 5, 21, 23, 153
Jamaica Hills, 148
Japanese, 19, 59–60, 70, 94, 95, 103, 107, 113
Jews (Judaism): in Bayside, 138; Bukharan, 130, 145, 146; in Cambria Heights, 137; and Congregation Tifereth Isael, 14; and Diversity Plaza rally, 154; and exclusionary covenants, 18, 25, 27, 34, 65; in Far Rockaway, 123; in Flushing, 127, 146; and Flushing Remonstrance of 1627, 17; in Forest Hills, 14, 146; in Fresh Meadows, 146; and Friends of the New Germany, 45; and Germans, 144; and housing projects, 73; Jewish centers, 55, 66, 95; and Ku Klux Klan, 42; in Middle Village, 136; Milner on, 93; in the Music Masters, 135; as "old" ethnic group, 103, 111, 120, 128, 143; Orthodox, 130; and Queens Fair Housing Committee, 70; and Queens General Hospital, 42; and Queens Unity Day, 117; Russian, 96, 100–101, 107, 112–113, 146; Sephardic, 112; war veterans, 44; writers, 92
JFK (Kennedy) Airport, 5, 7, 137
Johnson, Lyndon (LBJ), 19, 85–87, 151

Kew Gardens: Borough Hall, 145; and fourth ward, 23; and Genovese, 74; and Hiraoka, 60; and home building, 47; and LIRR, 14; and 1941 survey, 57; and 1970 census, 96; and 1939–1940 New York World's Fair, 45; and Queens-Midtown Tunnel, 54; and Soviet Jews, 100
Kew Gardens Hills, 127

Koch, Edward, 89, 116
Koreans: Community Action Center, 97–98; and condominiums, 107; in Douglaston and Little Neck, 143; in Elmhurst, 106; and Elmhurst Hospital, 107; in Flushing, 19, 95, 97–98, 103, 105, 107, 114, 146; in Kissena Park, 136; Kleiman on, 121; Lee on, 118; Moon (a.k.a. Silk), 153; and No.7 train, 120, 127; and PS 89, 107; and Reformed Church of Newtown, 107; in Richmond Hill, 112; in Sunnyside, 119; wedding ceremonies, 113–114; and Yun, 114
Korean War, 66, 68

LaGuardia Airport, 5, 8, 79
LaGuardia, Fiorello, 50
Laurelton: blockbusting, 126; block party, 56; civic group, 72; demographic transformation of, 123; and Gross, 19; as segregated, 88; and Steele, 88; as thriving, 146
LGBTQ, 154
Libyans, 146
Lindsay, John, 90
Little Neck, 11, 69, 73, 96, 114, 147
Long Island City: and African Americans, 28, 42, 72, 117; artists, 131; Brewster Aircraft, 58; Bridge Plaza, 33; Brotman on, 155; decline in population, 67; Gantry Plaza State Park, 144; Grace United Christian Church, 42; Isamu Noguchi Garden Museum, 138; and Italian Americans, 56; and Ku Klux Klan, 42, 117; luxury condos, 152; and Manhattanites, 114, 152; and Metropolitan Life, 32; Neighborhood Plan, 158; and 1970 census, 96; PS 1 Contemporary Arts

Center, 138; Queensbridge Houses, 117; Queensview, 67; settlement of, 11; Society of St. Paolina celebration, 56; Sunnyside Yards, 115; Thomas Hill section, 55; Tom Cat Bakery, 154
Long Island Railroad (LIRR): and Cambria Heights, 136; and Forest Hills West, 26; hiring of African Americans, 28; and Jamaica, 12, 28, 122; and Jamaica Estates, 21; and Kew Station, 14; as main transportation option, 40; number of stations in 1940, 55

Macedonians, 105
Malba, 60
Maltese, 94
Maspeth, 10, 57, 120, 136, 137
Merrick Mark, 64
Mexicans, 20, 127, 129, 137, 144, 146
Middle Village, 120, 136, 157
Mormons, 130
Moroccans, 146
Morris Park, 14, 23
Moses, Robert, 46, 49, 77–81
Muslims (Islam): in Astoria, 105; in Corona, 105; and Elmhurst Hospital, 144; in Flushing, 105; Jamaica Muslim Center, 148; mosques, 146; Ms. Marvel, 153; and Diversity Plaza rally, 154; Muslim Brotherhood, 151; and 9/11, 140; rising number of, 129; in Sunnyside, 128; taxi drivers, 130

Native Americans, 10–12, 132, 137, 138
Nepalese, 156
Newtown, 14, 111
9/11, 4, 20, 135, 140

1964–1965 New York World's Fair: advance tickets, 78; as celebration of global culture, 19; and CORE, 86; and Japanese, 95; and Koreans, 103; Moses, 77, 79–80; New York City Building, 139; and New York State Pavilion, 4; Space Park, 83; theme, 53, 76; Tirella on, 151; transportation to, 81; as unforgettable experience, 1–2; Unisphere, 3
1939–1940 New York World's Fair: as ambitious project, 45; and Catan, 83; financial loss, 77; Ford Motor Building, 47; MacDougall on, 49; and Moses, 46, 77–79; New York City Building, 68, 139; and 1964–1965 New York World's Fair, 19, 76; and real estate, 47–48; Trylon and Perisphere, 46
No. 7 subway train: and diversity of borough, 6, 144; and Elmhurst, 106; and Harlow, 126; as "the International Express," 8, 20; and Manhattan, 121; and ridership, 130; Shepard on, 120; and transportation grid, 16; and World Cup, 131

O'Dwyer, William, 64
Ozone Park, 14, 42, 111, 127, 132, 138

Pakistanis, 95, 126–128, 148
Peruvians, 102, 127, 129
Poles: and Calvary Cemetery, 137; and demographic transformation, 103; immigration in 1970s, 93; in Jamaica, 29; in Middle Village, 136; and 1970 census, 95; and 1960 census, 73; in Ozone Park, 127; and PS 89, 106; in Ridgewood, 144
Protestants: and Bunker, 124; churches in 1940, 55; in Flushing, 146;

Protestants *(continued)*
and "garden city" concept, 18, 22;
German Second Reformed Protestant
Dutch Church, 59; in Jackson
Heights, 25, 32; and Ku Klux Klan,
30; Reformed Church of Newtown,
111; and Robertson, 130
Puerto Ricans: busing of, 72; and
demographic transformation, 93; and
housing, 87; in Jackson Heights,
102; and Moses, 81; population of
in New York City, 70; post-World
War I immigration, 66; and White
flight, 73

Queensboro Bridge: Lieberman and
Lieberman on, 14–15; opening of
14–16, 21, 31, 37; and Queens-
Midtown Tunnel, 54; Roosevelt
Island Historical Society on, 5; and
trajectory of Queens, 33; Tyree on,
17; upper deck, 38
Queens-Midtown Tunnel, 38, 40, 54
Queens Village, 14, 43, 96, 99, 125

Reagan, Ronald, 112
Rego Park: Bukharan Jews, 145; and
dissolution of Soviet Union, 145;
and Ghent, 152; and Israelis, 93;
and Middle Village, 136; and 1970
census, 96; real estate, 152; rent
hikes or lease terminations, 61; and
Soviet Jews, 100, 107, 112, 130;
Stephen A. Halsey Junior High
School, 114
Revolutionary War, 12
Richmond Hill: and blockbusting,
101; demographic transformation of,
112, 138; development of 14; and
Ferraro, 111; and fourth ward, 23;
and Hindus, 153; and Indians, 147,

156; and Ku Klux Klan, 31, 42;
mural, 102; and 1970 census, 96
Richmond Hill South, 42
Ridgewood, 31, 60, 72–73, 131, 144,
151
Rockaways: and African Americans,
72, 88, 149; Breezy Point, 89;
demographic transformation
of, 123; Far Rockaway, 68, 88. 123,
149; foreclosures, 149; and Hudson,
11; incorporation into New York
City, 14; and Irish, 120; Jacob
Riis Park, 55; origin of name, 10;
Redfern Houses, 68; as "resilient
neighborhood," 158; Rockaway
Beach, 8, 9, 31
Rockefeller, Nelson, 53
Romanians, 73, 105, 119, 127, 144
Roosevelt, Franklin Delano (FDR), 44,
49, 56
Rosedale, 71, 96, 100–101, 146
Russians (Soviet Union): immigration
in 1970s, 19; Jews, 96, 100, 107,
112–113, 146; in Kew Garden
Hills, 127; in Middle Village, 136;
and 1970 census, 95–96; and 1960
census, 73; in Parker Towers, 103;
and Queens Public Library, 150; in
Rego Park, 145; subway ridership,
130

Scots, 90, 92
Serbians, 105
Seventh-day Adventists, 130
Shea Stadium, 5, 8, 11, 79–80
Sikhs, 132, 138, 144, 146, 157
Slavs, 101
Slovaks, 157
South Jamaica, 41–44, 49–51, 68, 101
South Ozone Park, 8, 74, 149, 153,
157

190 | INDEX

Spaniards, 114, 119
Springfield Gardens, 70–71, 73–74, 87–88, 101, 122
St. Albans: Addisleigh Park, 64, 66; and African Americans, 72, 122, 149; development of, 25; fair housing fair, 87; foreclosures, 149; and Native Americans, 138; as segregated, 88; underrepresentation of ethnics, 96
Sunnyside: and Armenians, 104; billboard, 131–132; Brotman on, 155; decline in population, 67; development of, 119; diversity of, 132; intolerance towards Blacks, 150; and Irish, 119–120; and Manhattanites, 114; and 1990 census, 132; real estate, 152, 157; Sunnyside Yards, 115; and Turks, 128
Sunnyside Gardens, 18, 24, 119
Surinamese, 153

Taiwanese, 103, 106, 111–112, 127–128
Thais, 127
Throgs Neck Bridge, 78, 155
Tobagans, 123
Triborough Bridge, 37–39, 47, 79
Trinidadians, 95, 123, 153, 154
Trump, Donald, 98, 117, 153–154
Tunisians, 146
Turks, 17, 103, 128

Ukrainians, 109, 135, 146
United Nations, 19–20, 63–64, 68, 106, 139, 144
Uruguayans, 102, 115, 120, 127
Uzbekistanis, 145, 146

Venezuelans, 99, 112, 147–148
Vietnamese, 100, 106
Vietnam War, 86

Wagner Jr., Robert F., 86
Welsh, 92
Whitestone, 17, 73
Whitestone Bridge, 79
Willets Point, 5, 6, 46, 158
Woodhaven, 12, 23, 31, 96
Woodside: and Calvary Cemetery, 137; Carter on, 110; and Columbians, 99; diversity of, 132; and Diversity Plaza rally, 154; and Filipinos, 156; housing project, 65; and Irish, 119–120; and Manhattanites, 114; and 1970 census, 96; and No. 7 train, 130; real estate, 157; settlement of, 12; Spanish-speaking immigrants, 93; and undocumented, 99, 106
World War I (Great War): and Black middle class, 18; and development of Queens, 18, 21, 24, 40, 48; and Germans, 144; New York City housing shortage, 32, 34; and O'Hara, 51, 63
World War II: and African Americans, 60; and civil rights movement, 18, 23; and demographic transformation of Queens, 57–58; development of Queens, 18; displays of patriotism, 56–57, 60; espionage, 58; and Flushing High School, 58; and Germans, 19, 58–59; housing, 51, 56; and Jackson Heights, 65; and Japanese, 59–60; rent control, 61; and serving the common good, 53; War Brides Act of 1946, 19; war plants, 40